Poor Numbers

A Volume in the Series
CORNELL STUDIES IN POLITICAL ECONOMY
edited by Peter J. Katzenstein
A list of titles in this series is available at www.cornellpress.cornell.edu.

POOR NUMBERS

*How We Are Misled by African Development
Statistics and What to Do about It*

MORTEN JERVEN

CORNELL UNIVERSITY PRESS
ITHACA AND LONDON

Cornell University Press gratefully acknowledges receipt of a subvention from the University Publications Committee's Rapid Response Fund, in the Office of the Vice-President for Research, Simon Fraser University, which assisted in the publication of this book.

First published 2013 by Cornell University Press
First printing, Cornell Paperbacks, 2013
Printed in the United States of America

Library of Congress Cataloging-in-Publication Data

Jerven, Morten, 1978–
    Poor numbers : how we are misled by African development statistics and what to do about it / Morten Jerven.
        p. cm
    Includes bibliographical references and index.
    ISBN 978-0-8014-5163-8 (cloth : alk. paper)
    ISBN 978-0-8014-7860-4 (pbk. : alk. paper)
    1. Economic development—Africa, Sub-Saharan—Statistics.
2. National income—Africa, Southern—Accounting.   3. Economic indicators—Africa, Sub-Saharan.   4. Africa, Sub-Saharan—Economic conditions—Statistics.   5. Africa, Sub-Saharan—Statistical services.   I. Title.
    HC800.J47   2013
    338.967—dc23   2012045248

Cornell University Press strives to use environmentally responsible suppliers and materials to the fullest extent possible in the publishing of its books. Such materials include vegetable-based, low-VOC inks and acid-free papers that are recycled, totally chlorine-free, or partly composed of nonwood fibers. For further information, visit our website at www.cornellpress.cornell.edu.

Cloth printing   10 9 8 7 6 5 4 3 2 1
Paperback printing   10 9 8 7 6 5 4 3 2 1

CONTENTS

ILLUSTRATIONS

Tables

Figures

PREFACE

How do they even come up with these numbers? That was the question
I wanted to answer. It was 2007 and I went to Zambia to do fieldwork for
my doctoral thesis in economic history. I wanted to examine how national
income estimates were made in African countries. I was struck by the derelict state of the Central Statistical Office in Lusaka. The planned agricultural crop survey was being delayed by the need for car repairs, most of
the offices were dark, and the computers were either missing or very old.
The national accounts division had three employees, of whom only one
was regularly in the office while I was visiting. No one at the office could
account for how the income estimates had been made more than a decade
ago. In the library there was a dearth of publications and no record of any
activity that may or may not have taken place in the late 1970s, the 1980s,
and the early 1990s.

The data and methods used to estimate Zambian national income had
last been revised in 1994. A short report on methodology had been prepared, but it was unpublished and was circulated internally as a manual
for the national accountants. It revealed the real state of affairs of national
income statistics in Zambia. I was surprised by the lack of basic data and
the rudimentary methods in use. Regular and reliable data were available

only on government finances and the copper sector. The entire agricultural sector was accounted for by observing trends in crop forecasts for eight agricultural commodities. For the rest of the economy there really was no usable data. The construction sector was assumed to grow at the same rate as cement production and imports. Retail, wholesale, and transport sectors were all assumed to grow at the same rate as agricultural and copper production, while business services were assumed to grow at the same rate as trade and transport.

"What happens if I disappear?" In 2010, I returned to Zambia and found that the national accounts now were prepared by one man alone. His question was not hypothetical, but one of real concern. Until very recently he had had one colleague, but that man was removed from the National Accounts Division to work on the 2010 population census. To make matters worse, lack of personnel in the section for industrial statistics and public finances meant that the only statistician left in the National Accounts Division was responsible for these data as well.

"It is awful," the economic advisor from a northern European embassy told me when I asked about the quality of the growth and income data in Zambia. After hastening to note that he or she did not want to be named in my report, the advisor went on to say that the statistical office in general was in dire need of reform. The per diem allowances mean that the statisticians earn very well when they are in the field collecting data, but they earn very little for working at their desks preparing estimates and reports. According to my informant this meant that the statistical office was always looking for excuses for why more data were needed, why more fieldwork was needed, and why people were pulled from other sectors to participate in data collection.

"The donors don't understand," a representative from the UK Department for International Development (DfID) had told me the previous day. "They are all over the Millennium Development Goals." The new development agenda is geared toward these targets and resources are readily available for collecting data in order to prepare reports on social indicators. This comment also illustrates the stark contrast with the previous development paradigm, which focused narrowly on economic growth. The priority given to data on economic growth and physical indicators of economic change is currently very low. As a result, the availability and reliability of data on economic development are poor and are getting worse, while the data on social development are getting better and better.

My meeting with the only person working on preparing income and growth data in Zambia was cut short. "I have a meeting with DfID," he told me. It turned out that DfID, whose representative the previous day had been lamenting that personnel were pulled away from compiling the very important economic statistics, had scheduled a meeting with the national accountant. DfID were concerned about a report they had funded that needed to be completed by the end of the year. The director of the unit in charge of finishing the report, called the Living Conditions Monitoring Survey, had left for Japan for further training. DfID now wanted the national accountant to finish the report for them.

These stories illustrate the kind of problems national accountants in Africa encounter in the production of income statistics and some of the stakeholders involved in that process. Similar anecdotes could be told from research visits I have made to other countries in sub-Saharan Africa since 2007. I was interested in trying to answer the question: How do they come up with these numbers? The challenge is to move beyond anecdotal evidence and provide a systematic explanation. The answer is multifaceted and complicated, and it varies from country to country. The process involves many stakeholders and is in part hidden in statistical jargon and technical procedures. This book is written for data users and provides an answer for development scholars and practitioners in the field to the question How good are these numbers?

The short answer is that the numbers are poor. This is not just a matter of technical accuracy. The arbitrariness of the quantification process produces observations with very large errors and levels of uncertainty. This numbers game has taken on a dangerously misleading air of accuracy, and the resulting numbers are used to make critical decisions that allocate scarce resources. International development actors are making judgments based on erroneous statistics. Governments are not able to make informed decisions because existing data are too weak or the data they need do not exist.

This book presents a study of the production and use of African economic development statistics. All of the central questions in development revolve around the measure of the production and consumption of goods and services. This is expressed in an aggregate composite metric called the gross domestic product (GDP) that is used to rank and rate the wealth and progress of nations, which I will refer to in this book as national income and economic growth. It is the most widely used measure of economic activity, yet little is known about how this metric is produced and misused in debates about African economic development.

This book provides what could be called an ethnography of national income accounting in Africa. Sally Engle Merry provides a definition of such work:

> Doing an ethnography of indicators means examining the history of the creation of an indicator and its underlying theory, observing expert group meetings and international discussions where the terms of the indicator are debated and defined, interviewing expert statisticians and other experts about the meaning and the process of producing indicators, observing data-collection processes, and examining the ways indicators affect decision making and public perceptions.[1]

In the period 2007 to 2011, I conducted interviews at statistical offices, central banks, and donor missions and had lengthy discussions with colleagues and country experts. I have collected and studied published and unpublished reports on the sources and methods used in national accounting. The book is based on research visits to Botswana, Ghana, Kenya, Malawi, Nigeria, Tanzania, Uganda, and Zambia. In order to get a continent-wide perspective, I have also collected data through e-mail surveys.[2] I have also assembled datasets from different international agencies and rigorously compared different versions of these. The book offers an assessment of the extent of the inaccuracy in development economics statistics, the policy implications of these data problems, and, finally, what can be done about it.

Before drawing some sweeping conclusions, it is appropriate to note a few caveats. The book is not about all statistics from all African countries. It is a book about the system of national accounts and GDP statistics—the fundamental framework for economic information about these countries. As the country list above indicates, the detailed information is mainly drawn from Anglophone Africa.[3] There is a tradeoff between breadth and depth in such a study that I have tried to minimize by relying on the richer information collected in the personal interviews and the summary information from the continent-wide survey I conducted. National income statistics present an extremely useful angle from which to understand how the statistical systems in these countries work, because the measure draws upon information collected in most subdivisions of statistical offices.[4]

It is important to show that African statistics are of dubious quality, yet my findings may be met with a shrug of the shoulders. In parts of the development community this is indeed old news, and many have already accepted the consequence of it and shy away from generalizations about patterns of economic development solely based on statistical analysis.[5] At the other end of the spectrum, the confidence of statisticians in the data they use will not be shaken until they are convinced that the inaccuracy of the observations is truly problematic. This book aims to bridge this gap in perspectives by giving both audiences tools for handling development statistics. Beyond showing why data quality matters, it provides a first-ever systematic analysis of the levels, direction, and causes of errors in African economic statistics. The book deepens our understanding of when the quality of economic and social statistics is poor and why that happens. It furthers a nuanced view of the importance of political pressure in the production of statistics. It examines the interplay between data producers and the main stakeholders who exert pressure: international organizations and domestic political leaders.

The book boldly takes a stab at the final difficult step. It is easy enough to show that numbers are wrong and that wrong numbers mislead scholars and policymakers, but it is more difficult to know what to do about the situation. What kind of reforms should be implemented? This book discusses what can and should be done to improve the guidelines for both producing and using statistics. It offers a perspective on the interaction between global standards or norms and how these are adapted and adjusted to local conditions. The basic lesson is that new baseline estimates are needed in most African countries, and these must be based on local applicability, not solely on theoretical or political preference. The policy advice is not simply more funds for data collection. There is a need to strengthen the legitimacy of statistical offices as providers of data—acknowledging the role that statistical offices can play in development is an important step toward enabling them to be providers of regular and reliable data for development planning.

Thus, this book hopes to bridge the unhealthy divide that currently exists between scholars who use qualitative methods and those who use quantitative methods. Scholars who use numbers should listen more carefully to those who criticize the use of numbers, and conversely, the skills of qualitatively oriented scholars may usefully be applied to the task of unearthing the sources of numbers and providing insights into how these numbers may be interpreted. There is a surprising gap between knowing innately that these numbers cannot be good and an unwillingness to study how bad they are. The first step is to acknowledge the problem.

ACKNOWLEDGMENTS

This book is dedicated to the honest and hardworking civil servants at statistical offices across sub-Saharan Africa. Without their contribution, this book could not have been written. Their professionalism and commitment in the face of bureaucratic and financial hardship continues to impress me. I hope that their openness and willingness to participate can be repaid by this book. I do realize that the title of the book may seem like an undisguised insult to these statisticians, and for that I apologize. But I believe that openness and attention to this important problem in development studies justifies this language. For a variety of reasons, the numbers we currently use are providing us with a poor guide to African economic development.

One example of the openness of African statisticians is the way I was greeted on a visit I made to the National Bureau of Statistics in Abuja, Nigeria, in February 2010. When I was introduced to the director of dissemination, he literally greeted me with open arms and a resounding "Welcome!" He explained that his office was in the business of providing information and that he considered this work a service. Without demand or consumers for the data his office generates, their product would not exist. His approach and attitude is instructive. The central problems

I identify have to do with how the interaction between data producers and data consumers is currently organized. We need to think more clearly about what we want to know and how we demand the information. This particular knowledge production function has problems on both the supply and the demand side. My book aims to deal fairly with both sides.

I was not met with equal enthusiasm at all institutions. In 2007, I was physically thrown out of the library of a statistical office in Eastern Africa. At that time, the "library" was just a room with disorganized piles of books on the floor, and I had been officially invited to see if I could find anything useful there earlier in the week. When the chief librarian returned to work later in the week, he was aggravated and declared that the library was in no state to conduct research in. I could do nothing but wholeheartedly agree. Four years later, I was assisted by the kind intervention of the national accounts division, which provided me with access to the information I needed.

One cannot just walk into a statistical office and ask: How poor are your numbers? One of the tasks of a statistical office is to stand by its numbers as far as is reasonable. At one office in Western Africa, I was reassured that the current GDP estimate was neither an underestimate nor an overestimate. The number was what it was, with no margin of error. This official knew very well, as did I (having spoken to a colleague the day before), that back-of-the-envelope calculations that had been made at the office indicated that the current GDP estimates were undercounts by at least 40–50 percent. The official was just following official protocol as she backed up the numbers generated at her office. My approach was to try to engage in an open communication and ask basic questions such as: How did you come to know? What was your method? The answers to these questions told me what I needed to know. Most of this information is never written down, and therefore much of the interesting information about the production of data is retrievable only through the type of research I have done. It relies on open doors, and I am grateful for all the doors that were opened to me.

As will become clear in the book, I am not equally generous in my thanks to the disseminators of data, particularly the IMF and the World Bank and their data sections. Here, as at the statistical offices, there were exceptions to the rule. I have had long and useful conversations with technical consultants and representatives on country missions. IMF and World Bank researchers who were trying to piece together empirical work that relied on these data sometimes shared their experiences and frustrations with me. In general, though, the IMF and World Bank are more concerned about maintaining the official validity of the numbers they use. This is especially true at the World Bank Data Group. They answered my standard research questions with generic references to data manuals and formulas or, as was often the case, they replied that they did not share this information.

My appreciation goes out to those representatives from the World Bank and the IMF data divisions who attended a talk I gave in November 2011 at the Center of Global Development (CGD) in Washington, D.C. I learned a lot from their questions, responses, and reactions. I am also grateful to the CGD for inviting me and to Alan Gelb for chairing the session.

I gave a similar talk at the Conference on Measuring National Income, Wealth, Poverty, and Inequality in African Countries, held in Cape Town, organized by the International Association of Research in Income and Wealth and Statistics and Statistics South Africa. I thank Liv Hobbelstad Simpson of Statistics Norway for putting the panel together and Derek Blades for very useful comments. In response to my paper, and in particular to the news of the upward revision of GDP in Ghana, Shantay-anan Devarajan, chief economists of the World Bank for Africa, blogged about "Africa's Statistical Tragedy."[6] While I disagree with Devarajan's characterization of the problem (as I argue later here, the problem is basic data availability, not methods of aggregation), his brave statement, which clearly rubbed his own institution's data group the wrong way, has helped pave the way for a careful rethinking of how we measure African economic development. At the conference I also re-met Magnus Ebo Duncan of Ghana Statistical Services, whom I learned a lot from.

I have benefited greatly from discussions and comments following my presentations of pieces of this book on several occasions since 2007. Twice I have been at the School of Oriental and African Studies (SOAS) at the University of London to present my work, once at the History Department in 2009 and a second time at the Centre of African Studies in 2011. I learned a lot from Deborah Johnston at SOAS, with whom I have been discussing measurement problems in African development since my graduate school days. Thanks also to Robin and Kevin Grier at the Economics Department at the University of Oklahoma, who invited me to give a paper there in 2011. Further thanks to Sue Onslow of the Department of International

Development at the London School of Economics and Max Bolt of the Anthropology Department at the same institution who invited me to give papers in 2010 and 2009, respectively. I am very grateful to Boris Samuel and Beatrice Hibou, who invited me to Paris for an interview about development statistics in May 2011. Thanks also to Morten Bøås, who invited me to present at the Fafo Institute for Applied International Studies in Oslo in December 2011. I am grateful to Catherine Boone for inviting me to join her panel and speak on agricultural statistics at the African Studies Association in 2011 and for collaborating with Anthony G. Hopkins to invite me to speak at Department of History and the Department of Government at the University of Texas at Austin in October 2011. Further thanks to Leandro Prados de la Escosura, who invited me to present my work on African growth statistics in Madrid in May 2012.

I have also had the opportunity to present my work on measurement of African economic performance at the Ratio Institute in Stockholm in 2006; at the History and Economic Development Group at the University of London in 2007, 2010, and 2011; at the Sound Economic History Workshop held in Lund 2007; at the Economic History Society in Nottingham in 2008; at the 11th Conference of Africanists in Moscow in May 2008; at the African Studies Association meeting in the United Kingdom in Preston in 2008 and at Oxford in 2010; at the Centre for the Study of African Economies at St. Catherine's College in Oxford in 2009; at the World Economic History Congress in Utrecht in 2009; at the Third European Conference on African Studies in Leipzig in 2009; at the African Studies Association meetings in San Francisco in 2010; and at Third European Congress on World and Global History at the London School of Economics in 2011. Many thanks for the numerous useful suggestions made at this occasions, and special thanks to my co-panelists and the co-organizers of panels at these events; Alexander Moradi deserves particular mention.

In addition, I have presented at the African Economic History Workshop, which has been organized every spring by Gareth Austin (at the London School of Economics from 2006 to 2010 and at the Graduate Institute in Geneva in 2011). Many thanks to the many regular participants at these workshops, who were patient as I have tested and tried different first versions of these chapters on them. Special thanks also to the members of the African Economic History Network, particularly to Erik Green, who hosted to the first meeting of the network at Lund in December 2011.

African economic history is an excellent starting point for learning the skill of probing numbers, tracing their provenance, and considering their historical and economic importance, and it is an even better starting point if you are to be introduced to the subject by Gareth Austin. I was lucky and honored to have been supervised by Gareth as I was writing my doctoral thesis on the measurement of African economic growth at the London School of Economics from 2005 to 2008. After he had supervised my master's thesis he urged me to visit some statistical offices and ask them how they come up with their numbers. The thesis was examined by Anne Booth and Howard Stein, both of whom provided the right pointers toward the questions I pursued in my postdoctoral research.

The research for this book has been funded by Social Sciences & Humanities Research Council of Canada with a Standard Research Grant. I would like to thank Patrick Manning, Daron Acemoglu, Stephen Broadberry, and Alan Heston for serving as external referees for the grant application. A pilot project was funded by an Endowed Research Fellowship and the President's Research Start-Up Grant at Simon Fraser University. Finally, the Simon Fraser University Publication Fund has provided support for editing and indexing. The many conferences and research trips I have made since 2007 have been made possible by contributions from the Ingegerd and Arne Skaugs Research Fund, a Professor Wilhelm Keilhaus Grant, the Erasmus Mundus Outgoing Mobility program, the Norway Bank Fund for Economic Research, an Economic History Association Exploratory Grant, the Radwan Travel and Discovery Fund, a Conradi Grant, and a Hambro Grant.

I would also like to thank the The Nordic Africa Institute in Uppsala, Sweden, and the Economic History Department at London School of Economic and Political Sciences for hosting me as a visiting fellow in 2011.

I have had excellent research assistance from Madeleine Hawkins, who has worked full time on the project since spring 2011, thanks to funding by the Vice President for Research Undergraduate Student Research Award at Simon Fraser University. I am grateful for her enthusiasm for the project and her attention to detail. In addition, Jake Madison, Pierre Nguimkeu, Awa Kane, Gerardo Serra, and Sabiha Jukic have contributed excellent research assistance to particular parts of the book.

I extend my thanks to my colleagues at the School for International Studies at Simon Fraser University, where I have been happily employed since the fall of 2009. Special thanks to John Harriss, Jeff Checkel, Alvaro Pereira, and Tamir Moustafa for reading earlier versions of the manuscript and providing extremely helpful advice. Thanks also to Martha Snodgrass for organizing our research colloquium and to the participants at the colloquiums for repeatedly volunteering useful comments on the many papers I presented to them on African development statistics. I am very grateful to Peter Katzenstein and Roger Haydon at Cornell University Press for believing in this book project. Thanks also to the two anonymous readers for their advice about preparing the final manuscript.

Even though they do not always know what I am up to on my trips to African countries and during the weeks I spend in archives, my family and friends have always believed in me and supported me, and for that I thank them. My beloved wife, Taraneh Ghajar, is a joyful fellow spirit in every aspect of my life. She is also an economic historian, a researcher, and a writer. Without her company on my trips and her help in every aspect of this endeavor, I could not have completed it. And finally, my thanks to our soon-to-be-born little daughter, who provided the best motivation I could possibly have for finishing the book.

INTRODUCTION

Poor Numbers is a book about the role of development statistics in academic debates and in policymaking related to African economic development. This issue is particularly important for developing countries, especially for African economies. Roger Riddel has suggested that "perhaps the most fundamental problem with the available Africa data is that these are widely known to be inaccurate but the degree of inaccuracy cannot easily be judged—itself a sign of the underdevelopment of the region."[1]

This raises a question: Are poor numbers a problem unique to Africa?[2] The famous phrase "lies, damned lies and statistics" should remind us that the problem is a general one.[3] Some controversy invariably surrounds the collection and compilation of official statistics in all countries.[4] The larger problem of the politics and accuracy of numbers is neither geographically specific to Africa nor exclusive to debates on economic development. However, a surprisingly small number of studies examine the role, power, and quality of the numbers applied to issues concerning African economic development. This is surprising because, as argued below, there are good reasons to be very skeptical about official statistics in poor economies. I hope to not only fill this gap in the literature but also contribute to the general scholarly debate about the use of numbers in the social sciences. This literature often notes how numbers have the power to both misinform and inform political debate. In the "least developed economies," and most of these are on the African continent, numbers not only inform politics, they also sometimes transcend political debate altogether. The circle of policymakers is often depoliticized. It is dominated by technocrats, donors, and international organizations that may abort, change, or initiate policies based on very feeble statistics.

African States and Statistics

According to most commonly accepted criteria, the African continent is home to the majority of the least developed countries in the world. All other things being equal, there are a priori grounds to believe that poorer economies will have lower-quality statistics. A poorer economy will have relatively fewer available resources to fund the functions of an official statistics office. Furthermore, the quality and availability and therefore the cost of collecting statistics depends on the record keeping of individuals and companies. In poorer countries, individuals and enterprises are less likely to be officially registered and to keep formal records of their economic activities.

There are additional characteristics pertaining specifically to African states that justify a special regional focus. The work of economic historians has emphasized that African polities were typically land abundant and that labor was relatively scarce.[5] This has implications for the property rights regime. Land has typically not been subject to private property rights and states have not collected taxes on land holdings. Some exceptions confirm this rule. As the work of anthropologists bears out, where land has been relatively scarce, private property rights have developed, but to this day, secure private land titling remains the exception on the continent.[6] This has direct implications for the power of the state. Political science scholars have established a link between historically low population densities and the contemporary weakness of African states.[7] Historians have encapsulated the manner in which colonial and postcolonial African states adapted to their inability to control access to land with the concept of the "gatekeeper state."[8] Unable to collect taxes on land, income, or production, states were reduced to collecting taxes at ports by levying duties on exports and imports.[9] The result is that in most African states the database for aggregating measures of income and growth is weak. For large shares of the economy we have little or no information and the figures involve a great deal of guesswork.

This should suffice to make the general point that statistical capacity in African economies is generally weak. This book shows how this weakness varies systematically through time and space. It is useful to start with the meaning of the word validity, a central term when evaluating evidence in the social sciences. It is most often invoked when the correctness or accuracy of an observation is in question, but it is often forgotten that the Latin root of "validity" means power.[10] The definition of validity as power provides the starting point for the historicization and contextualization of national income estimates in the second chapter. Furthermore, it is useful to remember that the word statistics is directly linked to the word state and refers to the "facts" states collect to get knowledge about their own economic or social conditions.[11] The validity of national economic statistics could thus be interpreted as varying according to the power or legitimacy of the state and/or the agency acting on its behalf. The ability to collect information and taxes are closely related, and the form and extent of monitoring and intervention states have undertaken has varied considerably. Meanwhile, the United Nations System of National Accounts has put a global standard in place. The challenge for a local national statistical office is to provide a measure of the economy. Statistical capacity, or the ability to adhere to the global standard, depends critically on the resources and information available at any given time and place. Activities such as tax collection, census-taking, creating a public record, and conveying statistical information are essential parts of "public politics" and are central to the activities of the state.[12] The capacity to collect taxes and gather information are closely related, and monitoring has been particularly constrained in African states.

In sum, in Africa, the normal predictions about the relationship between poverty and the quality of statistics apply, but in addition, several structural characteristics of African states put them in a weak position in terms of monitoring and collecting information on economic activities.

These structural characteristics are not static, and they do not apply uniformly. How the statistical capacity of African economies has changed, even deteriorated in some places at some times, and how it can be improved is the subject of this book.

Numbers in Social Sciences

So where does this book fit into other studies on "bad statistics"? Peter Andreas and Kelly Greenhill suggest that the social science literature on numbers can be categorized into three main strands.[13] These include studies that look at specific statistical problems and how numbers are manipulated. A second strand of work considers how and why users of data are misled, and a third strand of statistical literature helps consumers of statistics identify "bad" numbers. This literature draws on empirical studies to show how misleading numbers are produced and how and why they are so easily created. Andreas and Greenhill make the point that many studies stop short of pointing out actual policy implications and the mistakes that derive from the use of incorrect or poor numbers.[14]

I argue that poor numbers fundamentally shape what we know about development in sub-Saharan Africa, which in turn shapes how decisions are made. These processes are described more generally by Sally Engle Merry. She describes how the "production and usage" of an indicator may have a knowledge effect and a governance effect.[15] In the production process, the object of measurement is defined and standardized so that the indicator achieves an impression of certainty and objectivity. Merry uses the example of IQ measures to argue that categorization sometimes involves a process of producing the very phenomena that the indicator is supposed to capture.[16] GDP is an equally striking example. The process appears to be standardized and rule based,[17] yet the measurement of the wealth of a nation involves a range of discretionary and sometimes arbitrary decisions. This process goes beyond the gathering and organization of information; it is a distinct form of creating knowledge.

The governance effect is of equally great importance. In this book the term governance is used in the context of how numbers provide an opportunity for transparency and accountability, but it is also related to governance in its more direct sense: numbers provide evidence for decision makers. Indeed, it is often the imperative to govern that provides the rationale and the resources for producing the indicator in the first place.[18] The measure will form the basis for decision making. An indicator may determine whether a particular policy will be implemented, discontinued, or reinforced. Indicators such as income levels or economic growth are crucial for African economies in this context. Each indicator determines the possible ways to allocate resources not only for the state itself but also for the international development community.[19]

Organization of the Argument

The first chapter states and describes the problem. It introduces some of the basics that are essential for understanding the production of economic statistics in African countries and provides a guide to the different types of statistics and the central data providers. It also offers readers a map of the different stakeholders involved in the process. The rest of the chapter is devoted to an analysis of how much we currently know about income levels in African countries. Huge discrepancies and alarming gaps in the knowledge exist, and the chapter concludes with the observation that any ranking of African economies according to GDP levels is misleading.

The second chapter offers a short history of national income accounting in Africa and argues that income statistics need to be fully historicized and contextualized. While these data are often presented as facts, they are better considered as products, and the production of the data is subject to particular economic and political constraints. The statistical capacity of African states was greatly expanded in the late colonial and early postcolonial period, but was greatly impaired during the economic crisis of the 1970s. The importance the statistical offices was neglected in the decades of policy reform that followed—the period of "structural adjustment" in the 1980s and 1990s. In retrospect it may be puzzling that the International Monetary Fund (IMF) and the World Bank embarked on growth-oriented reforms without ensuring that there were reasonable baseline estimates that could plausibly establish whether the economies were growing or stagnating. For statistical offices, structural adjustment meant having to account for more with less: Informal and unrecorded markets were growing, while public spending was curtailed. As a result, our knowledge about the economic effects of structural adjustment is limited. More generally, the economic growth time series, or the cumulative record of annual growth between 1960 and today, for African economies does not appropriately capture changes in economic development.

The third chapter is a direct response to the question economists most commonly ask: "Yes, we know that there are measurement problems. But does it really matter?" The answer is yes, it really does matter. The chapter presents some basic findings about controversy and disagreement between the datasets used in development economics and shows that policymakers, nongovernmental organizations, and scholars draw different conclusions based the different datasets they use in their analysis. The chapter presents some numerical examples that underscore the dangers of ignoring data quality. Numbers we are currently using to allocate scarce resources are not good enough for these purposes, and the econometric models we currently use to explain differences in development performance are far more impressive than the numbers they set out to explain.

The fourth chapter builds on survey information and interviews conducted in field research to paint a picture of the current situation at statistical offices in sub-Saharan Africa. The chapter discusses the policy implications related to the future of statistical systems in sub Africa. The current development agenda is set by the Millennium Development Goals of the United Nations. This has led to some statistical capacity building in a number of countries, while in others there have been perverse effects when statistical capacity is diverted to data collection in order to monitor particular donor targets. At present there is no coherent global strategy for improving the provision of data for development. This is related to the general problem of accountability in development. Sometimes ignorance is bliss, for both the donor community and local political leaders. This book argues that putting a coherent global strategy for statistical capacity building in place is important and stresses that such a standard must be geared toward solving local problems. The book advances several useful and practical steps toward such an agenda.

This book develops some distinct arguments about African development statistics. In the conclusion, these arguments and the implications for the use of numbers in social sciences are discussed more generally. In some cases, it is better to admit ignorance rather than merely hope that either the errors in a dataset will cancel each other out or that the data points are within a reasonable margin of error. In most cases a useful analysis can be conducted if quantitative analysis is based in careful criticism of data sources and is supplemented by qualitative investigation. In order to employ the evidence usefully, one must know the conditions under which the data were produced. This is readily recognized in qualitative analysis, but somehow these principles have not been applied to quantitative evidence. They are readily forgotten in internationally available African development statistics. The numbers we use in development today are too poor for their purpose, and because they are so important, we must do a better job of using and analyzing them. This book shows why and how this is the case. It begins by asking how much we actually know about income and growth in Africa.

1

What Do We Know about Income and Growth in Africa?

What do we know about income and growth in sub-Saharan Africa? The answer is: much less than we like to think. The data are unreliable and potentially seriously misleading. The question is of great importance. Economic growth rates or per capita income estimates are commonly used in statements about development in Africa. Sometimes the data are used to buttress a claim, and other times they are the starting point in defining a problem. If income and growth statistics in Africa do not mean anything, a great part of development analysis and policy targets are similarly meaningless.

The most pressing problem with the quality of data is ignorance among those who use the data. The scholars who are best equipped to analyze the validity and reliability of economic statistics are often data users themselves and are thus reluctant to undermine the datasets that are the bread and butter of scholarly work. When concerns with data are expressed, they are usually limited to some carefully phrased caveats in footnotes. International institutions are the main providers and disseminators of the data, and their programs and plans are often tied to targets and indicators. Thus the pragmatic approach is to accept the data at face value. Privately or in technical consultations advice may be given or direct pressure may be applied during the process of producing the data. Finally, on the domestic political scene, there is little to no transparent debate about the issue. The lack of economic literacy is a problem, and when statistics become the centerpiece of domestic debates, technical discussions give way to political agendas. Thus, the issue of data quality is doubly blurred.

At the same time, both the dependence on and demand for economic statistics is increasing. The aims of development are increasingly stated as quantifiable targets, as they are framed, for instance, by the Millennium Development Goals. The buzzword in the development community is "evidence-based policy," and scholars are using increasingly sophisticated econometric methods, borrowing metaphors and methods from the medical sciences in their work, as if observations about economic development have the accuracy of laboratory experiments. The impression of measurability and accuracy is misleading, and that has broad implications across social science disciplines that deal with issues of African development.

This chapter starts by explaining the concept of national income accounting. It then presents a general picture of how national accounts are implemented in Africa. Empirical evidence shows that the quantitative basis for knowledge about African economic development is very fragile. Leading scholars know that the data are weak, but most data users are incapable of judging exactly how weak and how this weakness affects policy analysis.

What Is National Accounting?

National income measurement is governed by a global standard: the United Nations System of National Accounts (SNA). The foundations of this system were laid out by the Committee of Statistical Experts set up by the League of Nations in 1939. The committee produced a "Recommended System of Accounts," a paper written by Richard Stone. The first version of the SNA was created by the National Accounts Research Unit of the Organization for European Economic Co-operation.[1] This unit, chaired by Richard Stone, produced "A System of National Accounts and

Supporting Tables" in 1953. The standards of national accounts have since been revised three times, so that there are four versions:[2] in addition to the SNA 1953, there are also SNA 1968, SNA 1993, and SNA 2008. However, Michael Ward argues that "although they pay lip service to the subsequent revisions . . . many countries still adhere to the basic system and its corresponding accounting foundations as first set out."[3]

Many people are not familiar with this system and may scarcely have heard of it, but it is the framework that generates most of our basic information about national economies. Its main product is the most important development indicators of them all: national income and economic growth. In theory, this global norm is now followed by all members of the UN member states. Data is regularly collected by the UN Statistical Office and disseminated by its agencies to rate and rank all the wealth and progress of the nations of the world. In the words of Yoshiko Herrera: "The scope of the SNA as an international institution and the level of cooperation and coordination that it demands are nothing short of heroic."[4]

The resulting metric, and the object of study in this book, is gross domestic product (GDP), or gross national income (GNI), colloquially referred to as national income. This statistic is used to measure the size of an economy, and this is the data by which countries are ranked as developed or less developed. Economic growth is a measure of change in real GDP per capita. In theory, this measure is obtained by combining the value of all of the value-added activities in an economy throughout one year and dividing that total by the size of a country's population in that year. This outcome is then deflated by a measure of price changes, and finally the result is compared with the equivalent figure for the previous year. This assumes that the data fully covers all activities and that the outputs and inputs within each activity are properly valued and quantified. It further assumes that the population is properly enumerated from year to year and that the deflation measure is timely and correct. In practice, this measure does not reach that assumed level of accuracy, even in countries with developed economies.[5] Some economic activity is not measured, a population census is usually undertaken only once a decade, and the construction of comparable price indices involves compromises about which goods and services to include in the index. The disparity between the measure in theory and the measure in practice is the subject of this book.

National Accounts in Africa: The Main Problems

The central issue in national income accounting is deciding which economic activities and actors should and can be included in the official accounts.[6] This is often referred to as the "production boundary." Since the application of the United Nations Standard of National Accounts, there has been a discussion about where one should draw this line. In western economies, this means that the economic value of the activities of "housewives" are not accounted for. With specific reference to African economies, Brian van Arkadie noted that the "existence of a large amount of 'subsistence' activity (or, at least economic activity which does not result in a recorded marketed transaction) makes Pigou's famous quip about the national accounting consequences of marrying your cook much more than a mere curiosity."[7] In other words, if you marry your cook, the value assigned to the activity of preparing meals will move outside the production boundary and the service provided will no longer be considered as part of the domestic production of goods and services.

In all economies a distinction between recorded and unrecorded economic activity exists. In "developed" economies, unrecorded activity consists of illegitimate economic activity and economic activity within the family household. In most African economies, the unrecorded economy is so large and therefore so economically important that to leave it unrecorded is unsatisfactory. However, its inclusion in the national accounts has been constrained by the availability of data. This has resulted in a variety of innovative accounting practices at the individual statistical offices. This section provides a general picture of some of the basic methods used at statistical offices throughout sub-Saharan Africa. A more nuanced picture, showing which sources and methods were used at different times and places across sub-Saharan Africa is discussed in chapter 2.[8]

In theory, there are three distinct ways of aggregating GDP: the income method, the expenditure method, and the production method. Again in theory, these are supposed to be reached independently. and their respective results should be balanced. The first approach adds up profits, rents, interest, dividends, salaries, and wages. In practice, this approach has not been suitable for estimating the GDP of African economies. The main component of the method would be profits earned by farmers, and this information is not directly available. The expenditure approach is more feasible, at least at first glance. Its components are private consumption, investment, government consumption, and the balance of exports and imports. The problem here is personal consumption and the part of capital formation related to rural and small-scale economic activities. The production method totals estimates of value added (output minus intermediate consumption) per sector (agriculture, mining, manufacturing, construction, and different services) to equal total value added, or GDP. This method has been preferred in official national income accounting in postcolonial Africa. While the System of National Accounts suggests that all three methods should be estimated independently, thus providing a check on the accuracy of each estimate, this practice is not often followed. Postcolonial national accounts have typically been estimated using the production method, while expenditure on private consumption has typically not been estimated independently but has been derived as what is called a "residual." In practice, this means that instead of reaching an independent estimate of this important component, an estimate is reached by subtracting all other components of expenditures from the GDP estimate that was reached using the production approach.

GDP statistics from African countries, then, are best guesses of aggregate production. It is important to keep in mind that national income is a composite measure. Statisticians at the Kenyan central statistical office approach the issue pragmatically: "It is possible to use a number of criteria in order to assess the progress of the economy, but the usual measure of the rate of economic development is the estimate of gross domestic product. Estimates of domestic product are not, however, among those statistics which are a definite measure to which there can be only one precise measure comparable to the number of oranges in a bag. It is in fact an aggregation of numerous data which vary substantially in order of precision."[9] This was more clearly stated in an appendix to the national accounts for 1978 prepared at the statistical office in Lusaka. The report differentiated between two types of guesses; one asterisk indicated a "guestimate" and two asterisks meant a "guestimate with a weak basis."[10] These quotes highlight the importance of looking carefully at the individual components of this composite measure. The aggregate, here generically referred to as national income, is a result of pragmatic decisions at the statistical offices that are subject to the availability of data, financial resources, and political instructions.

The quality of a national income estimate is thus a result of the quality of the activities at a statistical office. National accounts divisions depend on data that are produced in different parts of a statistical office—particularly for data on population, agricultural and industrial production, and prices. The supply of data from these subdivisions is subject to the number of available data collectors and the level of funds available for collecting and processing data. Frequently statistical offices rely on data made available from other public and private bodies. For example, agricultural data typically comes from a ministry of agriculture or its equivalent. In some sectors that are dominated by a few large operators, such as construction, mining, electricity, water, finance, communications, and transportation, offices depend on the supply of data from these private or public entities.

There is a distinction between "survey data" and "administrative data." A survey is a specific tool the statistical office uses to collect responses from individual agents. Whether or not a statistical office is able to conduct surveys depends on its access to specific funding, as the normal budget allowance typically covers only the basic operation costs of the office. The administrative data are collected by public bodies to facilitate day-to-day governance and reflect the ambitions and extent of the activities of the state. The availability of data, which varies from country to country and according to the circumstances at a given time, determines the quality of the final estimates.

The basic questions that determine the quality of GDP numbers are whether the statistical office has any data, how good those numbers are, and what the national accountants do when data are missing. The first step in the aggregation process is to create a baseline estimate or a benchmark year, which is year 1 in the statistical series. If everything is accounted for in year 1, one can later safely assume that any additions of people, goods, and services are additions and thus are progress or growth. The most exhaustive instrument is a census in which everything is about a "population" is recorded. This can be a census of population of the country, agricultural production, or the transport sector. If a census is not available, a survey may be used. Surveys contain some information about a sample of the total. If there ever was a census, the data compiler can aggregate its results, assuming that the sample is representative. If there is no total population to relate this survey to, the statistician will have to make a guesstimate, literally making up the missing information without any official guidelines.

An example would be an informal sector survey. The survey will yield information on earnings of individuals in this sector but the statistician does not know the total number of participants in the sector. Often there is no data. When data on levels of economic activity are missing, GDP compilers have to rely on estimation by proxy, or assumed relationships. A classic example is when no data on food production exists and the statistician assumes a per capita intake of calories and then multiplies that by a guess of the farming population to get a measure of how much food is produced but not marketed in official channels or recorded markets. Data are usually missing for parts of the service sector, and a common method of estimating the value of that sector is to assume a proportional relationship with the production of other physical goods.

When an estimate of the level of national income for a given year has been reached, the wealth of the nation is measured. The next step is to measure economic growth, in order to monitor the progress of the nation. It is easy to get the impression that this would simply entail aggregating all available data once more and comparing the current year with previous years. However, the way this is done in practice is quite different. The estimates of levels for the individual sector form the starting point. In some categories of analysis, such as government expenditures and turnover for larger businesses, statisticians are able to compare the total for one year with another, but for large parts of the economy they usually rely on so-called performance indicators, or proxies. These indicators use annual data collected from public bodies and private businesses, supplemented by data on exports and imports. Typical examples of performance indicators use cement production and/or imports as a proxy for growth in a construction sector[11] or the number of new official licenses as proxies for growth in a transport sector.

There is a basic distinction between the process of aggregating an estimate of income levels and the process of estimating economic growth. One can think of it in terms of weight. The value assigned to a weight may be inaccurate. If the degree of inaccuracy was consistent, it would not matter much in terms of measuring change. That is, even if a weight shows you to be too heavy, if the weight is equally skewed in the same direction the next year, you would at least know with accuracy how much weight they have gained or lost. There is one mathematical caveat to this: since change is measured in percentage, you will appear to be gaining weight at a faster rate if the weight showed you to be lighter than you really were. Following from these principles, one could expect the following: the more the level of GDP is an underestimation, the more the rate of growth will be an overestimation. However, this isn't quite the way it works with complex statistical measures. It is mathematically true when one is measuring the weight of a person or the number of oranges in a bag but it is not automatically true when one is measuring GDP, because the GDP is a composite index with a base year.

The base year estimate is of crucial importance. It determines the proportional shares of different sectors of the economy. The issues that can follow when one uses composite indexes are generally referred the as the "index number problem."[12] The size of each individual sector in the base year determines the impact the growth in one sector has on the aggregate growth in the following years. In order to measure "real" economic growth, the economy is accounted for in the base year's prices. This is done by either deflating a sector with a measure of inflation over time (this method is often used for data from service sectors) or by expressing output in the base year prices directly using volumes, which are multiplied with the prices in the reference and/or base year. Generally speaking, the less "normal" and the older the base year is, the more misleading the growth series will be. For example, if the base year is a drought year, the growth in the ensuing years will be exaggerated (assuming that they are not drought years as well). This also means that if one part of the economy is underestimated, its contribution to aggregate growth will also be underestimated. Thus, it does not automatically follow that an economy that has an underestimated income level will display faster economic growth in the future. If the share of a rapid-growing sector—such as a new export crop, the informal economy, or a service such as telecommunications—was erroneously judged to be very small in the base year, growth will be underestimated in the years that follow, until a new base year is made and methods and data are revised.

Data availability and data sources are what matter most in terms of the quality of statistics. Statistical methods and models matter far less. For the uninitiated observer, the sophistication of the statistical techniques required to create an appropriately weighted index may seem complex. Yet it is not technical skills or sophistication of econometric software that is the constraining factor for computation. What matters is the availability of data. A statistician can do very little about a basic lack of data.

Once the data availability is determined, the right way to proceed is to pose two questions: Is the resulting measure is valid? Are the measures reliable? The concept of validity is related to whether the measure is accurate,[13] and the concept of reliability is related to whether the measure is similarly inaccurate or accurate each time. Thus, reliability differs from validity: when a measure has a predictable error, this error would make the measure invalid, but the measure would still be reliable. In terms of GDP per capita, if the level estimates are inaccurate but this inaccuracy is the same across time, the evidence can still be useful for understanding economic change. Similarly, if the national income all countries were incorrectly measured with the same error, one could still compare between countries. Unfortunately, this is not the case. African development statistics have both validity and reliability problems. The basic reason is that GDP aggregates economies that are, in large part, unrecorded. The statistical reasoning is that once you have a valid measure, or, in other words, once all economic activities are accounted for,[14] you will know that all "new" activities are "economic growth," not simply previously unrecorded economic activities. Exhaustiveness has not been reached, and it is probably not an attainable goal in the foreseeable future. Therefore, all GDP statistics have both reliability and validity problems. Another way of phrasing this is that we do not know very much about income and growth in Africa. Yet data purporting to measure these things are still produced, disseminated, and used. The next section surveys the validity and reliability of internationally available GDP estimates from sub-Saharan Africa.

A Survey of the National Income Evidence

So where do data users go when they want to know the GDP level of a country? There are three major sources of national income data: the World Development Indicators, the Penn World Tables, and the datasets of Angus Maddison.[15] Each is based on national account files as prepared by the respective national statistical agencies, but they differ in the modifications they use, the purchasing adjustments they use, and according to their currencies. The World Development Indicators database is maintained by the World Bank Group. It is the data source most commonly used in public domains such as politics and the media.[16] The second source is from a database maintained by economists at the University of Pennsylvania. This database has been updated since the first version was published in 1980. The most recent version was published in 2011 as version 7.0. These data are the ones most commonly used by growth economists in cross-country growth regressions. A third source of income data are the datasets produced by Angus Maddison. These datasets are commonly used by economic historians and economists and are regularly updated by the Groningen Growth and Development Center at the University of Groningen.

So what do we know about income levels in Africa? In table 1.1, the countries are ranked according to the reported GDP per capita for year 2000; the poorest countries are at the top and the richest countries are at the bottom. Only sub-Saharan African economies are ranked in the table, and the rankings include only countries for which GDP per capita data for the year 2000 is available from all three sources.[17] The table shows the resulting ranking from the three different data sources. The dollar values (as reported after each country name in the table) do not agree. This is not surprising. The GDP estimates have been converted into international comparable U.S. dollars using different formulas. In this particular exercise we are looking for coherence between the different datasets in the relative ranking of African economies.

The three sources agree on the ranking of some countries but disagree on most and in some cases with a large discrepancy. The sources agree unanimously that the Democratic Republic of Congo (DRC), formerly Zaire, is the poorest country. It should be noted that its income is probably grossly understated in the official statistics. MacGaffey noted this in 1991, and the extent of underestimation in DRC has certainly not improved since then.[18] Among the ten poorest economies, only six consistently appear in that bracket according to all three sources: the DRC, Sierra Leone, Niger, Burundi, Tanzania, and Ethiopia. There is better agreement among sources about which are the ten richest countries. There is wide variation in the relative ranking, but nine out of ten countries appear in the top ten groups of all three sources.

There are also large fluctuations in the rankings. When considering the lowest and highest rank of a country across the three sources, some stand out. The most uncertainty occurs with regard to the placement of Guinea, which Maddison ranks as the seventh poorest economy. But Penn World

Table 1.1. African Economies ranked by per capita GDP (in international USD)

Rank	Maddison	Per capita GDP	World Development Institute	Per capita GDP	Penn World Tables	Per capita GDP
1	Congo-Kinshasa	217	Congo-Kinshasa	92	Congo-Kinshasa	359
2	Sierra Leone	410	Ethiopia	115	Liberia	472
3	Chad	429	Burundi	139	Sierra Leone	684
4	Niger	486	Sierra Leone	153	Burundi	699
5	Burundi	496	Malawi	169	Ethiopia	725
6	Tanzania	535	Tanzania	190	Guinea-Bissau	762
7	Guinea	572	Liberia	191	Niger	807
8	Central African Rep.	576	Mozambique	191	Tanzania	817
9	Comoro Islands	581	Niger	200	Togo	823
10	Ethiopia	605	Guinea-Bissau	210	Madagascar	823
11	Togo	614	Chad	218	Chad	830
12	Zambia	645	Rwanda	242	Malawi	839
13	Malawi	656	Burkina Faso	243	Zambia	866
14	Guinea-Bissau	681	Madagascar	246	Burkina Faso	933
15	Madagascar	706	Nigeria	254	Central African Rep.	945
16	Angola	765	Mali	294	Gambia	954
17	Uganda	797	Sudan	313	Rwanda	1,018
18	Rwanda	819	Togo	323	Mali	1,047
19	Mali	892	Kenya	328	Sudan	1,048
20	Gambia	895	Central African Rep.	339	Uganda	1,058
21	Burkina Faso	921	São Tomé & Principe	341	Nigeria	1,074
22	Liberia	990	Uganda	348	Mozambique	1,093
23	Sudan	991	Gambia	370	Benin	1,251
24	Mauritania	1,017	Zambia	394	Kenya	1,268
25	Kenya	1,031	Ghana	413	Congo-Brazzaville	1,286
26	Cameroon	1,082	Benin	414	São Tomé & Principe	1,300
27	São Tomé & Principe	1,226	Comoros	436	Comoros	1,359
28	Nigeria	1,251	Mauritania	495	Ghana	1,392
29	Ghana	1,270	Angola	524	Mauritania	1,521
30	Benin	1,283	Lesotho	548	Senegal	1,571
31	Zimbabwe	1,328	Guinea	605	Lesotho	1,834
32	Côte d'Ivoire	1,352	Senegal	609	Angola	1,975

Rank	Maddison	Per capita GDP	World Development Institute	Per capita GDP	Penn World Tables	Per capita GDP
33	Senegal	1,358	Zimbabwe	620	Cote d'Ivoire	2,171
34	Mozambique	1,365	Cameroon	675	Cameroon	2,472
35	Lesotho	1,490	Cote d'Ivoire	739	Guinea	2,546
36	Cape Verde	1,777	Congo-Brazzaville	791	Zimbabwe	3,256
37	Congo-Brazzaville	2,005	Swaziland	1,538	Cape Verde	4,984
38	Swaziland	2,630	Cape Verde	1,541	Namibia	5,269
39	Namibia	3,637	Equatorial Guinea	1,599	Equatorial Guinea	6,495
40	Gabon	3,847	Namibia	2,366	Botswana	7,256
41	South Africa	3,978	Botswana	3,931	South Africa	8,226
42	Botswana	4,269	South Africa	4,020	Swaziland	8,517
43	Seychelles	6,354	Mauritius	4,104	Gabon	10,439
44	Equatorial Guinea	7,973	Gabon	4,378	Seychelles	10,593
45	Mauritius	10,652	Seychelles	6,557	Mauritius	15,121

Source: Alan Heston, Robert Summers, and Bettina Aten, Penn World Table Version 6.2, Center for International Comparisons of Production, Income and Prices, University of Pennsylvania, 2006; Angus Maddison, Historical Statistics of the World Economy: 1-2006 AD, 2009; World Development Indicators (World Bank, Washington, DC, 2007). Note that this table was created in 2009. These datasets are continually updated, and the numbers will have changed somewhat since then.

Tables lists it one spot short of the category of the ten richest African countries in GDP per capita terms. The World Bank ranks Mozambique as the eighth poorest country, while Maddison places it among the twelve richest economies. Across the three sources, Liberia jumps twenty places: Penn World Tables ranks it as the second poorest, yet Maddison ranks it as richer than most African countries. Angola, Central African Republic, Comoros, Congo-Brazzaville, Nigeria and Zambia all make leaps of more than ten places in the rankings from one source to the other, leaving the relative ranking of one-fifth of the countries as a matter of high uncertainty.[19]

What kind of agreement should one expect? Using the example of weight introduced above, it could be equated with measuring the weight of forty-five different bags of flour with three different scales. In this case one might assume some kind of systematic error. One scale might be off and thus would measure items to be a bit heavier or lighter than the other scales. This would mean a clearly discernible and stable plus or minus error attributable to the specific scale but an agreement in ranking that would be extremely close to 100 percent. GDP is, after all, a measure of the income of the same country in the same year, theoretically using the same method. It is obvious from this table that the issue is not just systematic error in measurement between the sources, as in the example of a faulty scale. Instead, it is as if each time the income is measured, it is done using a different scale with an unknown margin or direction of error.

A pressing question is whether this inconsistency in reporting in different datasets is common to all income data. It is true that there is always some variation between estimates, depending on which source of data was used and what method was chosen to express the data in international currency. However, the range of variation (and therefore uncertainty of the information) deriving from African economies is much larger. A similar comparison using income estimates of twenty-two Latin American countries from the Maddison and World Development Institute datasets showed that the sources agreed about the relative income ranking for the majority of the countries. Thus, the same data sources are more reliable on Latin American countries.[20]

Why is there so much disagreement in the African data? As mentioned, the systematic variation in cash values means that the income per capita measures are quoted in international dollars from different years: Maddison uses 1990, the World Development Indicators database uses 1995 and the Penn World Tables uses 1996. Furthermore, the income estimates reported in datasets provided by the Penn World Tables and the World Development Indicators differ because different formulas were used to calculate the international price estimates. The methods used to express the income estimates are quite similar and should not in themselves account for such differences in ranking.[21] Maddison notes that "the discrepancy between the World Bank and my estimates is bigger than can be explained by the bias of EKS [Elteto, Koves, and Szulc] measure."[22] The main problem lies with the primary source. The international GDP per capita datasets all take the national account files, as provided by the appropriate statistical agencies, as a starting point. Therefore, the datasets inherit all of the problems with data quality with the data from the country where the data are collected.

The dataset provider has a multitude of national accounts data files to pick from, and the process of splicing various series together involves some discretion. The process used to select and harmonize series is not accounted for in a specific and transparent manner in the data descriptions that accompany published datasets. In theory, the only difference between national data and international income and growth data is that the latter are expressed in international prices. But there are other, more important sources of disagreement. The data series provided by the national statistical agencies are subject to revisions, and various official series exist with different base years that cover the same time period.

This problem goes back to the nature of these datasets. These are not truly global datasets; they are national data from various states that international databases disseminate. The United Nations Statistical Office was the first organization to collect national accounts data through an annual questionnaire sent out to member countries. According to Michael Ward, this arrangement initially worked well, especially before the petroleum crises in 1973 and 1978, but thereafter "the practical work on national accounts both in UNSO and in the member countries got farther and farther behind. Increasingly other international agencies and the major donors began to express their frustration at the poor quality and timeliness of the national accounts data."[23] In 1981, Kpedekpo and Arya commented on the status of national accounts in Africa: "Reflecting the practice of the industrial countries, it focuses attention heavily on the main tables, especially the gross domestic product (GDP), and the international agencies reinforce this bias by requesting national statistics offices to provide data for aggregates long before the preparation is defensible, resulting in figures that are little better than random numbers."[24]

Ward describes how the World Bank in particular was concerned about the fact that some nations did not provide data in a timely manner. He notes that despite the fact that "the Bank never had a mandate to compile statistics and was never involved in actual basic data collection for the national accounts," in the 1980s it started publishing its own gross national income per capita numbers in U.S. dollars.[25] These estimates sometimes contradicted official data, but they became widely accepted "because they appeared more current and consistent."[26] Furthermore, country missions and "interactions with government at the highest level ensured that [World Bank] officials were granted access to data that others did not have. . . . Numbers that were subsequently generated . . . were, in some political sense, endorsed by those in authority."[27] There is no information about how, when, and why these numbers came about,[28] and the most recent tables of GDP estimates invariably include some estimates that have different provenance and varying degree of quality. How this has in turn led to contradictory numbers was clearly displayed in table 1.1.

Alwyn Young discovered the problem of absent data and unclear provenance when attempting to build up and revise a database for African measures of living standards. He argued that the underlying data supporting estimates for living standards are minimal or nonexistent.[29] Young reports that for twenty-four of the forty-five countries for which the Penn World Tables provides international price data, there are in fact no benchmark studies of prices that should form the basis of an international price data comparison. Although the UN reports national accounts in constant prices for forty-seven sub-Saharan African countries from 1991 to 2004, it has received data for less than half of these 1,410 observations, and for fifteen of the countries no underlying data has been received at all.[30] The World Bank Statistics Manual explains that when the data are missing, the bank uses "a method for filling the data gap, which is based on the assumption that the growth of the variable from a period for which data exists has been the same as the average growth for those other countries in the same regional or income grouping, where data exists for both periods."[31]

Possibly to reassure data users, it reports that "these gap-filling procedures are run automatically, with no human intervention."[32] It is important to uncover which part of the data are actually produced by the statistical offices and which are simply imputations, created with "no human intervention." This method is used to fill in the gaps when creating regional data. When data are missing for individual countries, the deliberations of the data group at the World Bank and advice from the country missions are used to generate recent country estimates.

This procedure results in discrepancies between GDP data provided from the national statistical offices and those generated at the World Bank. In turn, different scholars and databases report different growth and income numbers, and as time passes, the economic history of these countries, as written by numbers, is influenced as much by political negotiations as they are by actual economic change in the respective countries. In order to get a feeling for how serious this problem is, I gathered the most recent available data from the World Bank and the most recent available data available at the country level. This information is summarized in table 1.2. The country-level information was gathered through the respective national statistical office websites. Where possible, the data has been confirmed or gathered via personal communication and e-mails as a part of a survey of methods and sources in use at the national statistical offices in African economies.[33] These data make it possible to check for consistency between national statistical office information and the information provided by the World Bank and the statistical offices in sub-Saharan Africa. The first column records the year of the latest estimate that was prepared. The second column reports the base year for the constant price estimates, the third column reports the most recent GDP estimate at current prices as supplied by the statistical office, and the fourth column shows the same information as reported in the WDI database. The final column compares the latest estimates from the two sources.

The list shows great variation, testament to the confusion regarding sub-Saharan African economic growth and income. Only seventeen of the forty-seven countries had prepared estimates for the year 2009 or 2010 at the time of inquiry in 2011. Despite the absence of data, the World Bank provides data in both constant and current prices for all of these countries until and including the year 2009. This means more than half of the rankings of African economies up to 2009 may be pure guesswork. It is not clear from the World Bank database whether or when these data are official, official preliminary data, projections based on previous country performance, projections based on performance of neighboring countries, or conjectures based on "expert" advice. It also implies that about half of the underlying data for continent-wide growth statistics are actually missing and have been created by the World Bank through unclear procedures. The prevailing sentiment is that data availability is more important than the quality of the data that are supplied.

The base year is of crucial importance. It is interesting to note that the base year used by the World Bank is different from that reported by the respective national statistical office for Burundi, Central African Republic, Republic of Congo, Equatorial Guinea, Gabon, the Gambia, Guinea, Guinea-Bissau, Lesotho, Malawi, Mauritius, Niger, Nigeria, Rwanda, Seychelles, Sierra Leone, Sudan, and Uganda. In addition, it has not been possible to establish which base year is currently in use at the national

Table 1.2. Availability of national accounts data at statistical offices in Africa and comparison of country-level GDP and World Development Institute GDP

Country	Estimate	Base year	GDP from country[1]	GDP from WDI[1]	% difference
Angola	–	–	–	5,989	
Benin	2007	–	2,642	2,658	–0.6
Botswana	2004	1993/94	47	47	0.0
Burkina Faso	2005	1999	2,881	2,863	0.6
Burundi[2,3]	2007	2006	1403	1,060	32.4
Cameroon[2]	2009	2002	11,040	10,474	5.4
Cape Verde[2,3]	2007	1980	107	107	0.0
Central African Republic[3]	2003	1985	670	662	1.2
Chad[3]	2009	–	3,622	3,228	12.2
Comoros[3]	–	–	–	153	
Cote d'Ivoire	2005	1996	9,012	8,631	4.4
Democratic Republic of Congo[3]	–	–	–	3,366	
Djibouti[3]	2000	–	91	–	
Equatorial Guinea[3]	2002	1985	1,524	1,496	1.9
Eritrea[3]	–	–	–	18	
Gabon[3]	2008	2001	7,033	6,509	8.1
Gambia[3]	2008	2004	23	18	27.8
Ghana[2]	2009	2006	37	37	0.0
Guinea[2,3]	2008	2003	20,982	20,780	1.0
Guinea-Bissau[3]	2006	1986	172	303	–43.2
Kenya[2]	2009	2001	2,366	2,274	4.0
Lesotho[2,3]	2008	2004	13	13	0.0
Liberia[3]	–	–	–	59,840	
Madagascar	2009	1984	16,802	16,604	1.2
Malawi[2,3]	2007	2007	511	484	5.6
Mali[2,3]	2008	1997	–	3,067	
Mauritania[2,3]	2007	2005	915	734	24.7
Mauritius[2,3]	2010	2007	300	300	0.0
Mozambique[2]	2009	2003	326	280	16.4

Country	Estimate	Base year	GDP from country[1]	GDP from WDI[1]	% difference
Namibia	2008	2004	82	74	10.8
Niger[2, 3]	2010	2006	2,748	2,748	0.0
Nigeria[2, 3]	2008	1990	24,665	24,553	0.5
Republic of Congo[3]	2009	1990	3,870	4,523	−14.4
Rwanda[3]	2010	2006	3,282	3282	0.0
Sao Tome and Principe	2006	2001	1,445	1,546	−6.5
Senegal[2]	2009	1999	6,029	6,023	0.1
Seychelles[2, 3]	2008	2006	9	9	0.0
Sierra Leone[2, 3]	2007	2001	4,967	5,829	−14.8
Somalia[3]	–	–	–	1,347,900	
South Africa[2]	2010	2005	2,663	2,663	0.0
Sudan[4]	–	–	–	–	
Swaziland[3]	–	–	–	12,771	
Togo[3]	–	–	–	28,213	
Tanzania[2]	2010	2001	32,294	32,493	−0.6
Uganda[2, 3]	2009	2002	34,166	30,101	13.5
Zambia[2]	2008	1994	55,211	54,839	0.7
Zimbabwe[2]	–	–	–	5,625	

[1] In local currency, in billions.

[2] Information obtained from the statistical office personally.

[3] The base year used by the World Bank is different than that reported by the national government (or information not available).

[4] For Sudan, the WDI reported GDP in Sudanese pounds (9,871.88), while the official data are reported in the Sudanese dinars. Therefore Sudan is excluded on this table.

Source: World Development Indicators and national statistical office websites. I have adjusted the WDI data using the exchange rates reported for the year 2006.

statistical office in Benin, Chad, Comoros, Democratic Republic of Congo, Djibouti, Eritrea, Ethiopia, Guyana, Liberia, Mali, Swaziland, Togo, and Zimbabwe.[34] This explains some of the discrepancy between World Bank and official data, as reported in the last column in table 1.2.

Only ten of these countries have a base year that is less than a decade old. The significance of outdated base years was touched upon previously, but it might be reemphasized here with an empirical example. As explained previously, the base year determines the year for which prices are held constant when attempting to measure real economic change. In the case of Kenya, with a base year of 2001, one would account for coffee output for the year 2008 as it would be valued in 2001. This is done in order to distinguish economic growth from price increases. But the choice of base year has further implications. The index problem applies: the weight of each sector is also determined from its 2001 value. Thus, a sector that was small in 2001 but then grew would contribute proportionally less than its true weight to aggregate growth in 2008. A relevant example for Kenya would be the horticulture sector, which is larger today than it was in 2001. When GDP is revised and the base year is changed, the statistician can reweight the relative importance of the different sectors and change or reconsider methods and data sources.

A general rule of thumb is that the base year should be changed every decade to avoid major distortions. At the IMF Statistics Department, regional technical advisors remind national authorities that international best practice is to rebase every five years.[35] As seen in table 1.2, that is often not the case in practice. As far as it was possible to verify, only fourteen of the countries in table 1.2 have a base year from the last decade. How important is this variation? It is extremely likely that the income of the countries that use an outdated base year is severely underestimated. Ghana is one of the countries with an up-to-date base year: 2006. The revision using the new base year was done according to the global standards of national accounting. It was completed in 2010. According to the official report published by Ghana Statistical Services, GDP was 21.7 billion cedi in the previous 1993 series, while the national income was 36.9 billion cedi according to the new 2006 series.[36] The development community received this revision with some bewilderment. One headline of a blog post for the Centre for Global Development on November 5 2010 read: "Ghana Says, Hey, Guess What? We're Not Poor Anymore!" The author noted that this was good news, but also said that it raised questions about whether development numbers could be trusted: "Everyone knows that data is dubious, but this seems to add a whole new level of doubt."[37] Others took the revision as a fact. Bloggers and development experts Andy Sumner and Charles Kenny used the case of the sudden increase in measured wealth in sub-Saharan Africa as a prompting fact to explain to the readers of the *Guardian* "How 28 Poor Countries Escaped the Poverty Trap."[38]

In 2011, the World Bank accepted the new data series from Ghana, and it upgraded Ghana's status from a poor country to a lower-middle-income country. Up until last year, the base year for Ghana's national accounts was 1993. That is to say that all new information on economic activity was accounted for using the categories and weights from the early 1990s. The revised GDP estimate has been reached using new methods of accounting, and the new base year of 2006 has allowed the accountants to include new statistical material. Economies and societies can change quite a lot over almost two decades. For example, in 1993 the mobile phone had not yet arrived in Ghana; today it is widely accepted that the majority of Ghana's population use mobile phones.[39] When 1993 was the base year, this information could not be included: the communications sector was accounted for through the number of home phones and receipts from the national telecommunication company.[40]

When the current president, John Atta Mills, was campaigning in the presidential elections in 2008, one of his promises was to take Ghana to low-middle-income status by 2020. Was this sudden increase in Ghana's GDP a result of pressure to deliver on the president's electoral promises? On face value it could be easy to interpret the revision as politically motivated, but there are also incentives not to revise upward. Only countries classified as poor are eligible for loans on concessional terms from the International Development Association, the World Bank institution that provides support for the world's poorest countries. This classification depends on World Bank endorsement. When the World Bank gave the revised national income estimates its official stamp of approval, it reclassified Ghana as a low-middle-income country from its previous status as a low-income country.[41] The World Bank reported that the rebased national accounts followed a review of the nation's underlying statistical methodology by IMF advisors. This matches the information I collected when I visited Ghana Statistical Services in February 2010. An upward revision was expected, but at that time it was estimated to be about 45 percent. It was clear that using better data and better methods and thereby improving the coverage of economic activities in Ghana would create an upward revision.[42] Before the revision was announced, there were consultations between the statistical office, the IMF, the executive branch of government, the central bank, commercial banks, and think tanks in Ghana.

The data on national income in Ghana are certainly much improved. But the upward revision raises other serious knowledge problems: how should we now rank Ghana compared to other economies? Recall the previous example of different scales for measuring weight that I likened to the processes involved with base year measurements. While the measurement of Ghana's economy is probably more valid as a result of these changes—more accurately measuring its true wealth—serious issues of reliability are now appearing. It is difficult to assess to what extent our previous measures of Ghana were incorrect: when did Ghana really become a middle-income country? Previous accounts of recent and even long-term growth have been made on an invalid basis, and consequently our statements about the country's growth are unreliable.

What about making comparisons with Ghana's neighboring countries that are still using base years, statistical data, and methods that are out of date? The base year for Nigeria, the largest economy in sub-Saharan Africa, is currently 1993. While I am writing this there are reports that Nigeria is planning a rebasing and that Nigeria's GDP will be increased by at least 50 percent as a result.[43] Future revisions are likely to take place across many countries. Upon direct questioning in the survey, most statisticians in national accounts divisions replied affirmatively to the question: "Do you think that GDP is underestimated today?" Of the twenty-three countries I surveyed for this book,[44] only Namibia, Sierra Leone, and the Seychelles were satisfied that GDP estimates were covering the whole economy, while representatives from eighteen countries responded that GDP was underestimated.[45]

In the last column in table 1.2 the most recent estimate in local currency at current prices is compared with the same data from the World Bank.[46] This discrepancy is accounted for by the fact that national statistical offices and the World Bank often do not use the same base years for their accounts. For example, Burundi has updated its base year to 2006, while the World Bank series still uses 1980 as its base year. The result is that the World Bank reports a much lower GDP for Burundi, to the dismay of the national accounts division.[47]

In conclusion, rankings of African economies according to GDP levels should not be taken at face value. In large part, the information recorded in the databases is the result of automatic data permutations, preliminary estimates, or negotiated numbers. Thus, the differences in GDP levels that can be observed in the databases are as likely to be the product of statistical methods as they are to provide information about economic realities. The underlying data is so poor and there are so many different methods of measurement and aggregation that any upward or downward adjustment can find a technocratic or procedural justification. This makes it very hard to distinguish what can be classified as "better data" from what is more politically convenient data. Table 1.1 shows that any ranking of African economies according to GDP levels is misleading. Table 1.2 indicates a very uneven application of methods and data. Some countries are able to report data on a regular basis and have updated base years, while others are lagging behind. This information is obscured if one downloads the data directly from the international databases. The lack of transparency in reporting and the paucity of information accompanying the datasets mean that data users are easily misled. The lack of attention to the basis for the underlying data and to measurement methods means that current income and growth numbers are a poor basis for measuring development in sub-Saharan Africa. The final section of this chapter discusses the current knowledge about African development statistics and charts the road toward fully understanding the nature of the knowledge problem.

What Do We Know?

On August 8, 2009, *The Economist* reported that growth and income estimates from poor economies, especially those in sub-Saharan Africa, were considered so "dodgy" that some researchers had resorted to satellite data on light emissions from human settlements to estimate "growth from outer space."[48] Others have tried to correct for measurement errors by using meteorological data (rainfall levels), hoping to identify what part of the variation in growth statistics can be attributed to ups and downs in physical production, relying on the assumption that the output of the rain-fed agricultural sector will fluctuate with actual output and that other fluctuations may simply be the result of mismeasurement.[49] Dawson et al. asked whether the relationship between output volatility—measured as the standard deviation of annual growth rates—and slow growth is purely a product of measurement error.[50] Johnson et al. found that this volatility is inherent in the methodology of the most frequently used dataset for economic research, the Penn World Tables.[51] Despite such skepticism about measures, the *Handbook of Econometrics* highlights output volatility as a defining characteristic in developing countries,[52] and Arbache and Page echo this in their 2007 analysis using World Development Indicators, claiming that output volatility is a specific feature of growth in Africa.[53]

Statistics on African economies are widely known to be inaccurate, but the extent and nature of these inaccuracies and their implications for the users of the data have not been rigorously assessed. The previous section on income levels provides just a taste of the problems that data users face—most of the time unknowingly. Inconsistencies in the definitions of GDP and methods of measuring national income for African countries over the last half-century create problems when comparing income and economic growth. In turn, these problems undermine any general conclusions drawn about what stimulates or hinders economic development in Africa. For instance, it has been difficult to judge whether an improvement in growth following structural adjustment is an artifact of the data, if the difference in income per capita between two African economies is robust, or whether countries that are thought to have grown rapidly (or slowly) really have done so at the rates reported in the best available statistical compilations or according to national statistical reports. The World Development Indicators, the Penn World Tables, and the Maddison databases each report different growth rates for a given country.[54]

Concerns about the quality of African data are not new. In 1994, in connection with the trend toward econometric treatment of development issues and the increasing use of data from the Penn World Tables and the World Development Indicators, a special issue of *The Journal of Development Economics* published materials from a conference on the topic held two years earlier at Yale University. While several authors warned their peers to take more care in noting data deficiencies, criticisms of the data remained general. Srinivasan observed that researchers either are not aware of or, worse still, have chosen to ignore the fact that the published data, both national and international, suffer from serious conceptual problems and measurement biases and errors. In addition, it is not possible to compare within countries and across countries at any point in time.[55] Heston, one of the creators of the Penn World Tables, noted that since the landmark studies of five African countries by OECD economist Derek Blades in the late 1970s, seemingly little has been done to provide an overview of national accounting practices across countries. He called for the same type of study to be conducted across the whole spectrum of countries.[56]

Indeed, we must go back thirty years to the work of Derek Blades to find the last field- and archive-based empirical work on this topic.[57] He assessed official total income level estimates for Botswana, Kenya, Malawi, Nigeria, and Tanzania and produced a table with estimates of error range. The estimates were based on his own experience from statistical work in Africa, informal discussions with national accountants and experts from international agencies, and qualitative assessments provided by the five countries. Errors in the estimates of total GDP were in the 20 percent range, except for Nigeria, where they were found to be as high as 35 percent. Blades considered some sectors worse than others; his error range for modern agriculture varied from 25 percent (Nigeria) to 10 percent (Kenya and Tanzania), whereas for 'subsistence" agriculture the estimate was deemed to vary within an 80 percent band for all countries except Nigeria. Public administration, the sector with the best recorded statistics, still had a 10 percent error range, while small-scale operations were all considered to be poorly estimated.

Blades argued that there were high inaccuracies in the income level estimates, but maintained that estimates of growth were probably better. Still he warned that estimates of year-to-year variation should be treated with extreme caution.[58] He considered it unlikely that real GDP growth rates in developing countries would have errors of less than 3 percent. He concluded, "Thus an estimated year-to-year increase of 3 percent might mean anything from no growth at all to an increase of 6 percent." The size of this error band would remain guesswork, he noted, since "the GDP per capita growth rates published by developing countries have never been examined for their reliability."[59]

While scholars are well aware that the data are unreliable, no one has established whether this takes the form of "white noise" or whether there is a systematic bias.[60] In a recent think piece on the future agenda for development economics, Angus Deaton concluded that "the basic facts of economic development, such as the growth rates of GDP, come from measures that ought to be much more deeply debated than is the case."[61]

Blades's work was not detailed enough to establish a direction of bias in level or growth rates, and fifteen years after Heston's call to extend the investigation into estimation procedures and assumptions to more countries, this has not been undertaken until this book. The evidence reported in this book brings further support to the worries about growth and income estimates. Growth and income data are malleable, and different datasets support completely different versions of how to explain economic events. The error margins reported by Blades are on the conservative side. Per capita income levels are subject to revisions on the order of 50 to 100 percent, and discrepancies in growth rates are at times in the double digits. It should be noted that the Africa of the 1970s and Africa today are very different. In the 1970s, African leaders were presiding over states that were charged with formulating development plans and guiding African nations toward modernization and progress, and many of the states had successfully done so for a decade or longer.[62] Today, in 2010, most African states are still recovering from two decades of economic decline, state collapse, and a restructuring of the political economy.

Not enough research has been done to establish whether there is a particular bias in the data. Paul Collier is one of the few who has ventured a recent guess. He recently asked: "Is this dismal performance just an artifact of the data?" He answered his own question: "I think that, on the contrary, the genuine problems that afflict gathering of economic data in the poorest countries are likely overall to have caused an underestimate of their decline."[63] The information provided in this chapter has already shown that Collier got it wrong. On the contrary: data-gathering problems tend to cause an underestimation of income. It is correct that for some countries that are truly falling apart, no data is being reported, and thus through the "gap-filling method" the World Bank uses, very recent regional data report that sub-Saharan Africa is doing better than it really is. The discrepancy between the figures and economic realities elsewhere is not that easy to interpret. In order to gauge the size of errors and to evaluate the direction of bias in the evidence, the data needs to be fully contextualized and historicized. Because the international databases do not provide this information, the next chapter goes to the primary sources and studies how African economies have been measured at the national level.

2

MEASURING AFRICAN WEALTH
AND PROGRESS

This chapter provides an account of how African incomes have been measured over time and shows that the aims of producers and users of national income estimates have conflicted.[1] Politicians and international organizations seek income measures that reflect current political and economic priorities and achievements. Thus, the importance given to markets, the state, and peasants in the estimate will vary according to the current political environment. In contrast, statisticians aim to produce a measure that gives the best possible picture of the economy given the available data. Scholars prefer a measure that is consistent through time and space so that "progress" can be measured, compared, and analyzed. However, they have not being able to reach a consensus about how "progress" is best calculated or defined. The result is not an objective measure of progress but rather an expression of development priorities as determined by changes in the political economy and academic trends.

Thus, it is important to provide context about the history and context of the national income estimates. This chapter investigates changes in the priorities and power of African states and how they have related to central stakeholders. It first reviews some early debates about the value of initiating national income accounting for African countries, then it examines some early colonial estimates and looks at the changes and nuances in postcolonial accounting. It discusses revisions in accounting practices following structural adjustment and the growth of the informal economy. What William Easterly referred to as the "lost decades" in terms of economic performance were indeed "lost" in the sense that statistical offices documented economic activities in a limited manner.[2]

There has been a decided shift in how consumers of statistical data in academic and policy circles prefer to use data sources. Journal articles and monographs published on African economies in the 1960s, 1970s, and 1980s invariably referred extensively to official documents and used national accounts, economic surveys, and data from statistical abstracts to support scholarly analysis. In recent decades these data sources are almost entirely unused. This is due, in part, to the lack of availability and accessibility of these sources. Major competitors such as the Penn World Tables and World Development Indicators have become the preferred source of social and economic statistics. The World Bank reports official data as submitted to it by national statistical offices, with some modifications. Undoubtedly, the brand name of "World Bank" is better than the brand name of "National Bureau of Statistics," but the basic ingredients of the final product are the same. The fact that data users nevertheless prefer to use World Bank data provides a clear example of why, as Porter explained, we have come to trust some numbers over others.[3] A parallel development has taken place in development studies. The discipline is now dominated by economists who prefer econometric analysis using global datasets in cross-country regressions.[4] This has a built-in self-enforcement mechanism. Development experts are now first and foremost interested in economics, not economies. This means that often analysis is not conducted by country experts,[5] and these data users are not able to readily evaluate whether the statistics cohere with economic realities.

The review of the available estimates in chapter 1 showed that the distance between the producers and the users of economic statistics is an unhealthy disconnection. While data users take economic statistics at face value, the production of these statistics is subject to a range of contestable assumptions, variations in data availability, and sometimes nontransparent adjustments and revisions. A quantitative analysis can be fruitful only if it is based in careful criticism of the source and is supplemented by qualitative investigation. As the old motto says, "Back to the sources." In order to employ the evidence usefully, one must know under which conditions the data were produced. As Herring argues, research methods that recognize the social nature of data production are more likely to be reliable and valid than those that do not.[6]

According to the interpretation that sees data validity as an expression of social and political power, the disappearance of African states as valid providers of data for development in the 1980s clearly demonstrates the general demise of the state in sub-Saharan Africa. The developmental state in sub-Saharan Africa has usually been dated to the colonial period, beginning with the British Colonial Development and Welfare Acts of 1940 and 1945.[7] In the sub-Saharan African region, the state, with its bureaucratic structure and official institutions and, most importantly, its borders, is a colonial innovation.[8] Tax collection and government services such as health, education, agricultural extension services, and others all have their sparse beginnings in this period. With tax collection, government services and development plans came both the capacity and the need for some monitoring of the economy.

Independence provided a break with the colonial regime, but there were still many points of continuity,[9] of which statistical services were no exception. The developmental state expanded its scope and ambitions greatly,[10] and this meant that in the 1960s, national accounts became an integral part of development plans, both in terms of defining which areas and sectors to address as well as in terms of monitoring the success of a development strategy with respect to clearly identified targets.

Initial success eventually gave way to failure, and failure paved the way for structural adjustment and what Nicolas van de Walle has referred to as the "politics of permanent crisis."[11] The structural adjustment process meant liberalization reforms and a withdrawal of the state, not only through privatization but also by cutting back its role as a development planner. Structural adjustment was undertaken because it was believed that it would revive economic growth. As this book documents, the IMF and World Bank neglected to reform or fund statistical offices sufficiently for there to be a capacity to measure whether growth revived or not.

The growth records of sub-Saharan African economies are the accumulated results of efforts to estimate national income across the countries since
the 1950s. The whole record of each country is downloadable through international databases as a continuous series for most of the countries from
1960 onward.[12]

The dataset may appear to be readily interpretable as informative observations about income levels and economic growth, but it is in fact a range
of observations that vary considerably in validity and reliability. Many of
the observations in the datasets are not even data in the strictest sense of
the word because so much of the data are guesstimates or adjustments that
filled in gaps in data.

In theory, national income estimates are products that are produced by
a standardized, rule-based process. However, in practice, statistical offices
must use their discretion to create the final products. In an ideal world the
statistician would be able to say: "The data speak for themselves." This
chapter documents how the data are based on educated guesses, competing, and debatable assumptions, leaving the data on both trends and levels
open to question. It also provides a guide for how one should approach the
resulting numbers.

Colonial Experiments

In the exchanges among economists about the value of national accounting in Africa and other developing areas in the early 1950s one of the
pioneers of development economics, Dudley Seers, was decidedly pessi-
mistic about the rewards of instituting national accounting for the purpose of international comparisons of income and economic development.
"In the hands of authorities, such international comparisons may yield
correlations which throw light on the circumstances of economic progress, and they tell us something about relative inefficiencies and standards of living, but they are very widely abused. Do they not on the
whole mislead more than they instruct, causing a net reduction in human
knowledge?"[13]

As we know very well today, these warnings were not heeded, and
national income estimates were prepared in African countries following
World War II. In theory this was done according to the United Nations'

universal System of National Accounts. However, in practice, local application varied considerably. In 1945, the only African country to publish national accounts was South Africa. Southern and Northern Rhodesia followed suit beginning in 1949 and by 1958, Ghana, Kenya, Uganda, and the Congo had all published annual estimates. National income was estimated for Nigeria in 1951, but the next estimates were not prepared until independence in 1960.[14]

The first estimates made for the colony of Southern Rhodesia and the British protectorates of Northern Rhodesia and Nyasaland were characteristic of colonial accounting in that they did not initially include an estimate of the value added by "African" producers. From 1949 onward "a nominal figure of £5 million for African subsistence income was included in the value of national income of Northern Rhodesia."[15] This amount was reported as unchanged in the accounts from 1949 to 1953. The de facto assumption was that the value of total food production from African producers was decreasing quite rapidly (when population growth and inflation are taken into consideration). The first estimates ignored 'subsistence" production altogether; later estimates acknowledged it, but gave it a marginalized role in the accounts. During this time, there was a vigorous scholarly debate about the "subsistence economy" that is explored below.

Seers wittily referred to subsistence output as the "well-known morass which those estimating national income of underdeveloped areas either skirt, rush across or die in."[16] Reporting on efforts in Kenya, Donald Wood, Jr., offered a short and more accurate comment about why neither of the terms commonly used for this part of the economy are appropriate:

> There is no satisfactory name for this sector. The non-monetary sector is used in this paper because that is what it is called in the Kenyan National Accounts. The name is misleading since money is widely used in this sector. Other names which have been used to designate this sector are: the subsistence sector, although the standard of living is usually above the subsistence level; and the traditional sector, although social, economic and political institutions and behaviour are probably changing as rapidly in parts of this sector as they are elsewhere in the country.[17]

In this initial phase of experimenting with national accounting there was no agreement about how to integrate this sector into national accounts or indeed whether it was worth doing so. In line with a general optimism regarding the prospects for rapid growth in Africa, Peter Ady commented that it was "strange that some countries in Africa should be planning to devote so many of their scarce statistical resources to the more accurate measurement of this diminishing component."[18] The pessimism about national accounting, particularly about accounting for small-scale production, was accompanied by optimism about the future growth and "modernization" of developing countries. Seers provides a good example: "The fundamental difficulty is the same as it is for international comparison: in a few years an underdeveloped country may have changed so much that for the purposes of the underlying assumptions in economic analysis it can no longer be considered the same country."[19]

Others objected to the idea of measuring income and comparing income across countries. Herbert Frankel held that some economic behavior of Africans cannot be adequately explained by concepts drawn from market economics. He felt that some countries had such different concepts of income and welfare and were governed by such specific rules and laws that international comparisons would be meaningless. The concept of income or wealth varied from culture to culture to such an extent that efforts to maximize it could not be compared across cultures. Indeed, Frankel compared maximizing income to maximizing a game of chess. A game of chess is governed by specific rules, and these rules set the aim of the game. One could accept a scale of scoring points and thus maximize the outcome, but this sum or score would not capture the total utility of playing the game. Thus, the game itself cannot be maximized.[20]

Similar views were expressed by the economists who pioneered national accounting in the colonies. In a report on an experiment that prepared income estimates for Nyasaland, Northern Rhodesia, and Jamaica in 1941, Phyllis Deane noted that "when working out national income tables for Central Africa (as compared to Jamaica) it soon became clear that a more comprehensive and direct knowledge of the social and economic structure of Central African peoples was essential if a satisfactory framework was to evolve." Therefore, she felt it was necessary to discard the formal tables and envisage a new system that abandoned "the income classification according to profits, interest, rents, wages and salaries," instead substituting "a classification according to nationality."[21] This is why the final published accounts measured economic contributions by three racial groups:

Europeans, Africans, and Asians. The colonial accounts for Rhodesia recorded "normal" versus "African" output. The apartheid regime in South Africa used a similar accounting classification, providing different estimates for the "Bantu Homelands" and the "Black States."[22]

Alan Prest and Ian Stewart, who prepared income estimates for Nigeria in 1951, also noted problems with the application of "Western" concepts: "For a start, the distinction between production and living, the distinction between working and not working, is something reasonably tangible in the 'West'; it is often nebulous in Nigeria."[23] Prest and Stewart ended up accounting for transactions that took place within Nigerian households as market transactions, arguing that the extended household in Africa had to be interpreted differently than the Western household. They included intrahousehold services in the estimates, which even involved evaluating the value of the service of procreation wives for husbands. They used data on bridewealth as a proxy for the market value of this intrahousehold service. Pius Okigbo, who prepared estimates for 1950–1957, discarded this approach and favored a less inclusive approach than that of Prest and Stewart.[24] Eke, who reviewed the two estimation methods, noted that "this excursion by Prest could easily be dismissed as ludicrous, but it is much more serious than that."[25] He argued that it was a fundamental misconception that national accounts could fully capture all the processes that contribute to the welfare of human beings.

These colonial experiments could have had another outcome. Economists debated whether it was defensible to aggregate national accounts. Ady wrote: "The usual aggregates are certainly valueless, at present, for certain purposes: welfare comparisons using per capita income, for example, are obviously nonsensical when income estimates themselves are in part derived by multiplying up per capita averages of doubtful accuracy by population estimates equally subject to error." He added in a footnote that "there is at least one African country whose per capita income figures were revised upwards by 75 per cent in recent years."[26] Frankel likened the comparisons of national income aggregates from "underdeveloped societies" to "fiction."[27] Seers recommended that economists limit themselves to recording the sectors where they had data,[28] and refrain from misleading aggregation processes. But he realized that "the 'demonstration effect' of industrial countries is so strong that it is the rule, rather than the exception, for statisticians working in primary producing countries to treat national income estimates as the highest priority in statistical work."[29]

Prest and Stewart, who estimated the income of Nigeria, and Peacock and Dosser, who provided estimates of the income of Tanganyika, all argued that it was necessary to provide total aggregates because they would help inform governments and the international community about prospects for economic progress.[30] In the same vein, Billington argued that the United Nations System of National Accounts was the best approach to measuring the progress of African economies and that standardizing measurement was the right path forward.[31]

The beginning of the discipline of development economics is closely linked with the beginnings of national accounting on the African continent in the 1940s and 1950s. It is also during these years that the first estimates in the international datasets were made. Typically a data series starts in 1960, which is the artificially chosen year from which the economic growth stories begin. It is worth recalling the widespread skepticism about the use of these estimates and the misgivings expressed about their accuracy at that time. In Douglas Rimmer's retrospective review of fifty years of economic development in Africa, he commented on the early estimates provided for Ghana.

> I had the opportunity to observe the rough-and-ready methods by which national accounts were constructed in the Government Statistics Office in Accra. Much was guesswork. Much was also omitted; though not until later did I fully realize the significance of the parallel, unenumerated economy that is to be found everywhere and in some African countries has at times overshadowed the formalized economy. Also later I became conscious of the definitional and valuation problems that underlay the enumeration of economic output. I began to question the meanings that were read into the resulting totals of income. I realized the impossibility of determining percentage rates of change in these totals from one year to another when they undoubtedly contained the margins of error.[32]

These and other warnings such as those of Dudley Seers and other "development experts" were heard, but they did not have an impact on the development of national statistics gathering and compilation. As Merry has suggested, one can approach indicators as a knowledge problem or a governance problem. Although many questioned whether the estimates were intellectually defensible and argued that the final estimates were likely to decrease knowledge and mislead data users, it is clear that in the 1960s, the imperatives of governance proved more important. Pius Okigbo explained in the preface to his GDP estimates for Nigeria for the period 1950–57 that the GDP statistics were required and demanded as an input for national development plans. But he was careful to point out that "it is impossible to overstate the arbitrariness of the process of 'quantification.'"[33]

National accounts and the resulting income estimates and growth rates became the basis of most development debates. In practice, economic growth became the definition, the measure, and the target for "development" in the 1960s and the 1970s. GDP measures came under less scrutiny than had been the case for the early independently made estimates, arguably because they received an official stamp of approval.[34] Porter has argued that the objectivity of numbers is defined by context rather than by their actual content.[35] The formalization of national income accounting is an example of this process. While the accuracy and standardization of national accounting numbers did not improve significantly, the trust given to them improved greatly as they became a product and tool of the newly independent developmental states in sub-Saharan Africa.

Development in Practice

When national accounting was in its trial phase in newly independent African countries, Deane reviewed some of the new official estimates and commented that "what was once the happy hunting ground of the independent research worker has become the routine preoccupation of official statisticians and international Civil Servants." This might explain why there has been less scholarly attention to the subject of income measurement methods following independence. Methodology might have been assumed to be a task of standardization rather than a fruitful area for research. However, according to Deane, "the fact is ... that African national-income publications are as heterogeneous under the official stamp as they ever were when privately produced."[36]

Independence meant new priorities and new statistical needs. Before independence in former Northern Rhodesia, now Zambia, national accounts were prepared by the Central Statistical Office (CSO) in Salisbury. At the beginning of 1964, this responsibility was transferred to the CSO in Lusaka, where the national accounts for 1964 onward were prepared. The statistical office explained the rationale of the new estimates this way: "Economic Planning was an important task for the Government and the need for statistical information had therefore increased considerably."[37] In the context of the new economic and political conditions there was a need to revise the data on the level of private consumption and other categories of expenditure. Essentially this meant estimating the magnitude of total production as compared to estimating demand as measured by monetary transactions. In other words, the national accounts had to be based on the "production approach" rather than the "income approach" that had been used during the colonial period. This implied an upward revision, because non-monetary activities such as production for own consumption and smaller-scale transactions were included in the new national income estimates. A part of the population that had been neglected earlier was now seen as economically and politically (and therefore statistically) important.[38]

Despite the goal of establishing a new basis for the accounts, the available basic statistics were not sufficient. The estimates of agriculture in the first national account reports for Zambia covered commercial farming (non-African) and officially registered sales from African farms, while "African subsistence farming and hunting was estimated mainly in accordance with information given by the Food and Agricultural Organization (FAO) for per capita consumption of different kinds of commodity."[39] A similarly ambitious intent was evident in Tanzania. The Central Bureau of Statistics in Dar es Salaam attempted to include forty agricultural products, fifteen livestock products, and producers of government services in the estimates for agriculture. However, the bureau acknowledged that this effort was inadequate. Despite the importance of agriculture to the national economy, "the available information on crop acreage, output etc. is very meagre," except in the case of the export crops.[40] In Tanzania, data on production for own consumption were first available in 1969 through the implementation of a household budget survey based on a sample of 824 households spread throughout the country. For all other years annual consumption was assumed to grow at the same rate as rate of growth for the rural population, which was assumed to be 2.825 percent.

This assumption that agricultural growth increased at the rate of rural population growth was made in many African countries.[41] In one of the few empirical studies of African national income statistics, Derek Blades notes that for the growth estimates of subsistence agriculture, "the basic assumption is that output grows at the same rate as the rural population," thus assuming a 1 to 1 ratio of labor productivity in the rural sector.[42] Note that since rural population growth was slower than total population growth, this introduces a bias toward decreasing GDP per capita output. These estimates are not very sensitive to climatic variations or other factors that are assumed to affect agricultural productivity, though some ad hoc adjustment in the annual data was made in exceptional years: "In Zambia and Uganda annual variations around the trend are estimated on the basis of 'eye-estimates' made by agricultural experts in the main production areas."[43]

The data basis in Tanzania might seem meager, but it compared favorably with that of other countries. In Zambia, a pilot household budget survey was undertaken in 1972–73, whereas in Botswana a rural budget survey was first available in 1973–74. The latter provided the only survey data for agricultural production until a new survey was undertaken in 1986–1987.[44] In Kenya, estimates of agricultural output are based on an annual Integrated Rural Survey (IRS) and an annual census of large farms. The first IRS was undertaken in 1974–75, and it is not clear what source of information on small farms was used before this date.[45] In Nigeria, agricultural surveys have been conducted on a regular basis since the 1950s, but these had a very small sampling frame and covered an irregular geographical area. In fact, Gerald Helleiner notes that in the surveys conducted during 1955–60, "no one area was covered more than once" and "in no one year were areas in more than one region covered."[46]

Helleiner, who analyzed the general state of national accounting in Nigeria, wrote in 1966 that "the Nigerian national accounts remain in a sorry condition" and that changes in the estimation procedures made comparisons for the early years "unsuitable." He concluded that "the estimates inevitably involve so wide a margin of error that the lack of consistency in the aggregates need not to be viewed so seriously."[47] The main point was that although the aggregates had changed to include agricultural production, the data basis was generally not good enough to pinpoint year-to-year change.

Immediately following this evaluation, Nigeria experienced a destructive and long civil war.[48] When the Second National Development Plan (1970–74) was drawn up, the latest income estimates available for the planners were those that had been made for the year 1966, just before the civil war started. The primary purpose of this development plan was supposedly to address the consequences of this civil war—a difficult task considering the dearth of data on the national economy after the war.[49] In fact, the Nigerian national accounts were not revised again until a team led by Professor O. Aboyade completed a revision in the 1980s; their report was published in 1981.

Aboyade observed that "a number of critical estimates were based on highly tenuous assumptions." For instance, the estimate for the contribution of transport and trade was "based on the long standing but unverified assumption that distributive activities always account for one-eighth of Nigeria's gross domestic product."[50] The report noted some improvements and inherited weaknesses compared to previous methods and data, but it stressed that a fundamental weakness of this revision and of earlier ones was that it was done in an ad hoc manner. The team that had been recruited to complete it would likely disperse, and with it the value of the work it had contributed. What Aboyade described is a general problem: at different points in time, especially after independence (or in this case after a civil war), new estimates of levels would be drawn up, but a system ensuring the regular flow of administrative data needed for the computing of GDP and the adequate personnel to process these data were not sustained after the revision.

However, regular access to some data on economic change was improved upon. A notable change in many African economies, especially in Zambia and Tanzania in the 1970s, was a centralization of the economy and the growing power of parastatal companies. In both Zambia and Tanzania, this was paralleled by an emphasis on socialism. Thus, this change was more pronounced in these two countries (and other socialist countries). This does not mean that these countries should be considered extreme outliers. In other so-called capitalist countries, the state was also deeply involved in the trade, marketing, and transport of agricultural crops (both for food and for exports) and was engaged directly or indirectly in manufacturing and construction through newly formed development corporations.[51] This new structure eased economic recording. In Tanzania in the 1970s, the data used for the national accounts on the trade, finance, and industry sectors were largely drawn from parastatal enterprises, while data on crops were largely drawn from state marketing boards. This might be interpreted as a choice of convenience, but in the case of Tanzania, there was a correspondence between legitimate and recorded economic activity. It was illegal to market commodities outside state or parastatal channels, and marketing that took place outside those channels could not be thought of as making a contribution to the national income.

The Lost Decades

Progress soon gave way to decline, and in the 1980s and 1990s, economies collapsed in what are called the "lost decades." This turn of events redefined the task of development. It also affected development statistics: The convenient data sources became increasingly obsolete as parallel, black, and informal markets thrived. The new challenge was to account for this informal economy in the midst of a collapsing formal economy in which the statistical offices were firmly embedded. These decades were indeed lost in national accounting terms.[52] As historians Ellis and Nugent note, this makes the writing the history of the 1980s and 1990s difficult.[53]

In Zambia's national statistical office in Lusaka, the national account reports, other publications relating to accounting methodology, and most other relevant reports ceased to be available after 1973. Only an annex report to the 1973–1978 estimates was obtainable. This means that very little is known about the estimates and how they were reached in the 1980s. During my 2007 visit to the Central Statistical Office in Lusaka, neither the national accountants nor the persons responsible for library/data dissemination functions were able to clarify whether this was because the reports had gone missing or because they were never published.[54]

A similar problem was observed in Ghana, where the Ghanaian Statistical Services ceased publishing its annual economic survey in 1985 due to a lack of funding and qualified personnel.[55] The office attempted to reinstate this document as a regular source of economic information for Ghana in 2005, but it has not been published since that year. In Kenya, the only available document describing the methods and sources for the national accounts was published in 1977. Although I was assured at the Central Bureau of Statistics in Nairobi in 2007 that this publication contains "everything you need to know" about national accounting in postcolonial Kenya, many important changes have been implemented since then, including a survey of the informal sector.[56]

In Zambia, at the University Library Special Collection, which functions as a legal depository of official documents, and the National Archives, which has the same legal function, publications for the 1960s and early 1970s were present and catalogued, but after that there was a gap in the deposits. Librarians at both institutions lamented this fact. It was explained that while the libraries had the legal right to the documents, finances for the transport and acquisition of these documents were not available. The librarian in each place explained that the documents would have to be collected by them personally, and understandably this had not happened.[57] The onset of the economic crisis and the ensuing structural adjustment had serious ramifications for the provision of national income estimates. This situation damaged the credibility of national statistical offices as reliable providers of information. In Ghana and Nigeria, the statistical offices both underwent name changes: from Central Bureau of Statistics to Ghanaian Statistical Services and from Federal Office of Statistics to National Bureau of Statistics. In both cases this was a deliberate move to improve credibility, assert independence from politics, and distance themselves from previous controversy.[58] In Uganda, the formal economy collapsed in the late 1970s, and what Ted Brett calls the "untaxed economy" replaced it.[59] Muwanga-Zake describes the ensuing collapse of the statistical office:

> The main problem was the lack of investment in statistics production; the Department lacked resources and could not effectively carry out its role as the central coordinating body for statistics within government, let alone for the country as a whole. The Department lacked essential facilities: buildings became derelict; there was only one roadworthy vehicle; and there were no computers, so all statistics had to be manually tabulated and simple desk calculators used for calculations. Other agencies progressively took over aspects of the Department's data gathering and processing responsibilities. Inevitably, there was considerable overlap in some important statistics activities, such as price collection, estimation of GDP, and statistics on central government revenue and expenditure. Any published data had lost credibility.[60]

In the 1980s and the 1990s, all of the African economies (with the exception of Botswana) had to undergo "structural adjustment"—the policy reform programs that the IMF and the World Bank established as conditions for further financial support. This meant a reduction in the role of the state in all states, irrespective of whether they were referred to as "capitalist" or "socialist" in the 1970s and 1980s.[61] In many countries some of the basic functions of the state were privatized, and with this the capacity to record national data disappeared. Beatrice Hibou chronicles how customs collections were privatized in Mozambique and Cameroon and that because of this, "the national accounts do not record either the volume or the value of the exports, nor the tax and customs revenue."[62] These tax reforms can be seen as pragmatic attempts to increase revenue, and the appearance of autonomous tax collecting agencies have indeed been popular as a way of avoiding the fact that governments embezzle funds.[63] These reforms may or may not improve state capacity in the long term,[64] but the short-term effect on statistical services is clear. There is less direct tax revenue data for the statistical offices, and many statistical offices have not yet integrated the VAT data in their accounts. Integrating these new data sources into national accounts requires a rebasing and revision of the national accounts.

From Development to Liberalization

Statistical offices in some countries were not able to begin to adjust to new economic and political realities until the late 1990s. In that period, two national statistical offices, in Zambia and Tanzania, made major revisions to their statistical series. In Zambia, the report on the revision of national income estimates for a new series based in 1994 began by stating the obvious: "Inflation rates of more than 200 percent in the early 1990s had adverse effects on the provision of macroeconomic statistics."[65] The report noted that creating meaningful data about year-to-year real economic growth under such circumstances was complicated: structural adjustment entailed massive changes in the structure of production in Zambia, and "the break-up of the former large parastatals meant that previous sources of data were not available."[66] A revision and a rebasing were overdue; the accounts were still based in 1977 prices and the benchmarks were "becoming inadequate, and over time provided less accurate estimates."[67] The previous estimates had largely "excluded [the] informal sector and therefore impaired the value of GDP estimates over time, in all sectors except agriculture."[68]

After incorporating informal sector activity in the total GDP, the formal sector share of the Zambian economy was estimated at 58 percent in terms of value added, with a corresponding 42 percent share for the informal economy. To this estimate, the statistical office gave the following warning: "We wish to caution that including the informal sector activity in the Zambia National Accounts may tend to exaggerate the GDP of the nation, relative to other countries or even to the previous estimates which mostly excluded it. It must also be recognized that it will be difficult to up-date the sector relation based on indicators in the absence of surveys to monitor the activity in the future."[69]

In Tanzania, the report accompanying the new constant price series at 1992 prices held that "strong efforts were made to determine what is the story behind the figures, whether the data applies to what is experienced as happening in the industry. This has not been emphasised earlier." This statement was an indication that instead of letting the data speak for themselves, the statistical office had compared the revised figures to what was otherwise known or assumed about economic trends.[70] The statistical office noted that structural changes, especially in the late 1980s, were not reflected in the available statistics, resulting in an underestimation of value added: "Estimates of the size of this deficiency ranged from 30 percent to as much [as] 200 percent of GDP."[71] The new estimates of GDP levels were reached by incorporating all available data into the accounts, including the results of new surveys of the transport, trade and construction undertaken as part of the revision project. In the previous estimation methods of 1976 the "private sector was under covered—sometimes not covered at all—and the growing informal sector was not generally accounted for."[72] When the new GDP level was reached for 1992, a time series was developed by extrapolating these data on trends backward to 1987. When deciding how to calculate backward trends Tanzanian statisticians changed their assumptions for the revised GDP series: they expected the informal economy to increase when the formal sector was in decline instead of moving with it.

This question of how to relate the unobserved economy to the observed economy is analogous to the issues related to "subsistence" or "traditional" output that were raised in the 1950s. The "discovery" of the informal sector is usually credited to the ILO in 1972 and Keith Hart in 1973,[73] but the productive potential of this sector is still unknown.[74] Is the informal sector an independent source of economic growth, is it dependent on the formal economy for demand and supply, or is it a parasitic sector, profiting from the demise of the formal sector? The facts that are available in the national account statistics are expressions of assumed relationships between the measured and unmeasured economy, and the assumptions are often not transparent for the data user. The resulting figures therefore need to be questioned and treated critically as historical evidence rather than as raw data that can be used as empirical observations to, for instance, test the relationship between the formal and informal economy.

Thus, in the late 1990s both Zambia and Tanzania underwent a massive upward reappraisal of national income after structural adjustment. Both countries had followed a path of state-led development from the late 1960s until the crisis in the 1980s. During this period, as a matter of convenience and ideology, data on trade, services, and (by implication) production (through the state marketing board) were collected by the parastatal companies, which were assumed to represent the whole economy. When those state agencies were unable to offer services or unable to offer services for an acceptable price, economic actors turned to informal and parallel operators. That is why the national income estimates recorded a massive decline in the late 1970s and early 1980s. It is impossible to correctly gauge the movement and/or the size of this unrecorded component. Although Zambia and Tanzania have revised their economies to include informal sector estimates, the national accountants are unable to accurately measure this economic change. The resulting national income series is potentially misleading as scholars who wish to compare income across countries and across time approach per capita estimates.

Conclusion

In this chapter the national income statistics have been contextualized and historicized. I have described how the role of the state, and therefore the basis for national income statistics, changed with the power of the African states in the twentieth century. I have also discussed how some states were geared toward state-led development-led instead of market-led development and how that choice affected how economic activities were accounted for.

Three features of twentieth-century data collection in Africa deserve particular emphasis: the discontinuity between colonial data collection and
postcolonial data collection, the paucity of reliable data for the agriculture
sector, and the change from the developmental state in the 1960s and 1970s
to the liberalized state in the 1990s. The importance of these aspects will be
further substantiated in chapter 3.

As many historians have emphasized, patterns of continuity are evident when comparing the colonial state in the 1940s to the independent
developmental state in the 1960s and the 1970s. Nevertheless, independence also represents a clear discontinuity. Although some national income estimates were made first in the colonial context, these estimates
differed from the postcolonial ones in some crucial aspects. There was a
difference between the national income estimates made by independent
scholars and those that had an official stamp. In the official colonial accounts, the weight given to food production was nonexistent or negligible.
The annual colonial records of the British Empire, referred to as the Blue
Books, contained statistics on imports and exports, taxes and expenditures,
formal employment and the activities of public correction, education and
health facilities, but the pages on agricultural and industrial production
were blank.[75] As discussed earlier, the colonial estimates did not include
these activities within the category of production. In the system of national
accounts, there was provision to do so. All production that is marketed
should be included. After independence, statisticians working on behalf of
state authorities made an effort to include this production. Total population estimates followed the same dynamics; the example of the history of
population census-taking in chapter 3 will give a very clear picture of the
change in practices.

There are also some striking patterns of continuity, or path dependence,
across the colonial and postcolonial period in methods of statistical collection. In Eastern Africa the collection of official statistics started in 1948
with the creation of the East African Statistical Department (EASD),
which was headquartered in Nairobi, Kenya, and had subunits in En-
tebbe, Uganda, and Dar es Salaam, Tanzania. Statistics were collected on
trade, agriculture, migration, labor, and population. The different units
shared senior staff, who could be transferred between these units as determined by the High Commission. Following independence, the EASD was
split into territorial departments that were under the control of the local

governments, and a reduced EASD continued to exist under the newly created East African Common Services Organization.[76]

In 1976, the East African Community broke up, and with it the EASD. More responsibilities fell to the national offices. The task of compiling data on external trade fell to the Customs and Excise Department in Uganda, which in turn relied on electronic data-processing facilities in Mombasa, Kenya, to collect these data. Until 2008, external trade statistics for Uganda had been collected only on goods passing through the Mombasa port in Kenya,[77] even though Uganda has borders with Tanzania, Rwanda, Democratic Republic of Congo, and Sudan. In part, this is a surviving colonial priority: only officially recorded statistics of imports and exports with the non-African world mattered. But it has also been conditioned by the extent of collapse in the Uganda in the 1970s and early 1980s and the fact that the countries that Uganda and the countries that border it have been conflict zones until quite recently. Finally, since structural adjustment, no duties have been collected on imports or exports, so the Ugandan government has had little financial interest in documenting cross-border trade. When the Uganda Bureau of Statistics finally surveyed trade, it concluded that "the informal cross border trade is significant and contributes immensely to household welfare and the country's economic growth."[78] This opens up the possibility of a reorientation of economic regional policies for Uganda.

The second main feature, which I emphasized in chapters 1 and 2 is that the data on agricultural production are weak. Because these data are assembled using competing methods and assumptions, the outlook of the final data series is a matter of the discretion of statistical offices. This puts a statistical office in a weak position if the data series is questioned by stakeholders. In chapter 3 I will explore an example of controversy related to competing agricultural production data series. The third main feature emphasized here is the fundamental change in the outlook of the state following the period of structural adjustment policies introduced in the 1980s and 1990s. The mandate of the state was drastically reduced, and formerly interventionist states were liberalized and curtailed. Access to data changed, and so did political priorities. Statistical offices made some adjustment in their assumptions following revisions in accounting methods. The effect of these changes is discussed further in chapter 3.

It is important not to read direct causality into this argument. Statistical capacity deteriorated in line with the general economic and political crisis in the 1980s. The fault of the IMF and the World Bank is one of omission rather than one of commission. That is: statistical reform has been slow and incomplete—and some unintended consequences of some structural adjustment reforms include the deterioration of statistical capacity. It is clear that liberalization and decreasing the role of the state limits both the incentive and the ability of states to collect information. But the need for data has not decreased, particularly in the context of international monitoring of development trends. Thus, both the ability of and the incentive for states to monitor their own development has decreased.

When Killick wrote a new afterword to the new edition of his book on Ghana, *Development Economics in Action*,[79] he reissued the general warnings about the macroeconomic data. He also noted that "this condition has not improved over time. In fact, it may well be that in some areas the statistical services today are less dependable than in the early-1960s."[80] This mirrors Ward's observation that the World Bank was not ready to wait for the slow process of producing national income estimates and instead moved toward "the adaptation of these more fragile but 'up to date' figures" it had prepared.[81] These were "agreed upon numbers" and were results of negotiations between the bank and country representatives,[82] according to Ward:

> In effect, to many statisticians working "at the coal face," this development of data artifacts, which replaced more robust but time-consuming procedures in some countries, seemed dangerous because it rolled assumptions and hypotheses into official numbers. Genuine measurement took a back seat. In reality, there were no recent official GNP estimates based on actual detailed source data in many countries, especially the poorest.[83]

Thus, economic crisis correlates with poor data. In Africa, disruption shook administrative capacity and statistical systems. The response of governments and international financial systems was to withdraw from serious data collection and instead rely on negotiated numbers in order to draw up policy papers. However, these numbers did not yield good information on development.

What are the implications for data users? Killick feels that the researcher has to make the most of what usable data are available, because "the alternative is a silence that would not be justified by data deficiencies."[84] However, the growth record and the reported GDP estimates from the 1960s until 2010 need to be interpreted with variations in data, methods, and state practices in mind. This is where the first chapter in this book concluded, where I reported that Collier speculated that the data problems caused an underestimate of the decline in the 1980s and 1990s.[85] This is not likely to be correct. As I noted in chapter 1, the more dated the methods and data for the estimation of GDP, the higher the likelihood that income would be underestimated.

The result in terms of growth is also the opposite of what has been predicted. The decline was likely overestimated in the 1980s because most countries relied mainly on administrative data to assemble the national accounts. When states were less directly involved in buying and selling goods and transported fewer goods and people, provided fewer services, and in general had a policy of smaller state intervention, there was less data available that covered a declining proportion of the economy. As will be shown, income and growth were underestimated until surveys of the informal sector began to cover this growing part of the economy. It further follows that growth after structural adjustment has been overestimated. This will be demonstrated in chapter 3.

What about the early growth of the 1960s and 1970s? This is the period for which we have the best data. Most economies made new estimates following independence that were fairly inclusive and broad. This makes it less likely that early growth was seriously overestimated. The process of monetizing and formalizing economic activity was already well under way during the colonial period and continued into the early independence period. The most significant event to affect the reliability of data in the postcolonial period was the informalization of economic activities in the late 1970s, and this seriously undermines our ability to compare the wealth and progress of African economies today.

Does this mean that the data are not usable? It is clear that they are not usable for ranking economies, and it should be equally easy to understand that the most recent growth data are the result of negotiated prognosis rather than independent data estimation. Finally, long-term time series data across 1960–2010 or analysis of periods of growth within this timeframe can be done only with careful attention to the primary data. By this I do not mean statistical testing of the downloadable datasets; I mean an actual evaluation of the data series. This involves country-level knowledge and a familiarity with how statistics are produced.

The tendency in development economics since the middle of the 1990s has been toward large studies with cross-country regressions,[86] without any appreciation of problems with the data.[87] This is particularly likely to yield nonsense or misleading findings, resulting in inaccurate economic histories of postcolonial Africa. Currently, there are large gaps in the data coverage in the national accounts for African countries. These gaps have increased or have been reduced over time. These changes have not been value neutral;[88] they have been accompanied by a changing appreciation of the importance of the state, the informal sector, and the rural sector. The rebuilding of the statistical capacity of African economies, which will be discussed in chapter 4, needs to start with this acknowledgement. It is a process of agreeing upon who produces these numbers and who should be counted in them.

3

Facts, Assumptions, and Controversy

Lessons from the Datasets

The response from economists when presented with data quality problems is: Does it matter? The answer is yes, and this chapter presents some case studies showing how and why data quality matters. In the cases presented here, two or more datasets or several versions of the same dataset are in direct conflict with each other, and at face value, there is no obvious reason why one dataset has supremacy over the other. The cases also show that the datasets support competing scholarly interpretations that, in turn, have policy implications that are contradictory.

The case studies were picked for their particularly striking and well-documented disagreements regarding what are arguably the three most important variables for the economic and social analysis of African countries: total population, agricultural production, and change in national income. The examples are not only highly relevant, they are also representative of general problems, and they provide numerical evidence for the claim that measurement is not simply a technocratic exercise. The political economy in which the "facts" are embedded does matter.

The first case is taken from the attempts to conduct a population census in Nigeria. It shows how political contestation about total population data, perhaps the most important data for national policymakers, has rendered the data very difficult to use. The second case also relates to Nigeria but is taken from a controversy surrounding estimates of agricultural production since the 1980s. In the third case, the focus is shifted to Tanzania and the measurement of economic growth after structural adjustment. These three case studies show how malleable the data are and how political conditions and changes in measurement methods affect the data. Users are left to guess about which data to use, or worse, they choose one set of data without knowing about or acknowledging conflicting versions of the same data points.

Nigeria: Counting the Population

The basic starting point for estimating total income or trends in growth is a count of the population. The standard method at national accounting offices in sub-Saharan Africa is to use population data as a multiplier to measure the sectors of the economy for which data is not regularly collected.[1] Thus, for the informal sector and subsistence production, estimates may be made by using a per capita amount to account for these contributions to the national economy. Additionally, for these and other sectors, economic growth is often assumed to be proportional with population growth. Population data is of course the central factor in the most conventional measure of development—real per capita income—and without a correct count any statement on per capita trends in education and health is meaningless. Thus, data on population are vital for the measurement and practice of development. Population estimates also are relevant politically, and the census has a direct impact on electoral representation and fiscal spending. Consequently, population counts are prone to controversy, particularly in countries where power is heavily contested and the state's capacity to monitor is weak.

Unfortunately, the process of counting the total population in Nigeria has been subject to massive controversy and difficulty. Today, we can only guess at the size of the total Nigerian population. In particular, very little is known about the population growth rate. The history of census-taking in Nigeria is an instructive example of the measurement problems that can arise in sub-Saharan Africa. It is also a powerful lens through which the legitimacy of the Nigerian colonial and postcolonial state can be observed.

The first population census was held by colonial authorities in 1866 and only covered Lagos. The next censuses, which were held in 1871, 1881, 1891, and 1901, also only covered Lagos and the immediately surrounding areas. In 1911, the census covered the additional region of Southern Nigeria (which merged with the Lagos colony in 1906). In 1921, the first census was held that, in theory, covered the whole territory of what is referred to today as Nigeria. In practice, however, enumeration outside cities in the south and in the north was not rigorous.[2]

Locust swarms in the north and tax riots in the southeast (in Aba, Onisha, and Owerri) disrupted the completion of the 1931 census. Actual enumeration was conducted only in Lagos, five other townships, and 201 villages in Northern Nigeria. The final population estimate was made using tax records.[3] Hill argues that the estimates for 1931 were as much as 75 percent too low; indeed, she suggests that the population in the north was probably around 20 million rather than the 11 million that the census yielded.[4]

The most serious problems for contemporary measurement and analysis arose with the discontinuity surrounding the transition from colonial rule to independence. Between the population census held by the colonial authorities in 1953 and the population census held in 1962, Nigeria gained independence. In 1953, the Nigerian population correctly anticipated that the census would form the basis for estimating tax receipts. We can therefore safely assume that there was a significant downward bias of measurement in the 1952 census. In 1962, the situation was the opposite, and again, Nigerians most likely assessed the situation correctly. The 1962 census would provide the foundation for federal development expenditure and investment. Most important, the census would be the primary basis for future voting and the distribution of representational seats in the federal assembly.

The result was a high population count compared to the 1952 census, in both northern and southern Nigeria. Consequently, the political power of the north and the south became heavily contested.[5] The government, led by the Northern People's Congress, rejected the 1962 census, and another census was commissioned the following year. The population figures published in 1963 were again heavily discredited, this time by southern politicians (represented by National Council of Nigeria and the Cameroons) and, according to historian Toyin Falola, they are widely considered to be fraudulent.[6] The census results for 1973 were also rejected and are considered illegitimate.[7] No census was held during the military rule of the 1980s. Generally, in the postcolonial period the 1963 figures were used for planning purposes, and a growth rate of 2.5 percent from a 1963 base was adopted until 1976, when the assumed population growth rate was adjusted to 3.2 percent.[8]

A new census was proposed for 1991 as part of the return to civil rule by the Babangida regime.[9] This census was preceded by a publicity campaign and was well funded by foreign donors.[10] The resulting figures indicated that the total population was as low as 88 million. This would imply a very low population growth in the postcolonial period if the 1963 or 1973 data are used as base years. The World Bank did not accept this low estimate and the World Development Indicators dataset still reports 99.9 million for 1991.

The most recent census was planned for 2001 (the Nigerian constitution decrees that they should be held at ten-year intervals), but because of the transition from military to civilian rule, it was delayed until 2006. Preparation for the 2006 census was rigorous. A Census Awareness Study was prepared that indicated that about one-third of the population would not trust the numbers provided by the census. In southern regions there was a particular concern that in the north, goats and cows would be counted as part of the household, reflecting the widespread suspicion that the north's political leaders would tamper with the census numbers.[11]

In order to counteract the anticipated negative response, the National Population Commission (NPC) engaged in an advocacy effort to generate support for the census at the federal level. Members of the NPC informed ministers and members of the national assembly of the importance of the census, the chairman of the NPC called on state governors, and lower-level NPC commissioners contacted local government and other traditional and political leaders in order to provide information about the 2006 census and publicize its importance. The NPC credited the relative success of the census to this public relations exercise, a relatively more favorable political climate, and to the fact that both "in 2006 and 1991 the census was more scientific [than the previous censuses]. Both were conducted according to best practice. It was more accurate, better conducted."[12]

Despite these efforts by the NPC, the 2006 census was not executed without problems. In his report to the president of Nigeria, the chairman of the NPC noted that: "some enumerating staff deployed by the Commission were killed while some were assaulted and chased away during the current census in certain parts of the country."[13] The results were also fiercely disputed. The response from Nigeria's president, Olusegun Obasanjo, was to call "those who dispute the results 'confusionists,'" adding that when they saw the census didn't break the country, they sought to sow confusion. And he washed his hands of the issue: "If you like, use it, [if] you don't like [it], leave it."[14] One may be tempted to give similar cynical advice to academic users when it comes to interpreting the records of population size and growth in Nigeria for the twentieth century, but asserting the correct population size in Nigeria and its growth is far too important. Table 3.1 shows the official results of the censuses conducted from 1911 to 2006. The data vary to a surprising degree, and consensus regarding the plausibility of levels and growth is particularly hard to reach when the data have been so fiercely contested for political reasons.

Table 3.2 presents some implied annual population growth rates. The implied growth rates from 1953 to either 1962 or 1963 are both implausibly high. It is difficult to accurately determine to what extent this is due to postcolonial cheating or to colonial undercounting. On the other hand, the growth rate for the period 1973 to 1991 is implausibly low, which could be

TABLE 3.1. Nigerian population in census years (in millions)

	1911	1921	1931	1952/53	1962	1963	1973	1991	2006
North	8.12	10.56	11.44	16.84	22.01	29.78	51.38	47.37	n.a.
South	7.93	8.16	8.62	13.58	23.28	25.88	28.38	41.62	n.a.
Total	16.05	18.72	20.06	30.42	45.29	55.66	79.76	88.99	140

Source: R. T. I. Suberu, *Federalism and Ethnic Conflict in Nigeria* (Washington, DC: Institute of Peace Press, 2001), 169. Adapted from R. K. Udo, "Geography and Population Censuses in Nigeria," in *Fifty Years of Geography in Nigeria: The Ibadan Story*, edited by Olusegun Areola and Stanley I. Okafor (Ibadan: Ibadan University Press, 1998), 356; and "Report of Nigeria's National Population Commission on the 2006 Census," *Population and Development Review* 33, no. 1 (2007): 206–10.

TABLE 3.2. Estimating Nigerian population growth (%)

From	1911	1921	1931	1953	1953	1963	1973	1991	1911	1953	1963
To	1921	1931	1953	1962	1963	1973	1991	2006	2006	2006	2006
Growth	1.55	0.69	1.91	4.52	6.23	3.66	0.61	2.31	2.31	2.92	2.17

Source: My own calculations based on the data reported in Table 3.1. Percentage growth calculated as compound growth rates between census years.

interpreted as a sign of overcounting in the 1962, 1963 and 1973 censuses. The World Bank considers the 1991 census to be an underestimate.

As for the relative accuracy of these censuses, Polly Hill reported that the 1952 census yielded an estimate for the population in Kano of 3 million—a figure that in Hill's view should have been closer to 4.5 million, implying an underestimate of 50 percent.[15] The 1963 census counted the population in Kano at 5 million, and this census could be closer to the truth. This interpretation fits well with Caldwell and Okanjo's reading of the 1962 census. They argue that "it may well be that in some areas in Eastern-Nigeria there was an inflation of the population figures. But the magnitude of the population increases recorded is probably to be accounted for more by undercounting in 1953 than by overstatement in 1962."[16] Arthur Lewis agrees and suggests that if the 1953 result was an undercount by 20 percent, this would be consistent with about 45 million in 1963 (thus lending credit to the 1962 census).[17] But other scholars have found mistakes in the 1962 census. It was found that there were more men in the 20–24 age group than in the 15–19 age group. This is unlikely, but Umoh suggests one appealing explanation: Men above 20 years of age would automatically be registered as voters in the election that was to take place the following year. This suggests that the total population count may be correct but that many were reported to be older than they actually were in order to qualify as voters.[18]

Today, the NPC still suffers from a bad reputation. The National Bureau of Statistics[19] and the NPC remain separate institutions, and according to interviews made with public affairs officers at both institutions, the Federal Office of Statistics (FOS) has no desire to join forces with the NPC as it fears that would ruin the already-fragile credibility of its institutions. The NPC is unhappy with this arrangement and has said that the separation was a "shame," since they were "sister-institutions."[20]

This case has two conclusions: one with a positive note and the other with a neutral, if not negative, flavor. Recent censuses in Nigeria have taken place in a context in which the legitimacy of the NPC and other federal state institutions appears to be increasing. While the 1991 and 2006 censuses were problematic, in relative terms they can be viewed as small successes. This is probably due to the deliberate efforts of the NPC and the federal administration, but the general move toward transparency and democracy in Nigeria has likely also contributed to this development. The negative perspective is that for the purpose of estimating population growth, this evidence cannot be taken at face value. This has implications for the validity of any development statistics, in which population totals and population growth are two of the most used variables. Any statement—whether it is the number of people below the poverty line or doctors per capita—becomes guesswork. The implications for policymaking are striking, too: it becomes very difficult to make a guess about how many vaccinations or schools are needed and how many recipients are currently reached.

Measurement is not simply a technocratic exercise. The political economy in which the "facts" are embedded does matter. There is a clear trend of discontinuity in census-taking in Nigeria, from the colonial problem of evasion to the postcolonial race to be included. It is also a reminder of the importance and difficulty of getting "levels" right, and further, that the measure of change might be severely distorted when the levels are biased.

Nigeria: Counting Crops

In *Planning without Facts*, a book on Nigerian development planning published in 1966, William F. Stolper wrote that "the neglect of the subsistence production can lead to serious misunderstanding of the process of development and therefore to inappropriate policies and plans to accelerate development."[21] The problem of course was that information regarding this sector—in particular agricultural productivity—was inadequate, or indeed altogether absent.

Three decades later, in 1988, Paul Collier examined available datasets on food production in Nigeria with the starting point that in the 1970s and 1980s, "a combination of complex events and weak data" had yielded incompatible analyses. Data on food crops for the country were at this time supplied by four sources. Of these, the only source that was based directly on field surveys was the data published by the FOS. But Collier noted that these series are "frequently incredible" and, in particular, that they were often contradicted by the data from agricultural development projects.[22]

The data provided by the Central Bank of Nigeria are from the same source but report higher yields. As Collier notes, they "rather arbitrarily [scaled] up the FOS series for the more commercial crops by up to 30 percent in the belief that the FOS estimates for these crops are biased downwards."[23] The other two sources of data at the time of Collier's analysis were published by the Food and Agriculture Organization of the United Nations and the U.S. Department of Agriculture, both of whose data were indirect estimates that took "into account perceived trends in demand and imports, yielding production as a residual." Without justification, Collier concluded that although the data are "not being firmly based on observed production . . . these series provide the best guide to long-term trends in food production."[24]

The differences among the series in table 3.3 are striking. Generally, the series from the FAO and USDA are much more positive. The series from the statistical office indicates negative growth in all crops except for palm oil.

TABLE 3.3. Annual percentage growth in production of major food crops in Nigeria, 1970–1982

	FOS[1]	CBN[2]	USDA[3]	FAO[4]
Sorghum	−0.9	1.3	−0.5	−0.5
Yam	−3.5	−1.3	1.6	n.a.
Millet	−0.1	2.1	−0.1	0.0
Cassava	−8.5	−6.5	0.0	2.1
Palm Oil	2.4	2.4	2.4	2.4
Maize	−6.3	−4.3	2.5	2.5
Rice	−0.1	2.1	6.9	5.1

[1]Federal Office of Statistics
[2]Central Bank of Nigeria
[3]U.S. Department of Agriculture
[4]Food and Agriculture Organization
Source: P. Collier, "Oil Shocks and Food Security in Nigeria," *International Labour Review* 127, no. 6 (1988): 764. According to Collier, the data are from the World Bank, 1985.

For cassava and maize—two very important food crops—these growth rates would imply that the total harvest was halved over the decade. The FAO series implies that growth was between 2 and 3 percent, in keeping with a typical guess of the population growth rate in the same period.

Both the rate and the trend of growth in Nigeria's agricultural sector have been controversial. In "Policy Making without Facts," an article on structural adjustment policies published in 1992—the title referring to Stolper's book published almost three decades earlier—Paul Mosley wrote that the lack of data had "if anything increased in relevance."[25]

According to one dataset on agricultural production that was based on field surveys and was approved by the FOS, there was negative growth in food production in Nigeria after structural adjustment programs. Another dataset that was approved by the FAO and the Central Bank of Nigeria showed rapid growth in food production. The data are reported in table 3.4 and table 3.5. The policy implications of these two different datasets were completely opposite. The first implied that structural adjustment policies did not work, while the second implied that they were indeed effective. The problem is further compounded because both conclusions

TABLE 3.4. Total food crop production in Nigeria, 1981–1990 (% growth)

	1981	1982	1983	1984	1985	1986	1987	1988	1989	1990
CBN[1]	–	–	–	–	–	–	14.8	1.6	9.4	1.3
FAO[2]	1.1	4.6	–19.5	29.9	6.7	7.0	–8.0	0.7	60.0	–
FOS[3]	–0.4	9.1	10.6	–10.9	47.9	15.9	–35.4	41.4	5.7	–

[1]Central Bank of Nigeria.
[2]Food and Agriculture Organization.
[3]Federal Office of Statistics.

TABLE 3.5. Total cash crop production in Nigeria, 1981–1990 (% growth)

	1981	1982	1983	1984	1985	1986	1987	1988	1989	1990
CBN[1]	–	–	–	–	–	–6.4	9.0	30.1	2.4	8.8
FAO[2]	–1.7	–2.2	–22.4	14.9	7.6	–2.1	18.8	17.7	–1.6	–

[1]Central Bank of Nigeria.
[2]Food and Agriculture Organization.
Source: P. Mosley, "Policy-Making without Facts: A Note on the Assessment of Structural Adjustment Policies in Nigeria, 1985–1990," *African Affairs* 91 (1992): 227–40.

could make sense theoretically through two different interpretations. One could plausibly argue that a combination of the liberalization of internal food prices and reduced competition from imports led to a positive supply. Another equally plausible interpretation would be that the removal of fertilizer subsidies caused negative production.

Mosley's and Collier's study of the 1980s shows that there is considerable doubt regarding data on crop production, particularly for food crops. These troubles have not been solved. When compiling this dataset for Nigeria, I discovered a major difference in the published crop statistics. A comparison of the data reported in the 1995 *Statistical Abstract* and in the 1999 *Statistical Abstract* is shown in table 3.6.[26] It shows that not only is there variation from one data source to another but that the same institution is reporting radically different data for the same year: 1993/94.

Although these discrepancies might not significantly affect the national income estimates in the aggregate, the difference is huge in physical terms. A difference of 14 million tonnes of cassava and 7 million tonnes of yam could have a considerable influence on the transportation, distribution, and retail sectors in the country, not to mention the diet of the population.

The FOS has been supplying data on crop production since independence. These are based on the product of an acreage harvest estimate and a yield estimate for each year, which are reportedly based on annual sample surveys. Between the publication of the 1995 and the 1999 *Statistical Abstracts*, there was an upward revision in output data, as reported in table 3.6. Interestingly, the yield and acreage data were not adjusted accordingly. In fact, the yields were adjusted downward while the acreage

Table 3.6. Estimated output of major agricultural crops in Nigeria for the year 1993–1994 (in thousands of tonnes)

	Millet	Guinea Corn	Ground-nut	Beans	Yam	Cotton	Maize	Cassava	Rice	Melon	Coco Yam
SA 95[1]	3,595	5,413	2,008	1,946	15,861	263	4,505	17,261	1,303	490	2,100
SA 99[2]	4,738	6,145	893	1,463	22,709	214	6,816	31,005	2,943	108	1,164
% Change	31.8	13.5	−55.5	−24.8	43.2	−18.6	51.3	79.6	125.9	−78.0	−44.6

[1]Data reported in *Annual Abstract of Statistics 1995*.
[2]Data reported in *Annual Abstract of Statistics 1999*.
Source: Federal Republic of Nigeria, *Annual Abstract of Statistics 1995* (Abuja: Federal Office of Statistics, 1995); Federal Republic of Nigeria, *Annual Abstract of Statistics 1999* (Abuja: Federal Office of Statistics, 1999).

harvested remained the same, thus leaving only the totals adjusted. While the yields multiplied by the acreage did match up with the total in the 1995 *Statistical Abstract*, this was far from true for the 1999 abstract. Total physical production of all crops was revised upward by 42.8 percent—a substantial addition of more than 23 million tonnes of produce. As noted, the tubers yam and cassava, which are notoriously difficult to measure, accounted for 90 percent of this increase.

Tanzania: Accounting for Structural Adjustment

The available international datasets all take the national account files provided by the statistical agencies as their starting point. Expressing the estimates in international prices and using different primary data sources creates confusion about income levels. This has implications for growth estimates. This section uses the example of Tanzania to show how harmonization of growth time series across different base years creates illusory growth episodes. The constant price growth time series provided by the national statistical agencies are subject to revisions that affect growth rates. In addition, various official series with different base years cover the same years.

As a litmus test of how these methods affect reported growth rates, I constructed a correlation matrix of derived annual growth rate data from 1961 to 2001 from the Tanzanian official data, the Penn World Tables, and the Maddison dataset. The results are reported in table 3.7. Because

TABLE 3.7. Estimated correlation matrix of annual growth rates for Tanzania, 1961–2001

	Tanzania	PWT[1]	Maddison
Tanzania	1.00	0.23	0.75
PWT[1]	0.23	1.00	0.26
Maddison	0.75	0.26	1.00

[1] Penn World Tables.

Source: National Account Files of Tanzania; World Development Indicators, 2003; Alan Heston, Robert Summers, and Bettina Aten, Real GDP per Capita (Constant Prices: Chain Series), Penn World Table Version 6.2, Center for International Comparisons of Production, Income and Prices, University of Pennsylvania, 2006; Angus Maddison, Historical Statistics of the World Economy: 1-2006 AD, 2009.

the most current dataset from the World Bank does not report growth statistics for years earlier than 1987, the WDI data are excluded from this test. Although the Tanzanian official data series does not cover the whole period, a series can be produced using the growth rate from different constant price series. A correlation matrix is normally used to see if variables are moving systematically together. Table 3.7 compares annual growth rates for the same years for the same country. We would expect agreement to be high or perfect, which would indicate correlations of 1 or close to 1 between the sources.

The lack of agreement on annual growth rates in these sources is striking. There is so little agreement between the annual growth rates published by the Penn World Tables and the national statistical office that one would be forced to describe the two sets, which supposedly describe the same phenomenon using the same measure, as having no relationship with one another. Similarly, the Maddison data and the Penn World Tables seem to be unrelated. The agreement between Maddison and the official statistics is better but remains far from convincing. To get closer to patterns of variation, the highest annual growth rate and the lowest annual growth rate found in any of the three data sources is plotted for each year in figure 3.1. The difference between the highest (max) and the lowest (min) reported growth rates represents the range of disagreement for each year.

The average annual disagreement between 1961 and 2001 is 6 percent. It is not evenly distributed; there is serious dissonance regarding growth in Tanzania in the 1980s and 1990s. According to the Penn World Tables, the Tanzanian economy grew 20 percent in 1987. The following year, the Penn World Tables recorded a negative growth of 33 percent. Table 3.8 shows how these differences map out if averages are calculated for different time periods. In the table I have calculated averages of annual growth rates for different time periods according to the different data sources. Averaging fails to purge the data of uncertainty entirely. With the exception of the 1970s, throughout which all data sources agree that the Tanzanian economy was growing quickly, there is significant disagreement between the sources. Indeed, whether one finds that Tanzania experienced stagnation or rapid growth following independence in 1961 depends entirely on the data source one is referring to. It is open to speculation whether the 1980s were a period of modest growth, stagnation, or outright retrogression.

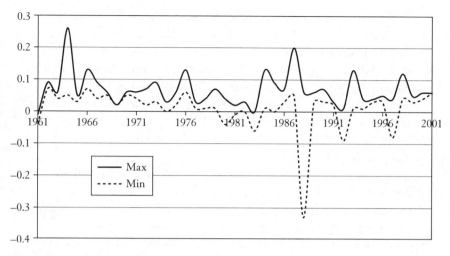

Figure 3.1: Annual range of disagreement in GDP growth rate, Tanzania, 1961–2001.

Source: Tanzania National Account Files; World Development Indicators 2003; Alan Heston, Robert Summers, and Bettina Aten, Penn World Table Version 6.2, Center for International Comparisons of Production, Income and Prices, University of Pennsylvania, 2006; Angus Maddison, Historical Statistics of the World Economy: 1–2006 AD, copyright Angus Maddison 2009.

TABLE 3.8. Average annual growth according to different data sources, Tanzania, 1961–2000

	WDI	Tanzania	PWT	Maddison
1961–1965	–	3.4	8.4	4.6
1966–1970	–	6.0	5.8	6.0
1971–1975	–	4.6	3.8	4.2
1976–1980	–	3.2	4.4	3.0
1981–1985	–	0.8	4.2	0.4
1986–1990	–	5.6	0.2	3.8
1991–1995	1.8	2.2	2.2	2.0
1996–2000	4.2	4.6	3.2	3.0
1961–1979	–	4.3	6.1	4.6
1980–2000	–	3.3	2.1	2.2
1961–2000	–	3.8	4.0	3.4

Source: World Development Indicators (WDI) 2003; Tanzania National Account Files; Alan Heston, Robert Summers, and Bettina Aten, Penn World Table, Version 6.2, Center for International Comparisons of Production, Income and Prices at the University of Pennsylvania, 2006; and Angus Maddison, Historical Statistics of the World Economy: 1–2006 AD, Copyright Angus Maddison, 2009.

The disagreement between the different data sources is caused by the fact that different versions of official data on Tanzanian economic growth are available to each dataset compiler for harmonizing growth series. The postcolonial official growth record of Tanzania is covered by four different constant price series. The first series, which was based in 1964 prices, was continued until 1982. The second series, which was based in 1976 prices, covers the period 1976 to 1993. The third series is based in 1985 prices and includes all years from 1961 to 1995. A fourth series is based in 1992 prices and covers the years 1987 to 2001.[27]

Figure 3.2 summarizes the aggregate growth rates according to the four different time series published by Tanzania's Central Bureau of Statistics. This figure shows how difficult it has been to harmonize the different versions of economic growth series in Tanzania, especially with regard to economic performance since the late 1970s. The difference between these estimates derives from the different ways of taking into account agricultural output that is marketed outside official channels. Conversely, the difference in estimates for the late 1980s to early 1990s revival period in growth depends on what assumptions were made to correct for the inadequate recording of output in formal and informal marketing channels. It was known that the informal markets were growing, and the different

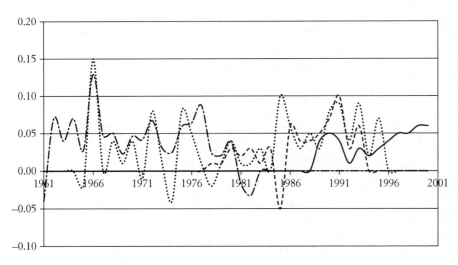

Figure 3.2: GDP growth at constant prices, Tanzania, 1961–2001.
Source: National Accounts Tanzania (various editions).

series corrected for this error in different manners. Moreover, the extent and timing of the decline in the 1970s vary considerably, creating uncertainty about the comparative economic performance of Tanzania across time.

Tanzania is one of the most intensively studied countries in sub-Saharan Africa, particularly by scholars interested in economic development.[28] The distinctive charisma of the first Tanzanian president, Mwalimu ("the teacher") Julius Nyerere, and the attractiveness of his ideas, especially his concept of *ujamaa* (togetherness, or African socialism), meant that from the 1960s onward, Dar es Salaam was an intellectual hub for development scholars. Similarly, the appeal of Tanzania for donors in the 1970s and 1980s stimulated research that focused on the efficacy of aid and economic development policies in Tanzania. Post-Nyerere Tanzania has retained the attention of scholars for several reasons, including anticipation of economic and political reforms and the vested interest of both researchers and donors. An indication of the degree of scholarly interest in Tanzania is the fact that there are two published monographs on the informal economy in Tanzania, a subject for which there is little research and data for other African economies.[29] Consequently, one would expect that the record of growth and development since independence in Tanzania would be fairly well established. But as the data in tables and figures in this chapter show, that is not the case.

In the 1970s, following the Arusha Declaration in 1967, Tanzania's economic activities were increasingly controlled by the Tanzanian state directly or through its parastatal subsidiaries. As a result, in the 1976 revision of national accounts, the majority of the data on trade, finance, and industry was drawn from parastatal enterprises, while data on crops was largely drawn from state marketing boards. The state was hit by external shocks that constrained public revenues and expenditures, and its capacity to maintain control over the marketing of agricultural products was weakened. Official prices were set too low and peasants turned to alternative markets. Initially, the state strongly resisted the growth of parallel and informal markets.[30] Pressure from donors, the IMF, and the World Bank resulted in structural adjustment policy reforms, which in turn changed Tanzania's political stance toward markets and initiated a trend toward liberalization. This resulted in a large structural shift from formal to informal activities, which took place at the same time that the nation's administrations were strapped for resources. The statistical office and later its database assemblers faced a choice. They could either report a dramatic reduction in overall economic activity as the formal sectors declined or they could assume that an increase in the informal sectors compensated for the reduction in formal activity. Until 1997, the statistical services in Tanzania had neither the data nor the resources to adjust to these new economic realities.

Thus, the growth effect from parallel/informal markets is largely missing in the official statistics before the 1997 revision. Collier et al. reported, "The country's informal economy has claimed much of the produce of the predominantly peasant agricultural sector. Peasants appear to have shifted from export and non-food crops to food crops for their own subsistence and for local informal trading."[31] Tripp emphasized the growth of the urban informal economy during the same period,[32] while Maliyamkono and Bagachwa estimated that in 1990 the unrecorded economy had "reached some 30 per cent of official GDP."[33]

In 1997, the methods and data used to estimate GDP were completely revised. The new series was based in 1992 prices and in used the methodology of the 1993 System of National Accounts. In this revision, statisticians noted that the decline of the formal economy and the growth of the informal economy were not reflected in the available statistics and that therefore the previous estimates of total value added were underestimates. "Estimates of the size of this deficiency ranged from 30 percent to as much as 200 percent of GDP."[34] The new estimates also include fresh surveys of transport, trade, and construction. The report noted that in comparison with the previous series, the "private sector was under-covered—sometimes not covered at all—and the growing informal sector was not generally accounted for."[35] The new series accounted for the informal sector and thus recorded a higher total GDP.

It is noteworthy that a World Bank publication records that the Tanzanian national accounts methods were modified in 1995 and that a revised series was published in 1997.[36] As pointed out above, these revisions only went back to 1987; consequently, the World Bank decided not to report growth data for the earlier period. Not all data compilers have been aware of the problem of reconciling the two series. Somehow, when the Penn World Tables, tried to reconcile the conflicting series, a large negative annual percentage growth rate (-33 percent) was recorded for the year 1988 in their data series. This has led to erroneous conclusions by data users. In the *Handbook of Economic Growth*, Durlauf et al. argued that negative output shocks are a typical phenomenon among low-income countries.[37] Not realizing that the "output shock" was a purely statistical artifact, they included the period from 1987 to 1990 in Tanzania on their "top ten list" of output collapses. It seems that when economic development experts are not country experts, the road from fact to fiction is short.

The recently published *Political Economy of Economic Growth in Africa, 1960–2000* is the most comprehensive and technically sophisticated study of African economic growth to date.[38] In the hands of country experts, one would expect that the growth of Tanzania would get a more careful treatment. Mwase and Ndulu are aware of the Tanzanian revision, and in a footnote to a figure for the econometric analysis it is noted that, "1988 is treated as a missing observation because the series shows an erroneous massive downward adjustment in that year."[39] However, simply rejecting the data for 1988 does not solve the problem of the Penn World Tables series; it actually makes it worse.

The resulting evidence, as shown in table 3.9, misleadingly supports the hypothesis of a sharp recovery in growth during the reform period. In 1987, there is massive growth in the Penn World Table data, but this increase is not supported by any other growth evidence. As a result, the revised Penn World Tables series seriously overestimates post–structural adjustment growth in Tanzania. Before rejecting the data for 1988, the data series measured growth from 1985 to 1995 at an annual average of less than 2 percent. After the year 1988 is treated as void, the annual average

Table 3.9. Annual rate of economic growth in Tanzania 1985–1995 (%)

	1985	1986	1987	1988	1989	1990	1991	1992	1993	1994	1995	Average
PWT 6.1	9	6	20	−33	5	3	3	−9	13	1	3	1.9
PWT Revised	9	6	20	–	5	3	3	−9	13	1	3	5.4
Maddison	0	3	5	4	3	4	2	1	1	2	4	2.6
Country data, 1976 series	−3	3	5	4	4	5	6	4	4	–	–	3.6
Country data, 1985 series	7	7	6	6	2	7	6	4	4	3	5	5.2
Country data, 1992 series	–	–	–	4	3	6	3	2	0	1	4	2.9

jumps to 5.4 percent. For the year 1987, the Penn World Table reports 20 percent growth, while Maddison and the official data report 5 percent.

As demonstrated by the evidence provided here, there is considerable uncertainty and room for misinterpretation about the Tanzanian growth record. The analysis of Tanzania's economic growth in the postcolonial period suffers from unreliable data, and claims of causal relationships between policy variables and periods of economic growth should be treated with extreme caution. Moreover, the implications of the findings from this case study go beyond this individual, national case.

Lessons from Data Controversy

I chose these three case studies of controversy regarding competing datasets because they are particularly well documented and striking cases. They have wide relevance. This section will discuss how they relate to similar situations in other countries. It will also further highlight that the different datasets support different scholarly conclusions and have contradictory policy implications.

Population

The case from Nigeria highlights clear patterns of colonial and postcolonial discontinuity or, more generally, how changes in political economy are reflected in national statistics. More specifically, in terms of census-taking, the Nigerian case illustrated the stark difference between a colonial-era problem of avoiding being counted in order to evade taxation and the postcolonial race to be included. The case also provides a stern reminder of the importance and difficulty of getting levels right, and further, that the measure of change might be severely distorted when the levels are biased. This question arises, with varying intensity, during each population census undertaken on the African continent.

The controversies surrounding census-taking in Nigeria are particularly noteworthy because Nigeria is probably the most populous nation in Africa—probably being the operative word. But they are also important because political and ethnic divisions have been so pronounced in the federal political system that has been in place since colonial times.

Underestimation of the population in colonial censuses and overestimation in postcolonial censuses is a general problem in sub-Saharan Africa.
To date, too little research has focused on verifying reported population
growth rates. It has been suggested that some colonial population estimates
may be as much as 50 percent too low,[40] but how this affects the acceleration in population growth rate that was recorded in the 1950s and 1960s
has not yet been clarified.

A recent example from Kenya shows how contentious taking a population census can be. The most recent Kenyan census was undertaken in late
August of 2009, and the results were released in August 2010.[41] The census
was undertaken in the context of relatively unstable political conditions
that included ethnically based postelection violence. Indeed, the inclusion
of tribal ethnicity on the questionnaire was seen as divisive at best, if not
dangerously inflammatory.[42] Furthermore, during the lead-up to the actual enumeration, certain groups began calling for its postponement, fear-
ing the deliberate distortion of figures and the importation of "outsiders"
into districts in an attempt to artificially inflate population statistics.[43] The
results of the census were used to draw new election boundaries—as provided for in the country's recently reformed constitution[44]—and to determine how to distribute Sh14 billion from the government's Constituencies
Development Fund.[45] The funds, which support development projects, are
distributed according to a metric that combines the population of each con-
stituency and results from the 2005–2006 poverty index.[46] A second government fund, the Local Authority Transfer Fund, is also dispersed based
on census results.[47]

During the release of the census results, the government—represented
by Planning Minister Wycliffe Oparnya—announced the cancellation
of the results from eight districts because exaggerated figures were reported in those districts.[48] All of the districts under dispute are located in
the northeastern zones of Kenya: Mandera Central, Mandera East, Mandera West, Lagdera, Wajir East, Turkana Central, Turkana South, and
Turkana North.[49] The planning minister argued that household size results were not consistent with population levels. "If there is growth in the
population, you expect households to increase. The per capita per house
is very high and the number of households very few."[50] Representing
the Turkana population, Assistant Minister Josephat Nanok called the
cancellation "illegal, unconstitutional, malicious and mischievous and

discriminatory and in bad faith."[51] Central to the argument of the Turkana community is the belief that the fault lies in the government's reliance on projections based on undercounted census results of 1999. "As everyone knows, the 1999 census was an overnight census exercise which could not capture the population numbers of all the pastoralists groups in Turkana who live a mobile nomadic life in an inaccessible terrain, thus the outcome of that census was not only inaccurate but also controversial," the assistant minister said.[52]

The numerical disagreement in Kenya was as large and controversial, if smaller in scale, than the example from Nigeria. The population of the areas under dispute was projected at 1.4 million persons. The census reported those areas as having 2.3 million.[53] It is also telling that one of the population groups involved in the controversy is engaged in transhumance activities and livestock rearing. The point made by the Turkana spokesman refers to two types of census-taking—de jure and de facto. In the latter, the enumerator records the answer to the question "How many people reside in this household?" In the former, the enumerator records how many are present on the day of the census—or overnight, meaning that the enumerator records the answer to the question "How many people spent the night in this household last night?"[54] Using the latter question tends to underestimate the count of pastoralists, and using the former question allows respondents to misreport. The claim the spokesman of the Turkana made, however, is misleading; both the 1999 census and the 2009 census used the de facto method.

The basic problem here is a lack of trust in the numbers. The validity of the numbers provided by official institutions—and therefore the power of the state—is in question. The weaknesses of the institutions are mirrored in a weakness in monitoring and recording. Population censuses can display the distance between theory and practice. In theory, counting the population is a straightforward activity; in practice it requires a range of discrete decisions about who should be counted, and the categories of belonging may be heavily contested. The question of ethnicity is much discussed in relation to sub-Saharan Africa,[55] but as has been shown here, economic categories or geographic belonging may also be contested.[56]

These social and political concerns about legitimacy of the data providers translate into vocal doubts about their numerical accuracy.[57] As mentioned, Manning has argued that the precolonial population of sub-Saharan Africa may have been as high as 150 million in 1850, as compared to the figure of 100 million that most datasets use. These revisions may mean that popular accounts of population growth (or even explosions)[58] may be based on very feeble statistics and that in many cases the acceleration in population growth in the postcolonial period is currently overstated in datasets.[59] These counting problems not only have policy implications but are directly related to politics and the legitimacy of the state in question.[60]

Crops

The controversy surrounding crop statistics shows how the basic question regarding the political economy—Who benefits?—matters. In the example of Nigeria discussed above, what was at stake was the fertilizer subsidy. The basic question was whether the removal of fertilizer subsidies had caused agricultural yields to fall or whether price liberalization had resulted in a positive supply response. Both interpretations had datasets to substantiate their claims. This case shows that agricultural crop statistics may be politically sensitive. Accurate total output data are not available but are reached using different methods of aggregation that are subject to assumptions that change across time and space. Without a standardized method, there is considerable room for uncertainty and discretion, thus providing opportunities for stakeholders to push for the adaption of measures in ways that suit their political goals.

The Nigerian case has contemporary relevance, specifically to the much-publicized introduction of fertilizer subsidies in Malawi since 2006.[61] Malawi's recently published agricultural census (2010) reports data that contradicts the previously published data from the Ministry of Agriculture that showed record high yields. The recent agricultural census (2006/2007) indicated a maize output of 2.1 million tonnes, compared to previous figures of 3.4 million tonnes.[62] The impressive growth data reported from Malawi in recent years has been supported by crop data collected by the Ministry of Agriculture and published in the Malawi Annual Economic Report. These reported crop data were based on the last census, which took place in 1992/93, and the annual projections of agricultural production were aggregated by multiplying yield and acreage observations from agricultural extension officers.[63]

A National Census of Agriculture and Livestock was undertaken in 2006/2007, but the report was not released until 2010. The census was funded by the Norwegian Agency for Development Cooperation (NORAD) and was conducted by Malawi's National Statistical Office. The delay was an issue of concern,[64] and when the census was finally published, the results were not accepted by the Ministry of Agriculture. The problem was that the agricultural census showed remarkably lower figures for the total output of all crops than those previously issued by the Ministry of Agriculture for the same year, including the prestigious maize crop. Notably, the maize figures reported in the census are much closer to national food needs, while the official figures in 2006/2007 would imply that either huge stockpiles of maize accumulated around the country or that a significant portion of the population was getting fat, neither of which are the case. Indeed, the caloric output of the official numbers would imply that the average Malawian consumes something in excess of 4,000 calories a day, compared to the commonly assumed figure of around 1,500 to 2,000.[65]

When the average yield figures from the two reports are compared, they show only a marginal discrepancy. The significant difference derives from how the data are aggregated. The issue of disagreement is the number of agricultural households; the Ministry of Agriculture used a figure nearly 1 million higher than that used by the census. Statistical officers diplomatically stated that this may have been due to the different definitions of the household that were used.[66] In other circles it was hinted that some farmers might have been invented in some cases in order to qualify for subsidies. It is not clear how these "ghost farmers" might have been invented, as both agricultural extension officers and peasants would have had incentive to inflate the number of farmers so they could qualify for subsidies. The agricultural subsidy was given as a voucher that could be redeemed for subsidized fertilizer. These vouchers therefore had a value.[67]

Although there is no direct evidence of tampering, the indications are strong, as were the incentives. The president and the ministry desired evidence of good, consistent performance in the agricultural sector to keep the electorate convinced that the nation's agricultural development strategy was working. Perhaps more important, they needed to be able to convince donors that their fertilizer and seed programs were working, thus ensuring that financial support would be forthcoming. The fertilizer subsidy program totaled 4.6 percent of GDP in 2008/2009, or approximately one-third of total aid inflows to the country.[68] It was also in the interest of peasants and agricultural extension officers to "increase" the numbers of farming households, not only to please superiors but also because the vouchers have a market value. There is some evidence and growing concern that the vouchers are not reaching the right recipients and that local officials are able to profit from them.[69] These worries aside, the situation of agricultural data in Malawi fits an established pattern of strong pressure from executives on statistical authorities to get the particular data the leadership needs. In such situations, the motivation is not to monitor the economy but to affirm success.[70]

The problem of agricultural crop statistics is not just an African one. A particularly well-documented and much-discussed example relates to the so-called Green Revolution in India, a supposed spurt in agricultural growth. Chambers noted that in hindsight, it was a mistake to believe that high-yielding seed varieties could have caused the significant increases in output that were recorded in the official statistics. The areas that were suitable for the high-yielding varieties were too small to have had an explosive impact on the aggregate growth rate. He argued that agricultural extension officers were given very ambitious targets for the supply of Green Revolution inputs, such as seeds and fertilizers, and that the officers "reported these [targets as] achieved when the reality lagged far behind." He also provided sources that indicated that the official statistics for some areas with high-yielding varieties were overstated by 3 to 5 times.[71] In addition, the Ministry of Agriculture in India questioned the crop output data produced by the statistical office because it did not reflect the data the ministry had on the usage of inputs in the agricultural sector. This well-documented story demonstrates how the Ministry of Agriculture in India in the 1960s and 1970 tampered with the official statistics in a way that reflected their own overstated statistics on uses of inputs.[72] Thus, the "Green Revolution" was not only overstated in statistics; it was artificially created before it really occurred.

The problems of monitoring and recording relate to more than state capacity. The challenge of recording is greater in some locations than in others. A number of authors have noted that agricultural statistics from developing countries, particularly African countries, are poor.[73] In an eloquent "prosecution" of development economics, Polly Hill explains that the main reason official statistics in poorer economies in the Southern

Hemisphere are in such a "calamitous state of affairs" is that the statistical methods are not suitable for how agricultural production is organized in the South.[74] The issue here is not only inaccuracies as such but whether there are systematic biases in the national accounting procedures. Hill reviewed the practices at the Food and Agriculture Organization of the United Nations and notes that the instructions in the 1980 world census of agriculture contain no specific advice for treatment of the particular problems of tropical countries, thus ignoring the fact that different techniques, such as mixing crops, are not only very common but are also more productive.[75] Hill argues that sampling methods were developed with the modern, specialized, capital-intensive agriculture practiced in the Northern Hemisphere in mind and that these methods are not transferrable to a nontemperate climate. In the South, total agricultural productivity per crop is complicated, and figures derived from an inappropriate methodology are misleading. A particular example relates root and tubers, known as cassava or manioc, to bananas and plantains. These crops, which are grown together on tiny plots, are not harvested until they are needed (the tubers only last for a couple of days). Although the FAO provides statistics on these crops, Hill argues that "no West African country can have the faintest idea as to how much is really produced."[76] Given how shaky these data on agricultural production are, it is surprising how many studies lend credibility to the FAO data series and make bold statements on long-term trends and short-term fluctuations.[77]

Ignorance of the methods in use at the statistical office may lead even cautious scholars astray. In chapter 1 I referred to a study whose authors were concerned about data problems, but they did not know the extent of the measurement errors or its causes: "Unfortunately, we are aware of no work that quantifies the extent of measurement error in African national income data or determines whether measurement errors are classical (i.e., white noise) at all, although the claim is often made that these errors are likely to be large."[78] The authors resort to the use of rainfall data as an instrumental variable in order to "control" for measurement error and they use only the variation in economic growth that correlates with or can be explained by variations in rainfall. The advantage, the authors hope, is that this would then only pick up growth that relates to food production and therefore living standards. The approach, which has been widely influential, has been imitated by many and criticized by some.[79]

The approach of using rainfall as an instrumental variable may make sense in theory. In practice, it is a bit curious when one studies how these production data are made in the first place. It is of course true that in agricultural societies rainfall is strongly related to income growth, but in terms of measurement practice, rainfall and income are not independent variables; they are linked by assumption in this case. As was noted in chapter 2, for the growth estimates of subsistence agriculture (and subsistence producers are the largest component of the work force in sub-Saharan Africa), "the basic assumption is that output grows at the same rate as the rural population." Thus these growth estimates are not sensitive to climatic variations. Instead, annual variations from the general trend in production were made on the basis of "eye estimates" made by agricultural experts.[80] Two main methods are currently used to aggregate food production trends at statistical offices in sub-Saharan Africa: Food production is assumed to grow with rural population, but it is "adjusted" for rainfall based on subjective judgments by statistical officers. Or food production is based on "crop forecasts" data from agrometeorologists. In this method, statisticians use an FAO model that projects crop outputs based on the level of rainfall during planting season.[81] This data may be adjusted, but in most years there are no resources for a representative crop-cutting survey. Thus in effect, when Miguel, Satyanath, and Sergenti use rainfall to control for measurement error, they are redoing the same exercise that was done to create the agricultural production series in the first place.[82]

In conclusion, the state of agricultural statistics leaves a lot of uncertainty. There is room for scholarly misinterpretations, and furthermore, as the case study showed, for political controversy and contestation of these very important data. Given the weakness of the evidence, the data are malleable and there is ample room for a negotiation of the agricultural data, or picking the data trends that are most convenient. Nigerian policymakers could pick the series that suited their political purpose in the 1980s, whereas the record high harvest data from Malawi made it to the pages of the *New York Times*.[83]

National Income Revision

The controversy surrounding growth statistics in Tanzania derives from a complete revision of the sources and methods used to estimate national income that was conducted in 1992, after structural adjustment. Until that year, national income data was largely derived from state and parastatal agencies and the informal economy was assumed to grow or decline in tune with the formal economy. In contrast, the new data series, which started in 1987, was compiled using the opposite principle: when the formal economy was in decline, the informal economy was assumed to be growing. In addition, new levels were estimated using data from a survey of the informal economy and a household budget survey. As a result, the "new economy" was measured as being 62 percent higher than previous estimated and the underlying growth dynamics were judged to be completely different than previous series indicated.

The break in the statistical series occurred between the years 1986 and 1987. The basic question is: How can we integrate this into a coherent development narrative? The formal economy in Tanzania has been in decline since the late 1970s, and there is ample supplementary evidence to suggest that economic actors turned toward the informal economy. The available data imply that the Tanzanian economy was in rapid decline until 1986 but that there was growth from a higher level from 1987 onward. The timing of this shift reflects changing assumptions at the statistical office. It is likely that the decline in the early 1980s was overestimated and that the improvement in growth in the 1990s was overestimated. The exceptional aspect of the revision in Tanzania is that it was so well documented and that these documents were still available when I visited there more than a decade later.

Writing generally on structural adjustment, Paul Nugent comments that "the statistics which constitute the basis on which structural adjustment is conventionally evaluated are especially problematic. Aside from the larger question of the relationship between the numerals and reality, there is the simple fact that African governments have lacked the means to gather reliable statistics."[84] The case of Tanzania has wide applicability. Economic decline in the late 1970s followed by structural adjustment in the 1980s and 1990s is the dominant pattern in sub-Saharan African. Changing economic realities were not reflected in the official economic statistics, and the effect of revisions raises questions about the efficacy of structural adjustment programs and the commitment of the IMF and World Bank to evaluating these programs. This issue will be expanded on further in chapter 4.

The case also points to another general problem that transcends the evaluation of structural adjustment policies. As I discussed in chapter 1, the problem of dealing with ad hoc revisions remains with us. Ghana's income was recently revised upward by over 60 percent, and upward revisions are likely to be forthcoming from other countries. Perhaps most surprising, upward revisions like these are in line with global standards of national accounting. The problem is that so many countries have not revised their national accounts yet. Some countries are still following the 1968 Standard of National Accounts, while others have already implemented the 1993 or 2008 standard. The problem is not with the standards but that they are unequally adapted at the local level depending on data availability and the quality of these data. When the data are available that show statisticians that current estimates are out of line, there can be many hurdles in the way before an actual revision is undertaken. The first one is technocratic. As Heston suggested in a survey of national income problems in 1994, "often officials who use national accounts for growth purposes . . . may resist improvements in level estimates of output because it will introduce breaks in national accounts series."[85]

Statistical offices are dependent on ad hoc funds from donors to do these kinds of revisions, a situation that is unfortunate. The situation might be improved if governments themselves made the resources available, but the ultimate approval of new estimates necessitates coordination with the IMF or the World Bank data divisions or both. In Ghana, the revision process started a decade ago, but it was interrupted because of disagreements and the unavailability of technical advisors.[86] A similar problem was noted in Zambia, where the funding application for a revision of the accounts was not processed by the World Bank.[87]

The Nigerian director of statistics announced a pending 50 percent increase in GDP in November 2011,[88] but when I consulted with the World Bank and IMF data sections in the spring of 2012, the technical advisor had not yet travelled to Abuja to oversee the rebasing. According to the information I gathered on a visit to the bureau of statistics in Abuja in 2010, the base year for the constant price series is still 1990, and the 1993 SNA is still to be implemented. This does not mean that no revisions have been done. A recent revision of the basic data was undertaken during 2004 in collaboration with the IMF: "We did some compilations with some copious data and compared it with the 2003 estimates. There was a huge jump from 2003 to 2004."[89] The national accountants were advised by the IMF consultant to retroactively splice in the upward revision instead of accepting a break in the series. Following this advice, the Federal Office of Statistics series gives an impression of growth for the period up to 2004 that may be not justified, and there is no report confirming that these data were added or spliced into the original series. Thus, the method for revising these estimates was informal and wholly nontransparent.[90]

There is no agreement on a method for dealing with the growth effects of these revisions. Other national income accountants in the countries I visited reported that IMF representatives had recommended substantial upward revisions of the national income estimates. As in the case of Nigeria, the IMF consultants recommended that statisticians in other African nations "splice" in the increase retroactively, thus creating an illusory acceleration of economic growth in the most recent years. Essentially this means that instead of adding a big increase of 40 or even 60 percent in one year, the increase is divided into separate parts and added to the estimates for earlier years.

The data supplied through the international databases are a result of splicing together time series that show different growth rates. The end result is confusion when comparing growth across time or between countries.[91] As a result, the data used to assess development is in a precarious state. What can be done to about this? The next chapter suggests some practical steps toward better measurement of development.

4

DATA FOR DEVELOPMENT

Using and Improving African Statistics

This chapter provides an overview of the current state of affairs at statistical offices across sub-Saharan Africa. It supplies some important insights for the members of the development community that may enable them to become better data users. It emphasizes some deficiencies in how international data are supplied and discusses the policy options available for building the capacity to produce better data for development.

The chapter relies chiefly on interviews conducted during visits to statistical offices in Ghana, Nigeria, Uganda, Kenya, Tanzania, Zambia, and Malawi from 2007 to 2010. The main focus in these interviews was to understand the current situation in national accounts divisions. In order to achieve this objective, I conducted further interviews with central stakeholders, such as representatives of central banks and think tanks and independent scholars. I also met with representatives of donor country missions and advisors from the IMF and the World Bank. These semi-structured interviews are supported by e-mail surveys to provide a continent-wide picture.[1]

The uneven quality of development statistics, the scarce resources for statistical offices, and other, more specific, types of problems may seem to vary somewhat idiosyncratically from country to country. It is more difficult to apply the global standard of national accounting to some economies than to others; that is why all final products from national statistical offices should be considered local measures. Local adaptation depends on the financial resources and capabilities available at the local statistical office and is further shaped by national and international political and economic priorities. This chapter examines the findings of chapters 2 and 3 and develops ways of thinking systematically about the local variation in the final products.

Does Data Quality Matter for Decision Makers?

The problem with development statistics is both a knowledge problem and a governance problem. The statistics tell us less about African development than we would like to think. The discrepancy in methods and sources across time and space is large enough to compromise most quantitative analyses, whether they rely on simple descriptive statistics or on more advanced inferential statistics. This knowledge problem impacts scholarly work as well as international or national policy evaluation, and these evaluations in turn have direct implications for issues of governance. This lack of knowledge might be perceived as particularly striking. But should we be surprised? There are some good reasons not to be. It depends on the kinds of expectations we have for national policymakers and international development organizations.

Most authoritative scholarly voices in development economics perceive most African governments as corrupt and incompetent and as part of the problem, not the solution.[2] Indeed, this has arguably been the dominant view since the 1980s. In particular, the writings of Robert Bates and the application of rational choice perspectives to analysis of the behavior of African leaders and states have been hugely influential.[3] Understood in this manner, the leaders, and therefore the states,[4] are self-serving rational actors. They are interested in their own political survival and power and are not technocratic agents pursuing development per se.[5] According to this perspective, the accuracy of data will, in most cases, be a very low priority for politicians. Thus, if we expect African states to be "developmental," we should also expect states to be interested in measuring development. But if the political priorities of African states are more similar to those we expect in a "neopatrimonial" state, predictions about statistical priorities will be less optimistic.

As a general rule, political priorities signal statistical priorities. Political priorities can be hard to observe empirically, but data availability is a good indicator of political commitment. A country that is serious about agricultural development is more likely to invest seriously in agricultural statistics. Thus, when or if agricultural development is a high priority, this is reflected in the frequency and coverage of agricultural survey data. This has been frequently and persuasively pointed out to me in meetings with scholars, members of think tanks, and central bank officers in many countries; political commitment is often mirrored in the type of data that is available.

Unfortunately, policy targets often turn out to be empty political promises. If employment in the informal sector was a real policy target, as political leaders in many countries indicate, it is reasonable to expect that a labor market survey would be implemented. But data on this sector are typically not available or are very outdated. It is therefore telling that many political leaders campaign on promises of improving employment opportunities, because virtually no labor market data exists.[6] In many cases, there is little or no knowledge base for making governance decisions. Data collection is often done in accordance with a governance imperative: statistics are collected and compiled in order to facilitate particular policy agendas. Conversely, a lack of data may signal and facilitate inaction. This link has been strong throughout the time period analyzed in this book.

Agricultural statistics were not collected before agricultural extension services were begun in the late colonial period and the early postcolonial period. The appearance of industrial statistics coincides with the beginnings of strategies for industrial development. Similarly, patterns of statistical capacity follow the broader trajectory of African economies. Typical "gatekeeper" states limit data collection to records of the duties they collect at their borders, while developmental states are often more ambitious about the scope of data they collect. The ability to collect statistics— as is most clearly exemplified in the process of conducting population censuses—also reflects the power of the states. Porter notes that because the process of reaching an agreement on a "valid" number is subject to political contestation, "it requires a massive exercise of social power to establish valid numbers."[7] Furthermore, accounting for an economic activity can be read as a mark of approval by the authorities, and whether or not such accounting is done is indeed often how we distinguish between what we perceive as "formal" and "informal" economies. Extending the boundary of which parts of production are measured is an important marker that indicates which economic activities are recognized as economically and politically important.

In the first chapter, the example of a man marrying his cook was used to explain the importance of the production boundary and the treatment of the non-monetary or unrecorded economy. In this example the marriage would mean a reduction in national income because the service of food preparation would move out of the production boundary. This scenario has further implications as well: the former cook, now the wife, would be ineligible for social services and would not liable to pay taxes. Thus, it is primarily the contribution of women to the economy that is made invisible in developed countries. This is why the recognition of unpaid housework in the GDP measure has been called for.[8] The United Nations System of National Accounts has been revised to be gradually more inclusive of non-monetary activities. Although provisions were minimal in the 1952 standard, the 1968 version included important rural activities such as road building, land clearing, and house building.[9] In the 1993 and 2008 versions, allowances have been made to include more non-monetary activities, such as water carrying.[10] However, local application of these provisions is constrained by local factors. For those who are being counted, official inclusion within the production boundary is not only a matter of monetary gain, it is also a signal of political appreciation.

Does a high income level or a high rate of economic growth reliably determine the quality of the statistical services in a given country? Causation runs both ways. A high income level may be conditioned by a number of factors. Estimates of income level and economic growth rate are themselves dependent on the methodology used at statistical offices. For example, a more recent base year will produce a higher income measure.[11] In turn, we would expect, all other things being equal, that a richer country would have better statistical capacity. Without specific information about the methods used to produce the data, it is hard to judge whether a higher rate of growth or higher income actually imply good development performance or whether these measures have statistical causes. There is considerable room and opportunity for government or development officials to exert pressure on statisticians or to question both the data and the methods statisticians use in order to change estimates in one direction or the other. The discussion of Malawi's production of agriculture statistics in chapter 3 showed one instance of this. In that case, fertilizer subsidies created the opportunity and the incentive for both peasants and politicians to manipulate numbers upward. During interviews with the employees at the national accounts division, it became clear that there was a considerable amount of pressure to report high numbers. This was fairly well known, to the extent that the Malawi Reserve Bank and the IMF in Malawi did not view the numbers as accurate estimates of economic growth.[12]

But there is also some evidence that better numbers are indeed higher numbers. Uganda, which just finished its first agricultural census, found that the previously used livestock numbers were 60 percent too low.[13] The higher numbers have secondary effects on other numbers, meaning that capital formation data has been too low (increased stock in cattle is considered as investment)[14] and that the level of consumption of meat and milk could have been much higher than previously thought. This upgrade in the value of the livestock economy is a direct result of funding for the agricultural census. Without that resource, livestock would still be accounted for as contributing only 40 percent of the true value it added to the nation's economy. It should be noted that even though the level of information in Uganda has improved, this is no guarantee that such information will be reliable in the future. In 2010, Muwanga-Zake noted that in Uganda, "there is still no system for regular collection of annual agricultural statistics."[15]

There is other evidence that better methods yield higher numbers in the agricultural sector and that the method of data collection matters. In principle, many measurement instruments are available to the statistical office. At one end of the range are basic guesses and proxies. One proxy that many countries rely on is crop forecast data. These proxies are the result of regular projections using estimates of rural population and total acreage and are supplemented with meteorological data; in other words, they are adjusted for rainfall. Crop-cutting surveys are occasionally conducted in which statistical officers cut and measure a sample of crops to arrive at an estimate of yield per acre. These yield estimates are aggregated using the existing sampling frame. Household budget surveys are based on interviews. The main problem with the information obtained in these interviews is that it is based on recollection. In other words, household surveys rely on the respondent's ability to correctly estimate his or her past consumption and production, which he or she usually has not recorded.

Klaus Deininger and co-authors discuss the use of different methods to measure agricultural production.[16] They found that when Ugandan peasants recorded their daily harvesting of all crops in diaries, the numbers for production were far higher than numbers based on recollection. This is particularly true for tubers, roots, vegetables, and fruits that are typically harvested on a daily basis depending on recurring needs. The data from the diaries generated a production value that was 60 percent higher than that reached using the responses from the National Household Survey.[17] If measurement instruments like these were used regularly on a small scale, states would be aware that the contribution of smallholder peasants to the wealth of the nation is currently underappreciated.

The developmental states that appeared across sub-Saharan Africa after independence relied upon development plans that in turn relied on statistics. One criticism of these developmental states is that they overestimated their own capacity. The World Bank emphasized this in the 1981 publication often referred to as the Berg report.[18] This document famously provided the justification for the structural adjustment reforms that the World Bank and the IMF sponsored and endorsed in the 1980s and 1990s. The goals of structural adjustment were to limit state involvement and liberalize the marketing of agricultural products in the hope of accelerating economic growth. The main evidence of the need for reform was that growth had been slow and that food production in particular was stagnant. Berg acknowledged that the statistics he used in his report were only approximate, as statistical resources were lacking.[19] He also pointed out the weak capacity to estimate food production.[20]

Berg's general policy recommendations regarding liberalization were acted upon, but the arguments about statistical capacity were seemingly neglected, or at least they did not inform policy interventions. The report did state that African states lacked the capacity to monitor and implement good development projects and, in particular, that data collection and analysis were needed over the long term. Berg argued that short-term assessments with specialists are often not enough for the purpose of addressing the larger problems of economic development.[21] The report further recommended that donors should provide greater resources and infrastructure for statistical analysis and data collection. It also suggested that the international experts should be paired up with local analysts. The report suggested that the World Bank could play a big role in that regard.[22]

Instead of improving state capacity through the reforms recommended in the report, the activities of statistical offices were curtailed. Comprehensive national planning is largely a thing of the past on the African continent, and statistical offices are, with a few exceptions, in a worse situation today than they were three, four, or five decades ago. At the same time, the reduced role of the state means that public bodies have less access to information. It may be argued that such states also have less need for administrative data, but that would be a mistake. Data on development are central to political accountability, not only in domestic politics but also at the international level. The state still has an important role to play in communicating with development donors. Good governance, defined as accountability and transparency, depends on the quality and availability of the knowledge that contributes to decision making.

But does data quality matter for international development organizations? Banerjee describes the general problem among donors and the aid community as "resistance to knowledge."[23] He states that "aid thinking is lazy thinking"[24] and argues that this is because it is more gratifying to hand out aid than to fill out forms and figure out what really works. In a book on the social sciences and international development, Packard and Cooper note that "there is no notion of 'field economics' comparable to the status of fieldwork in anthropology, so that economists work with data mediated through state collection apparatuses and categories that are not fully examined."[25] This may have been a true statement a decade ago, but it does not apply as readily today. We have seen the rise of an increasingly vocal group of development economists who favor the increased use of randomized controlled trials to determine what kind of development policy works.[26] This trend circumvents the issue of macro data entirely and relies on microlevel tests to determine whether interventions such as providing vaccinations, textbooks, school lunches, or uniforms have a positive outcome on educational attainment and which of these interventions are the most cost effective.

One example is Esther Duflo, Michael Kremer, and Jonathan Robinson's study of the effectiveness of fertilizer subsidies in Kenya. The study conducted some demonstration experiments in which treatment and control plots were randomly selected. Not surprisingly, the study found that "fertilizer, when used in appropriate quantities, is highly profitable."[27] Thus this study gives a valuable answer to the question: Is the use of fertilizer profitable? In turn, the answer to this question can guide us in judging whether a fertilizer subsidy is justified or necessary or even point us to how much fertilizer should be subsidized. These types of randomized laboratory-like studies receive a lot of attention and are increasingly supported, but they reveal no understanding of how the political dimensions of providing fertilizer affect agricultural production in the aggregate or how the returns from fertilizer use are distributed. It is useful to have an idea about the returns on such investments, but for governments and donors, it is the macro question that really matters. Studying these issues in laboratory-like experiments may misguide scholars and policymakers; arguably it is the differences, not the similarities, between the political economy and the laboratories that are most important.

Randomized tests may have some applicability and may solve some bits and pieces of the knowledge problem in development studies. However, these microlevel experiments cannot and should not substitute for macroeconomic data. Central banks, ministries of finance, policymakers, and other stakeholders need to consider policy options with regard to the macroeconomic situation, however messy and limited the data basis.[28] This is not merely a technocratic concern. Accounting for the national economy is fundamental for government accountability. Without reliable macro data, political transparency is hard to imagine.

An example from fiscal spending in Uganda demonstrates this very clearly. Reinekka and Svenson report that surveys of central government expenditures on primary schools in Uganda from 1991 to 1995 showed that only 13 per cent of the funds allocated actually reached the schools. In response, a campaign was started that advertised in local newspapers how much public funding was allocated to the schools, thus enabling local schools to compare allocations with actual funds received. It was estimated that this intervention reduced graft considerably, and by 1999, 90 percent of the funds were reaching their destination.[29] Quality in the production and dissemination of data is crucial for accountability. How likely is it that a statistical office will get the necessary funds and political support needed to play this role in sub-Saharan Africa?

The Office of Statistics in the Policy Circle

As already indicated, statistical offices across sub-Saharan Africa are generally in poor condition. Even relative to their own surroundings, the statistical offices often seem to be in a particularly derelict state. Perhaps what is most striking is the contrast of this situation with that of another pivotal stakeholder in the economic policy process with much greater resource endowments: central banks. While statistical offices are located in rundown offices, often with limited computer facilities, as is the situation in Ghana, Malawi, Nigeria, Kenya, Tanzania, and Zambia, the central banks of these countries are located in new high-rise buildings with all of the modern facilities. Employment positions in the central banks command higher salaries and prestige, and central bank employees are in a better position both symbolically and physically to provide timely and useful advice to policymakers.

The policymaking process involves representatives from different groups. These parties may not be physically present during the process, but at the very least they are consulted for their input.[30] The formal decision makers are the representatives from the executive branch of government: the president, the ministry of finance (or the equivalent), and perhaps a specialist from the relevant ministry (such as the ministry of industry or agriculture). The role played by the statistical office in the process is to provide the information and facts required to define new targets and goals and to evaluate the efficacy of previous policies. These facts are provided by the central banks as well as by the statistical offices, and sometimes ministries have their own data collection and research capacities. The final major player is often a representative of the donor community, perhaps a technical advisor from the IMF, economists from the World Bank, or representatives of individual country missions. In many cases, donor missions that are providing funding for the project in question will use their own country economists and fund their own data collection.

National statistical offices, specifically national accounts divisions, are seriously constrained in terms of physical resources, staff, and basic data.

The accountant often has little or no information about large parts of the economy and must rely on assumptions and guesses about the "non-observed economy." The OECD has published a handbook that provides guidelines for measuring the non-observed economy that includes ways to define and account for these activities.[31] The handbook offers guidelines on how to classify economic activities, how to use survey instruments to record such activities, and how to triangulate estimates when certain data points exist. These guidelines are useful only if there are resources available to actually implement the guidelines, and, most pertinently, when data actually do exist.

Faced with a paucity of data and guidelines that leave a lot of room for discretion, the national accountants are in a weak position during the process of data production. The formal legal independence of statistical offices varies in sub-Saharan Africa. The statistical offices in Uganda, Nigeria, and Ghana are legally separate from the ministry of finance, but of course they still rely on public financing. In Kenya, Tanzania, Malawi, and Zambia, the statistical offices described themselves as semi-autonomous; they formally reported to the ministry of finance and planning as a subdivision of that ministry. In contrast, the independence of the central banks in these countries has been assured.[32] Finally, autonomy depends not only on legal and financial provisions but also on the quality of the numbers produced and the standardization of the production process.

Whether the statistical office is independent or semi-autonomous, the publication and approval of the final GDP numbers is a matter of consultation mainly between four parties: the statistical office, the ministry of finance/the executive, the central bank, and representatives from international organizations providing technical assistance. These parties may meet formally or informally during the process that leads to the final publication of the numbers. It was frequently related to me that the statistical officers preferred consulting with international organizations early on in the process in order to insulate themselves from political pressures.[33] In other cases, the central bank, the ministry, and the statistical office will meet together before meeting with the IMF representatives so they can compare notes and discuss the preliminary estimates. In these meetings quite substantial changes can be made: both the data and the underlying assumptions are up for discussion.[34] In cases where the ministry and the executive exert considerable pressure on the statistical office, the final numbers can be negotiated fiercely in meetings.[35] Regardless of how the national numbers are reached, more often than not, the World Bank disseminates different numbers than the ones reported by the national statistical office.

The World Bank invests considerable resources in the production and dissemination of "knowledge" and has since 1996 fashioned itself as a "knowledge bank."[36] Devesh Kapur has argued that the bank should consider spending its budgetary resources on financing rather than on the production of knowledge.[37] Some analysts disagree with Kapur. Christopher Gilbert and his co-authors, who argue that the World Bank is ideally placed to be a knowledge broker in development.[38] But Robert Wade sees the dangers of the World Bank's role as a knowledge broker and has likened it to the role Phillip Morris played as a broker of research on the health risks of tobacco.[39] William Easterly has pointed out that the World Bank is far better at distributing knowledge than it is at acquiring it.[40] Elaborating on this point, David Ellerman argues that the bank's emphasis on disseminating information is related its power. In order to maintain its authority, it is important that the bank seems to be speaking with one voice. That strategy effectively puts a constraint on the extent to which the bank can engage in learning from its clients.[41] In a study of the interactions between the international development community and Lesotho, James Ferguson has forcefully and convincingly argued that the World Bank and the international "development" project is a standardized process in which local conditions are ignored and empirical realities are overlooked.[42] These interpretations cohere with my observations about the process of producing the numbers the World Bank uses. The emphasis is on agreeing upon numbers, and, as Michael Ward put it, measurement is in the backseat.[43]

This pattern of one-way communication also fits well with the impression I gained about how national accountants interact with technical advisors from World Bank and the IMF. While national accountants often voiced their appreciation of the technical skills they learned from these consultants, they also expressed some disappointment. A "consultation" with an international expert often meant that the expert would give local statisticians a list of things to do, without any indication of how the tasks could be achieved or any appreciation of the difficulties involved.[44] Some international consultants even described the current training provided to statisticians as harmful.[45] Other consultants were suspicious that national accountants feigned ignorance in order to qualify for weekend seminars and training courses and the per diem allowances that follow with them.[46]

The impact of the consultations and the training, which is geared toward international standards and software packages, is often that the local accountant is scared and feels inadequate. My informants suggested that each national accountant gets an average of three training courses per year in which the focus is on how to operate advanced software. Unfortunately, the real challenge—dealing with absent or deficient data—is not touched upon in detail in these courses.[47] For example, in Malawi, a three-year program funded by the Norwegian Aid Agency has succeeded in upgrading the national accounting systems to make use of the same software used in Norway and Germany. Because of the high rate of turnover in national accounting divisions, statistical offices may be left with a software system that no one knows how to use if trained personnel leave.[48] This particular capacity-building program also focused on developing better macro modeling tools for policymakers. The modeling efforts were viewed skeptically by representatives at the central bank in Malawi for two reasons. First, it was too complicated for most of the personnel at the ministry of finance to understand and use, and second, the data needs for the model overestimated the actual data availability on the Malawian economy and thus the model relied too heavily on assumed relationships to be useful.[49]

After structural adjustment programs of the 1980s, the IMF and the World Bank shifted the focus to redesigned policy reform programs called Poverty Reduction Programs. The policy targets of these programs were set out in Poverty Reduction Strategy Papers (PRSP) for each country. The motivation was to involve the country subject to the reform in the policy formulation process—the World Bank and the IMF referred to this as "ownership"—and to answer the criticisms of those responsible for administering structural adjustment programs who had pointed out their negative impact on the poor. Critics of Poverty Reduction Programs have pointed out that the actual changes to both process and content were minor,[50] but they did make a difference to the statistical offices: they created a new demand for data about poverty.[51]

David Booth and Henry Lucas argue that the Poverty Reduction Programs led to improvements in the quality and availability of household survey data. They argue that although some serious concerns over the sustainability of this level of data collection remain, at least the importance of the challenges involved with household surveys are now better recognized.[52] They also note that while the issue of data availability is discussed in the PRSPs, the country capacity for data analysis and collection is neglected.[53] Thus, although the new development agenda created a new demand for information, it did not have clear strategies for how this demand should be filled. Poverty monitoring has been complicated by this deficiency, and the existing data series, which is needed to evaluate progress toward Millennium Development Goal number 1—poverty reduction—currently relies on inconsistent and therefore unreliable data.[54]

Currently the international development community has embraced the idea of "evidence-based policy." The principles of "results-based management" are related to this new concept. This has inspired the development community to set out quantifiable targets such as the UN's Millennium Development Goals (MDGs).[55] This has also put the issue of statistical capacity of poorer countries on the policy agenda. The eight MDGs are supported by eighteen targets and forty-eight indicators that encompass most aspects of economic development. Interestingly, indicators of political governance were not included in the list of quantifiable targets. One of the justifications in a United Nations Development Programme (UNDP) report was that this would put too much pressure on the statistical capacities of poorer countries. The UNDP argued that while the concept of governance indicators is gaining favor at the national and international levels, statisticians have shied away from measuring this indicator due to a lack of data, a perceived lack of experience, and the political sensitivity of the endeavor.[56] This admission highlights the precarious situation of the statistical offices and raises a question: If such concerns apply to governance indicators, what are the effects of the data demands of the MDGs on national statistical offices?

The response from national accounts divisions, statistical offices, and international and national stakeholders is clear. Statistical offices do not yet have the capacity to respond to the pressures the MDGs have placed upon them. A discussion paper by Gonzalo Duenas Alvarez et al. provides a list of all the available data relating to twelve MDG targets for each sub-Saharan African country for the period 1990 to 2009.[57] The availability of data varies: nine countries have data at least as recent as 2005 for all but one of the targets (Liberia is the only country with recent data for all targets), and most countries have at least some data over the time period for all but

one target. Somalia and Sudan have no data at all. The indicators for poverty data are where we find the least recent observation. Most likely this
is because the survey instruments used to measure poverty involve more
costly data collection and analysis.[58] It is important to note that this study
surveys only a subset of the twelve MDG indicators. The data availability situation for all forty-eight indicators is likely to present a more pes-
simistic picture. The latest MDG progress report briefly mentions issues
of data availability, but it does not discuss how issues of statistical capacity
may affect evaluation.[59] Jan Vandemoortele claims that statistics have been
abused to fabricate evidence of success regarding the MDGs. He also argues that the use of quantitative targets has furthered a one-dimensional
view of development and that this process has strengthened the "money-
metric and donor-centric view of development."[60] Dimitri Sanga says of
the MDGs that "a major weakness is the assumption that data would be
available. Countries have been struggling to build their capacity to collect,
process and disseminate the requisite data."[61]

   In some cases the monitoring demands of the MDGs have meant a
windfall of economic resources for statistical offices. National accounts divisions have complained that this means that personnel from already understaffed divisions are being transferred to sections that collect data for
the MDG indicators. National stakeholders, such as central banks, have
said that they suspect that the quality of the important economic growth
data has been decreasing. In my meetings at statistical offices it has frequently been pointed out to me that because more resources are allocated
for data collection, analysis and dissemination have suffered. These concerns have been echoed by representatives from the IMF and the World
Bank. The concern is that the limited capacity of the statistical offices is
further constrained by the Millennium Development Goals agenda.

Capacity and Constraints at the Statistical Office

Data users have no a priori basis for judging which of the datasets are better than the others. Only seasoned country experts can reasonably judge
the quality of a country's data. Data users should know to what extent the
dataset they are relying on coheres with what is otherwise known about
a country. This would enable them to judge whether a large fluctuation

reflects economic change or a statistical error. Data users might also be interested to know how the data quality in a particular country compares with the quality of the data from another country. A data user who sees that that Ghana just revised its income upward by 60 percent may feel cautious about comparing the income of Ghana with that of Cote D'Ivoire or Nigeria. How should data users navigate the databases?

The term for this kind of information is metadata. This information should, ideally, accompany the statistical series. It should contain definitions, sources, and other information the data user needs to be a confident user of the data. I made this point in a presentation to the World Bank Data Group in November 2011, and to their credit they have since started using better country-level metadata with their datasets. This is an important step on the road to full transparency about data quality, though there is still a long way to go. Disseminators of international datasets offer very little of this kind of information. The only metadata that is included in the World Bank's online databank is this definition: "GDP is the sum of gross value added by all resident producers in the economy plus any product taxes and minus any subsidies not included in the value of the products. It is calculated without making deductions for depreciation of fabricated assets or for depletion and degradation of natural resources." The databank provides information about whether the data are in constant or current currency or local or international currency and says that the base period "varies by country."[62] The data manual contains only the generic mathematical formulas and definitions that are used to compile the data.[63]

In 2009, I contacted the Development Data Group at the World Bank to inquire about the availability of metadata and the raw data underlying the calculation of the time series of national accounts. The Data Group responded that "raw data provided by the National Statistics Agencies are not available for external users and only a handful of people at the World Bank have access to it."[64] At a second query I was referred to the data files available through the United Nations data division.[65] This data series goes back to 1970, and it provides better metadata for some indicators. However, for national accounts the sources and methods listed contain very little information. The metadata on national accounts merely describe whether the data is "official data"—that is, supplied directly from a national statistical office—or whether it is derived from World Development Indicators. This meant that I had come full circle. On my third query about the underlying national account files and the sources and methods used for the World Development Indicators, I got a similar response: "At the Data Group, we do not have the information you've requested. National account data we receive are electronic files either from the Country offices or from the IMF. May we suggest that you contact the National Statistics Offices directly?"[66]

I contacted the IMF, which replied in a similar vein: "We do not have statistical bulletins or any national source publications. Country authorities send data to us electronically in files that we do not share with the public."[67] In a last attempt to break the circle I contacted the compilers of the Penn World Tables for access to the underlying data series, but I was informed that "For African countries, we got the national account data from the UN."[68] I was thus referred back to the same place that the World Bank had sent me on my first query. Since the UN database includes data only from 1970 onward, I asked which sources were used before this date. I was told that "For the data before 1970, we applied the growth rate of the variable from our old national data to the new data of 1970 to extrapolate the missing data. E.g. Tanzania, we used the national account for PWT6.2., which had been extrapolated by using the national account data for PWT6.1. Before PWT6.1, we lost the track of the original source of the data."[69]

When I have contacted national statistical offices directly, I have been able to gather more information, but it has not always been possible to retrace the history of national accounting for all of the countries. There are crucial gaps in both the data series and the metadata. I had conversations about this lack of transparency and metadata with data consultants in Zambia and Tanzania.[70] One issue that was easy to agree upon was that it was difficult to get a sense of the relative quality of the different country estimates and the extent to which the national income of certain countries was underestimated. I was advised to get in touch with the East AFRITAC, the Africa Regional Technical Assistance Center of the IMF, which provides technical assistance to statistical offices in East Africa. I contacted their macroeconomic statistics advisor to get an insider's view of the relative state of affairs at statistical offices in East Africa.

On my first attempt to get some information I was told that the advisor had not yet spent enough time in the region to give an opinion. On the second attempt, the advisor replied: "I cannot add anything to the official responses given to you by the relevant statistics offices. As I currently provide technical assistance to these countries and have access to information provided to me on a confidential basis, I am not in a position to answer your request."[71] I countered that I had already been able to get some information from the World Bank, the UK Department for International Development, NORAD, and the IMF on these issues and explained that "one of the central aims of this study is to demystify the processes behind the production of income and growth statistics in the region. Taking the position that the IMF's role in this process is 'confidential' raises more problems than it solves."[72] In response, the IMF representative wrote, "You need to understand that I work for the Statistics Department of the Fund and provide TA [Technical Assistance] directly to the national compilers. I am allowed access to information on the basis of non-disclosure so that I can help them. If I or any other TA provider in the same position then provides the information to a totally unrelated third party, it is a breach of that trust and future TA offers would never be accepted."[73]

When I made a third request, the same IMF representative was able to provide some general advice: "In general terms, applying to all East African countries you mention, there is a need to strengthen source data for national accounts. However, these countries are poor with inadequate revenue to fund regular ongoing data collections for NAS purposes. In general, there is a need to strengthen data collection for agriculture, fishing, informal sector and services activities. There is also scope to improve price collections (agriculture, producer prices). Compilation staff and resources are also constrained, due to budget, limiting the range and quality of the statistics produced. Existing staff need further training and development. The constraints in compilation are reflected in the limited dissemination."[74]

The IMF and the World Bank provide some country-level information on the state of the statistical services in their Reports on the Observance of Standards and Codes (ROSC), which provide an overview of the extent to which countries adhere to internationally recognized standards and codes that pertain to private and financial sector development and stability. The initiative was established in 1999 as a way in which to improve financial stability at national and international levels. These evaluations are performed by the IMF and the World Bank at the request of the country under review. The IMF is largely responsible for evaluating data dissemination and fiscal transparency, while the World Bank takes the lead on issues of corporate governance, accounting and auditing, and insolvency regimes and creditor rights. The reports are highly standardized. This may make it easier to read the reports, but it precludes specific country-level information.[75]

Only sixteen countries—Botswana, Burkina Faso, Cameroon, Chad, The Gambia, Kenya, Malawi, Mauritius, Mozambique, Namibia, Niger, Senegal, South Africa, Tanzania, Uganda, and Zambia—have been evaluated since 1999.[76] The reports are not readily accessible to the lay reader. They contain a great deal of technical terms and abbreviations and give the distinct impression of being meant for circulation among technocrats rather than for the development community at large. In my earlier correspondence with representatives of the IMF and the World Bank, data division staff would sometimes refer to these reports,[77] but I have not been referred to them in my most recent queries, probably because they are now mostly outdated. My impression is that these reports are not widely read at the statistical offices, ministries of finance, or central banks. I found a hard copy of a report in only one of the statistical offices (Tanzania 2007; when I returned in 2010 it was missing).

The most common problem noted in the reports on the general state of statistical services is a lack of resources, including staff, infrastructure, and funding. This is also often cited as the greatest concern in terms of the sustainability of improvements in statistical capacity. In some cases, significant gains have reportedly been made, but there are concerns that these gains are not sustainable in the long run without improvements in the national provision of resources, as in the case of Tanzania. Other problems of note include issues with timeliness and periodicity, as mentioned in the reports on Botswana, Cameroon, Gambia, Mauritius, and Senegal; use of unreliable data, as in the cases of Tanzania, Senegal, and Chad; and inadequate dissemination and coordination of statistical production, as in the cases of Uganda, Senegal, and Cameroon.

Table 4.1 indicates which standards each country has either met or failed to meet. The IMF reports used "not observed" (NO), "largely not observed" (LNO), "largely observed" (LO), and "observed" (O) to assess each standard. In table 4.1, an X in the respective category signifies that the criteria are ranked as either "largely not observed" or "not observed" in the report. The countries that have the least number of X's are ranked highest. South Africa and Uganda have reached all of the standards set by the IMF (as indicated in the reports by rankings of "observed" or "largely observed"

TABLE 4.1. Summary of data provided in IMF and World Bank reports on national statistical capacity in sub-Saharan Africa

Rank	Country	POQ[1]	AI	MS	AR	S	A
1	South Africa						
1	Uganda						
2	Mauritius				x		
3	Tanzania				x		x
4	Botswana			x	x	x	
4	Namibia	x	x		x		
4	Senegal	x	x		x		
4	Kenya	x		x	x		
4	Zambia	x			x		x
5	Burkina Faso	x		x	x		x
5	The Gambia	x		x	x		x
5	Mozambique	x			x	x	x
5	Niger	x			x	x	x
6	Malawi	x		x	x	x	x
6	Chad	x	x	x	x		x

[1]POQ = Prerequisites of Quality; AI = Assurances of Integrity; MS = Methodological Soundness; AR = Accuracy and Reliability; S = Serviceability; A = Accessibility. The criteria for each category are set out as follows: POQ refers to the basics such as the legal framework, the available resources, and the relevance of statistical programs; AI covers the criteria for professionalism, transparency, and ethical standards; MS covers issues such as concepts and definitions of terms, scope of projects, classification of systems, and recording mechanisms; AR refers to the observance of standards for quality source data, statistical techniques, revision studies, and intermediate data; S addresses the periodicity, timeliness, consistency, and revision of the data; and A provides the criteria for data/metadata accessibility and user friendliness. This information is not available for Cameroon.
Source: IMF country reports.

for each standard). Chad and Malawi, on the other hand, are still falling short on a number of accounts, which suggests that their statistical capacity for producing acceptable national accounts is largely nonexistent.

These reports do provide general information that could be of interest to data users, but these metadata are not reported with the actual data series. It is striking that only South Africa and Uganda meet the required standards for Accuracy and Reliability (AR)—meaning that the source data and the statistical methods used to aggregate GDP estimates in these countries are neither accurate nor reliable. There is no note to that effect when users download the data series through the World Bank database.

How does this match up with my observations on the current situation at the statistical offices in sub-Saharan Africa? According to my own survey, there is a lot of variation. My survey was based on unstructured interviews with statistical officers and important stakeholders in offices in Ghana, Nigeria, Uganda, Kenya, Tanzania, Zambia, and Malawi from 2007 to 2010. This was supplemented with a survey of national income accountants in Burundi, Cameroon, Cape Verde, Guinea, Lesotho, Mali, Mauritania, Mauritius, Namibia, Mozambique, Niger, Senegal, Seychelles, Sierra Leone, and South Africa. All in all, I established direct contact with statisticians and/or stakeholders in twenty-three of forty-eight countries in sub-Saharan Africa. For sixteen of the remaining twenty-five countries, only summary data is available from the official websites, while for Angola, Comoros, the Democratic Republic of Congo, Eritrea, Liberia, Somalia, Swaziland, Togo, and Zimbabwe, I was not able to obtain any direct or indirect information.

On one end of the spectrum one finds Uganda. Here the statistical offices have a higher priority than in the other countries. Part of the explanation lies in the country's particular history. In 1986, the national statistical services in Uganda were completely depleted after a civil war.[78] The country seized the opportunity to build a statistical office that not only physically outshines others I have visited in the region but is also better staffed and delivers a better final product. Another reason that statistical production in Uganda is better than in other African countries is that leaders in the central bank and the Ministry of Finance have demanded better statistics and have provided the necessary resources to produce them.[79]

At the other end of the scale of the offices I visited is Zambia. The national statistical office is in disarray, and the national accounts division is severely understaffed. Employees at donor missions, the central bank, and the statistical offices were all very frank about the deficiencies in the data the statistical office produced and in the methods it used. No technical assistance has been given since the mid-1990s, and national strategies for statistical capacity-building have failed. In confidence, it was related to me that there had been a fallout between the national statistical office and the World Bank representative in the late 1990s and that in response, Zambia's applications for funding for the statistical office under the World Bank STATCAP scheme had been "blackballed."[80] STATCAP is a new World Bank lending program that is supposed support statistical capacity-building in developing countries.[81] At the time of writing, Uganda was the only country that had completed the application process, although Burkina Faso, Kenya, and Tanzania had prepared the initial project appraisal document. Pilot studies were under way in the Democratic Republic of Congo, Ghana, Nigeria, and Rwanda. According to the STATCAP website, the rationale for the program is that "many national statistical systems are caught in a vicious cycle where inadequate resources restrain output and undermine the quality of statistics, while the poor quality of statistics leads to lower demand and hence fewer resources."[82] It seems that this vicious circle describes the situation in Zambia quite well, but so far the difficulties of preparing the required documents to qualify for support has not been overcome.

Statistical officers who want to revise and rebase the national accounts series invariably rely on external consultants and funding. Since 2007, a technical assistance program supported by Norway that includes a resident statistician from the Norwegian statistical bureau has ensured that the methods used in Malawi (though not necessarily the raw data) meet European standards, and the base year and statistical methods have been updated at Malawi's statistical service. While the methods are now state of the art, the bigger problem in Malawi has been serious concerns about the independence of the statistical services.[83] Zambia, Nigeria, Tanzania and Kenya all have outdated base years and it is just a question of time before new baseline estimates will increase incomes in these countries, as has already happened in Ghana.[84] As I mentioned in chapter 1, respondents from eighteen of the twenty-three countries I surveyed stated that they believed that the GDP for their country was currently underestimated. Respondents were reluctant to make any guesses about how much. Representatives from only ten of the national accounts divisions I surveyed knew the size of their country's GDP adjustment at the time of the most recent GDP revision; the revisions ranged from as low as 5 percent to as high as 35 percent. The reasons for upward revision were reported to be general changes in methods and data and in the structure of the economy; the informal sector and the telecommunications sector were frequently mentioned. I further inquired whether the office had specific information about the informal sector and "subsistence" output, but apart from a few countries that had a specific informal survey, respondents invariably told me that a household budget survey was the only source of information.

The key lesson here is that the best indicator of the underlying data base for the estimates is how recently there has been a household budget survey and how frequently this survey is done. The caveat to this lesson is that without a revision that changes the base year and thus creates a new growth series, the new information obtained in the survey cannot be directly added to the GDP estimates without causing distortions. As documented here, the data is sometimes added in an ad hoc manner. How this affects development statistics and when it is done are matters of guesswork for data users, as the metadata do not provide information about these issues.

Data for Development: What to Do?

Most studies of economic statistics show how numbers are wrong and how they lead to misunderstandings, thus describing a knowledge problem. Data users need more metadata from the data disseminators, and data producers need help with capacity building, which extends beyond funding data collection. Neither data users nor data producers are getting the assistance they need.

The degree to which statistical offices are independent depends on legislation, funding, and the quality of the data. In some countries the statistical office is autonomous or semi-autonomous, in others it is directly under the ministry of finance. The legal structure determines the ability of the agency to publish its figures without the approval of the government and the ministry of finance. Most statistical offices have limited funding from the national budget that barely covers upkeep and basic salaries. Upgrades of facilities and data collection are entirely funded by international sources. In some countries, this has meant that the statistical office is increasingly becoming an agency for hire for specific high-profile data collection exercises.

Is data politically important enough for leaders to attempt to use statistics to lie? This book has documented that there is ample opportunity to tamper with national statistics. In most instances the statistics are not important enough in terms of domestic politics to motivate political leaders to influence the data. Leaders can adjust or choose statistical series at their discretion when it fits their political aims. A low level of economic literacy also reduces the incentive to tamper with statistics. A report from the UN

Economic Commission for Africa concluded, "For countries in the developed world, passing judgement may, indeed be left to the users who may have the statistical know-how to make an objective evaluation. However, the situation in Africa is radically different since statistical literacy is still at its infancy even in government circles."[85]

There is a lack of knowledge about which statistics do matter politically. We also know too little about the degree of statistical literacy in these countries. We need research about which indicators matter to whom and why. With the exception of some instances of crop and population statistics, economic and social statistics are mostly produced for the consumption of the development community, especially for donors and the IMF and the World Bank.

Statistical officers and technical advisors have generally not attested to having witnessed much political pressure during the process of producing statistics. Of course, this pressure is applied in negotiations and consultations behind the scenes, and participants in such negotiations are reluctant to contribute to transparency in the production of statistics. The process by which the final numbers are negotiated and the very weak data basis on which the estimates are made conditions what type of data we get. Typically the issue is not fabricated data; according to my informants, statisticians often self-censor.[86] If the data do not show anything controversial, the statistical officer will not have to answer difficult questions.

The Millennium Development Goals have increased political pressure on the statistical offices. Evaluations of progress toward the targets are based on statistical reports, and donors make funding dependent on completion of these quantitative targets. The positive outcome of this process is that more attention is being given to the statistical office, compared to the neglect of statistical offices during the period of structural adjustment. Currently, more funds are being made available to statistical offices than in the previous three decades, but this is being done in an uncoordinated fashion. Typically, support has been ad hoc and has been directly linked to particular donor-funded projects. In this way, donors distort data production instead of building up statistical capacity. This stretches current staff and infrastructure resources. Statistical officers are richly remunerated with per diem allowances when they are engaged in data collection in the field, but this leaves fewer people and resources for analysis and dissemination back in the statistical offices.

What is needed and is long overdue are new baseline estimates for African economies. This becomes clear from the discrepancies in the current methods used to compile national income estimates and the differences in the base years used for aggregation and deflation. As isolated cases it is of course good news that Malawi has updated its software and base year methods to European standards and that Ghana has been able to rebase the estimate of its economy to reach a more correct evaluation. However, these improvements in the methods of data production raise issues about comparing Ghana and Malawi with other African nations. Based on the statistical material alone, it is hard for data users to judge which of the African economies are developing and which countries are experiencing more economic progress than others. As disseminators of these statistics, the data divisions of international organizations have an important informational role to play here, but the emphasis in such divisions is on communicating clearly and powerfully rather than on worrying about the accuracy of the information that is being disseminated.

What type of support is needed? Best practices should be based on local conditions and not solely on international standardization, and the advice that follows should be read with this caveat in mind. In general, an effort to transparently record which particular data deficiencies pertain to each country specifically is needed. Drawing attention to data deficiencies is not only a first step toward solving them, it will also reduce the chance that scholars and practitioners of development will draw incorrect inferences from poor statistics.

The monitoring of specific projects should be tempered by a realistic assessment of the capacity of the statistical office to deliver information on the basis of which national leaders can confidently govern. The Millennium Development Goals agenda is committing the same mistakes that were committed at independence, during structural adjustment, and during the recent era of poverty reduction. In each of this eras, targets and policies to reach those targets were identified, but less thought was given to where the information should come from that would measure progress. It might be useful to turn an important development question around. Rather than asking what kind of development we should target, perhaps the question should be: What kind of development are we able to monitor?

I would argue that ambitions should be tempered in international development statistics. The international standardization of measurement of economic development has led to a procedural bias. There has been a tendency to aim for high adherence to procedures instead of focusing on the content of the measures. Development measures should be taken as a starting point in local data availability, and statisticians should refrain from reporting aggregate measures that appear to be based on data but in fact are very feeble projections or guesses. This means that it is necessary to shift the focus away from formulas, standards, handbooks, and software. What matters are what numbers are available and how good those numbers are. Comparability across time and space needs to start with the basic input of knowledge, not with the system in which this information is organized.

In data collection there is a tendency to aim for high validity—an emphasis on full coverage of the economy rather than reliability of the data. Thus there is a preference for aggregating data, conducting censuses rather than surveys, and making estimates of levels rather than measuring change. These preferences come at the expense of frequent survey data that tell data users something useful about changes. In practice, this means that funding is available for large one-off data collection projects.[87] Both statistical offices and donors share this preference: the statistical office gets access to per diem funding for data collection, and the donors fulfill globally demanded standards of statistical sophistication.[88]

Thus, a change in the structure of funding for statistical offices is needed. We need not only more funding but funding that is geared toward reliable, frequently disseminated surveys. It is better to survey fifty minibuses each year and thereby get an impression of earnings and services provided in the small-scale transport sector regularly than to have one transport census every thirty years and hope that change before, after, and in between roughly follows the number of license plates issued in the country. We also need a change in funding so that statistical offices are rewarded for dissemination and analysis of data. This relates to the independence of statistical offices, which derives from the ability of an office to survey, analyze, and disseminate and not just from legal structures. More regular survey funding would give statistical offices a better capability to collect data independently of government or donor projects.

Income and growth data users are currently given very little help from the data providers. The metadata—information that accompanies the data files—are absent or are insufficient. In order to best judge the quality of the estimates, the user needs to know when the last revision of the baseline estimate was undertaken. The availability of data on the informal sector will depend on when a household budget survey was last conducted. Finally, to avoid misunderstandings, data users should be informed about structural breaks in the series. In an ideal world the statistician would be able to say: "The data speak for themselves." This book documents that the data are based on educated guesses, competing observations, and debatable assumptions, leaving both trends and levels open to question and the final estimates malleable. This undermines the integrity of the statisticians and leaves them vulnerable in meetings with central stakeholders. Transparency in reporting, meaning that international databases acknowledge their sources and report metadata appropriately will be helpful in turning the attention of the development community to the important role local statistical offices play. Global standards for new baseline estimates must be based on local applicability, not just on theoretical preferences and wishful thinking in the development community.

Conclusion

Development by Numbers

More than five decades have passed since the publication of a bestselling book called *How to Lie with Statistics*. "Correlation does not imply causation" was one of the principal themes of that book. Luckily, this concept caught on and became a widely accepted and oft-repeated truism. Of course this does not hinder the capacity of social scientists to routinely commit the logical fallacy of arguing *cum hoc ergo propter hoc* ("with this, therefore because of this"), but at least most literate consumers of statistics have been imprinted with this basic response when presented with statistical results.

About the same time that book was published, the phrase "garbage in, garbage out" was coined. It refers to the fact that a computer or a model will process any logarithm and produce a result no matter what basic inputs are fed into the process. The basic defense of inferential statistics is that garbage, or errors in the data, as statisticians would surely prefer to call it, will bias the results toward zero. A statistician may say: "In fact your objection to my data is misguided; if the data were perfect, my results would be even stronger. Bad data weakens my findings." This could for instance apply to an investigation of the relationship between corruption and economic growth data or the relationship between official development assistance and economic growth. All of the datasets reviewed here have serious measurement errors, and thus you are not likely to find a statistical relationship using these real world data, even if one hypothetically does exist.

There are many reasons why one should not accept this defense. First of all, it does of course not apply if the errors are systematically, rather than randomly, distributed. Errors attached to numbers are indeed often systematic, and thus we may have serious measurement bias, particularly when approaching policy questions in poor countries. Second, whether the end result is that the analysis finds no relationship or the analysis finds the wrong relationship, poor numbers will mislead us. Finding no relationship is often publicized as a result, for example the finding that official development assistance has no proven average effect on economic growth in a cross-country regression.[1]

This book is first and foremost about descriptive rather than inferential statistics. It investigates the numbers that enter the models used in inferential statistics.[2] Getting these numbers right matters for scholarly analysis, but as has been emphasized here, descriptive statistics matter too. While "garbage in" does indeed influence the final product, numbers and aggregates are not just inputs in statistical models. They enter directly into decision-making models and have direct impacts on policy. They are fundamental to the operation of international and national political systems. The ranking and grouping of countries according to income is perhaps the most striking example of this in the international arena. Furthermore, data on recent economic performance have a direct impact on current politics and economics on the national arena.

The state of the scholarly literature today, particularly in African studies and International development but also more generally in the social sciences, is deeply and doubly unsatisfactory. To date it has either neglected the issue of data quality and therefore accepted the data at face value or dismissed the data as unreliable and therefore irrelevant. Numbers are too important to be ignored, and the problems surrounding the production and dissemination of numbers are too serious to be dismissed.

The book has searched for and ultimately found some firm middle ground in this divisive issue. In essence, my message is that the skills of qualitative scholars are needed to assess and assert the usefulness of numbers. Numerical expressions of social, economic, and political phenomena are all, to various degrees, social, economic and political phenomena themselves. Seldom do these numbers provide the untainted, objective observation through which societies can be gauged, analyzed, and evaluated in the manner that much statistical analysis seems to presume. The qualitative skills of historians, anthropologists, political scientists, and other scholars are much needed in tracing where these observations were made, what conditions affected their collection, and what influential factors prevailed when decisions were made regarding what was counted and how the counting process took place. This, then, is a call for qualitative researchers to pay more attention to numbers instead of dismissing them entirely.

It is of course fundamental to remind ourselves of the famous quote from Albert Einstein: "Not everything that counts can be counted; and not everything that can be counted, counts." The second part of this quote is particularly instructive. Because statistical data are powerful, much qualitative rigor has been sacrificed in order to quantify political and social phenomena beyond the basic economic metrics discussed in this book. This concluding chapter broadens the scope to provide an overview of existing datasets. Many of the points I have made about income statistics also apply to other metrics such as those that rank political systems or quantify happiness.

GDP and Other Numbers

How do we situate GDP among other numbers in the policy and academic domain? It is a curious measure. It is not like counting the population or summing up total exports. At the same time its definition is not as contestable as other measures, such as a quantifiable definition of political freedom. A long-standing and solid body of theory justifies the existence of GDP as a statistical measure. In addition, the collection of GDP estimates at both the national and international levels has firm institutional foundations. Presently, there is no clear substitute for this metric when it comes to ranking countries and determining their relative monetary weight and therefore their political weight in institutions such as the IMF and the World Bank.

The importance of GDP to economics can be likened to the importance of measures of temperature and pressure in physics and the natural sciences. Economics does aspire to be a science in the way that the natural sciences are sciences. To complete this ambition one needs general laws such as the laws of thermodynamics. The field of economics, for instance, offers John Maynard Keynes's general theory of macroeconomics. GDP plays a central role in the equations set out in the theory, as for instance when it captures aggregate demand or aggregate supply.[3] The key difference between economics and the physical sciences is that economists do not have an instrument for measuring movement in the aggregate of GDP like scientists have for measuring changes in density, pressure, or temperature. Moreover, there is no straightforward agreement about what causes changes in GDP.

But we do know its constituent parts. In the same manner that we know that population growth is a function of mortality, fertility, and migration, we know that GDP can be expressed in three ways: as a function of profits, wages, and rents (the income approach); as a sum of the value added in all sectors of the economy (the production approach); or as a sum of all private and public expenditures on consumption, investment, and exports minus imports (the expenditure approach). On a relative scale, this makes the task of quantifying economic growth or national income much more straightforward than summing up the level of democracy in a system.

Yet the number of difficult decisions that have to be made when aggregating the measure is still underappreciated. Many of these decisions are also highly controversial and politicized—who counts and what counts as value added in a specific time and place are contestable decisions. In this book I have discussed how the measure may be interpreted as an indicator of the power of a state. It expresses how much a state knows about itself, and this ability to know and to monitor is a direct measure of state power and may also be related to state legitimacy.

Some states know less about their own economy and the activities of their inhabitants—a plain descriptive statement that may be related to their political systems (the importance of state versus market), geographical characteristics (dense versus sparse population), and other factors as well as their relative level of development or poverty.[4] Yet the goal is to aggregate a measure that allows us to compare income and growth over time and space. This goal leads us into stating that some economies are more poorly measured than others.

The main problem of poor economies is the size of the unrecorded economy, but this is not just a problem related to poverty. One very complicated issue for comparisons of income levels across more developed economies is the valuation of the real estate sector. For different social and political reasons, the proportions of renters and homeowners vary quite a lot from country to country. The simplest way to measure GDP is to measure only recorded economic transactions. This would mean that only renters' expenditures for housing would be counted. Thus, the ability of renters to consume and produce would be measured, whereas homeowners would be left out. A similar misrepresentation comes from measuring the "market price" of services. In some countries, these services are subsidized, while in others they are arranged privately. Examples of such services include education and health care.

The principle of invariance means that GDP compilers need to make imputations to correct for these systemic differences from country to country that may lead us astray when using the measure to compare living standards.[5] In a recent report from the Commission on Measurement of Economic Performance and Social Progress, a group of expert economists from governments, universities, and nongovernmental organizations, there is an enlightening discussion about adding household work and the value of leisure to the conventional GDP measure:

> But imputations come at a price. One is data quality: imputed values tend to be less reliable than observed values. Another is the effect of imputations on the comprehensibility of national accounts. Not all imputations are perceived as income-equivalent by people, and the result may be a discrepancy between changes in perceived income and changes in measured income. This problem is exacerbated when we widen the scope of economic activity to include other services that are not mediated by the market. Our estimates below for household work amount to around 30% of conventionally-measured GDP. Another 80% or so are added when leisure is valued as well. It is undesirable to have assumption-driven data so massively influencing overall aggregates.

It is worthwhile to remember that this is very much the state of play for national accounts estimation in many sub-Saharan African economies.

The year-to-year estimates rely heavily on imputations. But only very occasionally can the process of going from scanty observations to a time series of numbers actually be retrospectively observed. One opportunity is provided thanks to Pius Okigbo, the Nigerian economist commissioned by the Nigerian government to prepare the national accounts for Nigeria for 1950–1957. Commenting on his own imputations, he wrote: "It is impossible to overstate the arbitrariness of the process of 'quantification.'"[6] As he prepared the estimates of agricultural production, he had only a few unreliable observations from agricultural officers' subjective reports, which varied in detail: "An occasional officer ventures a guess at the total acreage and yield since the previous year. Others guess at the percentage changes in acreage and yield since the previous year. Most restrict themselves to such remarks as 'average,' 'no change,' '1952 plus,' '1954 minus, or even 'very poor.'"[7] Based on these data, Okigbo prepared a time series for 1950–1957.

Okigbo warned that the series should not be used for comparisons of living standards, because it contained so little information about the most important sector of the economy.[8] Admirably, Okigbo further noted that it "would be unfair to the officials who have responsibility for statistics if we ended on a critical note," and therefore he emphasized that he had no doubt "that many of the gaps indicated in this report will be filled in the very near future." Just a few years later though, as I discussed in chapter 2, Helleiner wrote that "the Nigerian national accounts remain in a sorry condition" and that the changes in the estimation procedures made comparisons with the early years "unsuitable." This evaluation was expanded upon in a report prepared by a team led by Professor O. Aboyade, who revised the Nigerian national accounts in 1981. Aboyade was unusually candid about the shortcomings of statistical methods:

Our experience has shown that in a setting where weights and measures are amorphous and in a highly variegated landscape with contrasting political geography, the more mundane nuts and bolts approach of the economic anthropologist may advance the course of development of economic statistics more than the sophisticated discourses of the systems designer and sampling theorist.[9]

This recommendation of interdisciplinary approaches is very sensible. A final judgment on development must of course be tempered by an appreciation of the inherent limitations of quantification. As John Harriss argued while making a case for interdisciplinary methods in development studies, the quest for quantitative resolution in development studies must be enriched with qualitative rigor.[10] States need GDP and other metrics to function, but as scholars of development we must remind ourselves not to ask too much of the measure. The lesson is that GDP is too important to be ignored and the numbers are too poor to be trusted blindly. This means that the study of development cannot be limited to the use of economics and statistics. Interdisciplinary approaches are required.

Correlates of Growth: Development by Other Numbers

While the main focus in the book has been on GDP, the canvas has been broadened. Intermittently, I have looked at agricultural statistics and population statistics, which together with external trade make up most of the GDP metric in sub-Saharan Africa. I have also touched upon the new measurement agendas deriving from the shift of focus to poverty reduction and, more recently, to the Millennium Development Goals. The approach to measuring poverty and the design of the Millennium Development Goals are two large debates that go beyond the scope of this book.[11] This section will briefly extend the perspective from the previous section to discuss development by other numbers, with a particular look at some of the numbers that appear as causes that might explain development rather than outcomes.

Growth economists are of course the scholars who are most occupied with GDP figures. The basic model of the work of growth economists in the early years, growth accounting, was introduced by Robert Solow in the mid-1950s.[12] In this framework, the left side of the growth equation contains change in income, or economic growth, and the right side of the equation contains increments in labor and capital (population growth and investment), which economists would call the factors of production. If you assume that all countries have the same production function, this equation can be solved in a cross-country regression. Changes in economic growth that cannot be explained by increases in labor and capital is then referred to as residual, the unexplained contribution to economic growth.[13]

In the 1980s, this basic neoclassical growth model was expanded upon with the new growth theory, or "the endogenous growth model."[14] The goal of this model was much higher; it attempted to explain the large differences observed in economic growth across the world, which were not explainable by the neoclassical model. To do so required quantifying other factors that may affect economic growth beyond labor and capital, such as institutions, in order to eliminate the unexplained residual.

Barro provided the seminal article in this endeavor.[15] He presented a cross-country growth regression model that used global data on growth in GDP per capita from 1960 onward.[16] One of his central findings was a large and significant negative dummy variable in Africa.[17] Barro's interpretation of the dummy variable was that the analysis had not yet fully captured the characteristics of a "typical country" on the African continent.[18]

Over the following decade, a range of contributions attempted to "solve" the global economic growth equation by finding quantifiable variables that could explain the apparently anomalously slow growth of Africa. While the immediate focus was on factors of growth, such as the availability of capital and the quality of labor, these new growth models included measures that captured policy, such as inflation rates, black market premiums, and proxy variables for institutional quality. The new models identified 145 explanatory variables that were statistically significant. The voluminous literature this method has generated has been called the "growth regression industry."[19] Increasingly, it was perceived that these particular policy choices and matters of institutional quality needed explaining.[20] A chronic failure of growth in postcolonial Africa became an accepted fact.[21] It was not the growth rates themselves that needed explaining, but rather the parallel outcome of failed policies and a permanent shortfall in growth. According to this assumption, a lack of growth in the past is manifested in a low income today. Thus, the growth literature moved to focus on explaining cross-country inequality, as measured by per capita income today, rather than observed patterns of past per capita growth. This is how growth economists came to focus on the importance of history and institutions in explaining current differences in development.[22] This has in turn meant an expansion of quantification in the social sciences. The new categories on the right side of the economic equation demand new datasets, which in turn raises the issue of development by numbers with increasing urgency.

The number problem identified in this study of African development statistics relates to a much larger and pressing problem within the social sciences. Over the past couple of decades the use of global datasets of all sorts to rank and measure political development, social welfare, and conflict has become widespread. Although this spurt in quantitative research has brought about many positive contributions to the study of socioeconomic and political development, a number of serious shortcomings continue to limit the validity and applicability of these measures. The issues extend from how data is collected to conceptualization and methods of aggregation. These datasets are typically privately produced and disseminated. This is because they collect information on issues that states typically do not want to record, such as corruption or battle deaths.

Precisely because these data are not official and because they do not have the polystate status that most development statistics do, their validity is more readily drawn into question. This has at times caused lively debate. In this book I have shown that even when the same methods and sources are used to measure the same phenomena, very divergent results in income statistics have been produced. One of the areas where these debates have been perhaps the most clearly pronounced relates to data that measures war and conflict. Here the main issue is where to draw the line that establishes how many casualties are required to constitute a war, which inevitably becomes an arbitrary decision. There is also the inherently difficult decision of distinguishing between a civil war that spills over borders and an international war.[23] Thus, many results may be sensitive to decisions during the measurement process.[24] In addition, the problem that these datasets are not peer reviewed before publication has been raised.[25] The multitude of datasets used in the study of war is certainly confusing, but most of the time, this competition ensures that the right questions are being asked about the underlying data.[26]

One issue that has relevance beyond GDP statistics is a general lack of transparency in sources and methods. There is too little metadata, and aggregation methods are not made public. This problem is particularly prevalent with privately produced datasets.[27] It is compounded when there are disagreements at the conceptual level, and these issues are particularly pressing when datasets are produced for indicators of economic and political governance. While "economic growth" or even "war" are quite straightforward phenomena, when it comes to governance there are many competing definitions. Political indicators, particularly those that measure democracy, are perhaps the most controversial. The problems begin at the conceptual level: definitions vary. The two most used datasets,[28] the Polity IV dataset and the Freedom House dataset, differ in that the Polity dataset considers democracy primarily in terms of regime type and institutional change, whereas the Freedom House focuses on political rights and civil liberties. Consequently, the trends in the datasets differ.[29]

One report from the UNDP discusses seven datasets that capture corruption in one way or another: Transparency International's Corruption Perceptions Index, the World Governance Indicators, the Ibrahim Index of African Governance, the Global Integrity Report and the Global Integrity Index, the Open Budget Index, the Performance Measurement Framework, and the World Bank Governance and Anti-Corruption Diagnostics.[30] This list is not exhaustive. Stephen Knack adds six more: The Business Environment and Enterprise Performance Survey, the World Economic Forum's Executive Opinion Survey, the Institution for Management Development Survey, the World Values Surveys, the International Crime Victimization Survey, and the African Governance Indicators.[31] Other scholars would dismiss all of these and other measures of corruption as unreliable because they are subjective and do not objectively record instances of corruption. Studies that record corruption are subject to their own problems. In particular, it is reasonable to expect that people who are interviewed will understate their own experiences with corruption, particularly if they have actively participated in corrupt activities. And of course, such studies show lower levels of corruption than perception-based indices. How one would interpret this divergence between datasets that clearly biased in each direction is not clear.[32]

Most of these datasets come with warnings that state that they are picking up perceptions and are therefore endogenous and thus not suitable for causal explanations. In other words, a current perception of poor governance may well be related to a perception of poor economic performance, but that does not mean that one caused one or the other. Despite such warnings, the datasets are frequently used in empirical testing. Many of the indices also warn that the underlying data does not justify a ranking of countries according to these metrics. This of course does not stop data users from ranking them.[33] Despite these well-known issues of subjectivity and the problems of comparing the results from one place to another, data collected in surveys such as the World Values Survey, the Afrobarometer, the Eurobarometer, the Latinobarómetro, and the Asian Barometer are frequently used to establish general perceptions about the political and social situation in individual countries. Measurement errors will occur because of design and semantic and cultural influences; different questions will be understood in different ways in different social and political contexts.[34] Classical measurement issues associated with perception-based studies include the ability of study participants to accurately recall information, the long-term applicability of the findings (perceptions changes slower than reality), and obtaining a representative sample.[35] Moreover, published results that rank countries according to how corrupt they are may be more than just a product of the actual situation; they may influence perceptions that shape future rankings.[36]

These numbers, which are primarily used as correlates of growth in development economics but also as outcomes in other disciplines, have some obvious problems. For a historian, many of these sets are not "data" sets.[37] They are a collection of perceptions or the results of scholars' coding of variables to build up a dataset and thus are not observations. There are some common themes: the methods of aggregation are not explained and the sources of the data are obscure, sometimes withdrawn from the public eye, and in most cases this ends up misleading data users. It is also overwhelmingly clear that despite the warnings they come with, datasets are like guns: If they are left lying around, someone will use them. A reoccurring challenge is that different datasets that supposedly represent the same thing are used to support different interpretations. The measurement errors are not random; standards of measurements result in systematic biases in different settings. One final thing that these numbers have in common is that scholars pay great attention to defining the concepts and devote great effort to theorizing the existence of the phenomenon and spend comparatively little time critically probing the numbers that are supposed to represent them.

Conclusion

The general distrust of national income and economic growth data from sub-Saharan Africa is warranted. Some have called the metrics "random numbers,"[38] but in these chapters I have pinpointed systematic variation in errors and biases. The general problem of knowledge remains: we are un-certain about how well the numerals match up with the reality. Since the standard against which the validity of the data should be measured re-mains immeasurable in practice, the extent of inaccuracy of the aggregate economic observations remains obscure. And data users often get it wrong. Part of the blame lies with the nontransparent way these datasets are made available, and part of it lies with the uncritical way the data are consumed. Scholars need to ask themselves the same questions when confronted with numbers as they would when they are confronted with research findings: How did you arrive at this result?

Sarah Berry was indeed correct in her general dismissal of African agricultural statistics. She said that "the data are simply not good enough to warrant clear or firm conclusions about national (let alone continental) trends in agricultural output."[39] Polly Hill's claim that, despite the pub-lished statistics on cassava and other tubers, "no West African country can have the faintest idea as to how much is really produced" is also correct.[40] Roy Carr-Hill aptly summarized the current knowledge on social condi-tions in sub-Saharan Africa: "The assessments depend crucially upon the statistical series available. . . . These are so unreliable that whilst changes in some aggregate data series can be monitored, it is almost impossible to draw any conclusions about per capita social trends."[41] These concerns have been firmly substantiated by the research presented here.[42] We need to do better. Scholarship can help here; there have been more hands at work in the study of agricultural statistics in South Asia or in the study of demographics of Europe than there have been in the study of Africa.

Getting at reliable and valid data through experiments, natural or ran-domized, is very much in vogue in the social sciences and in the scholarship on economic development in Africa. It is the nature of social science inves-tigation that these methods are not applicable to all questions. Precision in answering in some of these questions such as "How large was the popula-tion?" or "How important was the subsistence economy?" or "How did an institution—such as private property rights—influence choice of produc-tion technique?" must sometimes be tempered with an appreciation of the limits to quantification. The answer is not always that "any (quantitative) data are better than none." Often scholars rely on very few observations of questionable provenance, and care must be taken when considering the quality of the evidence—be it qualitative, quantitative, oral, or of any other nature. This is particularly important for scholars who rely on data mediated through state collection apparatuses or through the eyes of external observers. We have already discussed how disillusionment with the quality or the lack of aggregate development official statistics has been met by some scholars. Alternative sources of information may help in a few questions, but these methods are unlikely to be sufficient and cannot fully substitute for official statistics.

This book has shown that the most basic metric of development, GDP, should not be treated as an objective number but rather as a number that is a product of a process in which a range of arbitrary and controversial assumptions are made. As a result, the metric should be used with the utmost care. The quality of this number depends on the state of the system that produces the statistics, and this system is deficient in many poor countries. The policy implication is not to ignore numbers. The implication for our knowledge of development is that we need other skills than statistics to interpret numbers. The implications for the practice of development are that we need to do better when we use numbers and that we need to rethink strategies that are supposed to support the production of these important numbers. Capacity for development is strongly linked to statistical capacity, and both virtuous and vicious circles are in play. States need macrolevel data to be able to make a rational policy decision. Numbers are essential for identifying and monitoring problems and evaluating solutions to problems. Therefore, statistics, statistical offices, and the problem of knowledge in development—how good the numbers are—need to take a more central place in future development policies.

The final note of this book is an encouragement to further scholarship, echoing the sentiment that was expressed in the preface. Histories of development are written with these numbers; decisions are made because of these numbers. Scholars who already are critical of how numbers are used in both scholarship and policy should use their critical skills to further engage with the numbers. Numbers should and will continue to be important for the study and practice of development. Decisions about what to measure, who to count, and by whose authority the final number is selected do matter. I hope this book leaves us better equipped to take on the task of taking part in these decisions, because poor numbers are too important to be dismissed as just that.

APPENDIX A

A Comparison of GDP Estimates from the World Development Indicators Database and Country Estimates

This appendix documents a comparison between the GDP estimates of the World Development Indicators (WDI) and those provided by each country's official national statistical office for the sub-Saharan African region as summarized in table 1.2 in chapter 1. The initial comparisons were made in late July 2011 with data downloaded from the World Development Indicators Databank databank on July 16, 2011, and country estimates made available through direct contact or an official government website. This information was updated with data drawn from the WDI databank on November 22, 2011. The dates of the country estimates are given in the "Comparison by Country" section below.

I used the WDI indicator of GDP (current local currency units) for both the July and November data downloads. For the country estimates, I used the most recent official estimates available; they are not preliminary or initial estimates unless otherwise noted below. I have also made base year comparisons using available country base year information and the World Development Institute's GDP deflator indicator (in which the base year varies by country). I gathered the base year data on July 16, 2011, and I verified them on November 24, 2011.

Although I intended this analysis to cover all of sub-Saharan Africa, it is not possible to include all countries in the analysis because of poor data availability and inconsistency. Because estimates for Sudan and Ethiopia are reported in different currency units and because of broken web links and other inconsistencies, I did not include the country estimates from those two countries. I also excluded Djibouti because it is not covered by the WDI databank. I was unable to find country estimates for Angola, Comoros, the Democratic Republic of Congo, Eritrea, Liberia, Mali, Somalia, Swaziland, Togo, and Zimbabwe, despite attempts to acquire information through direct contact and an exhaustive Internet search.

It should be noted that it may be, and indeed has been, quite difficult to navigate between preliminary and official estimates from the country sources. Where I have been able to ascertain which estimates are official, the comparison has been made using these observations. Another difficulty is that the datasets, both from countries and the WDI, are continuously being updated and revised. This means that data that were found in July 2011 were changed in November 2011. Where I have been able to verify that this was indeed an update of the data, I have used the data updated in November 2011 rather than date collected in July 2011. It is also worth noting that when I double-checked some of these entries during copyediting of the manuscript in August 2012, the WDI had again reported new updated country data for a number of countries. I have not updated the tables to reflect these changes, as I would find myself in a never-ending process of continuous revising. In 2012, the WDI was reporting estimates for 2011 for all of these countries, but the data reported in table 1.2 and the data reported in this appendix are the data that were available to me in November 2011.

All estimates are expressed in billions of local currency units.

Comparison by Country

Benin

In July 2011, the most recent country estimate available online was for the year 2005: 2,309.1 CFA francs. On July 16, 2011, the estimate from the WDI was 2,261.5 CFA francs. However, on November 22, 2011, the most recent official estimate for Benin, at 2,641.7 CFA francs, was for the year 2007. The 2007 estimate from the WDI was 2,658.1 CFA francs on November 22, 2011.

Source of country-level information: Institute National de la Statistique et de l'Analyse Economique, "Chapitre 11: Comptes Nationaux," in *Annuaire, 2005–2007* (Benin, 2007)

Base year reported by country: No data

Base year reported by WDI: 1985

Botswana

The preliminary estimate for Botswana for the year 2009 is 83.2 pula; this compares well to the WDI estimate of 83.3 pula for the same year. However, the country estimates for 2005–2009 are provisional. The most recent official estimate was 47.16 pula for 2004. The WDI estimate for this year was the exact equivalent on November 22, 2011.

Source of country-level information: Central Statistics Office, "Quarterly National Accounts Statistics Report–2009," Central Statistics Office, Gaborone, Botswana, December 2010

Base year reported by country: No data

Base year reported by WDI: 1994

Burkina Faso

In July 2011, a country estimate from 2005 provided a GDP of 2,881.4 CFA francs. The WDI databank reported GDP at 2,862.8 CFA francs. These figures were verified on November 22, 2011.

Source of country-level information: Burkina Faso, Institut national de la statistique et de la démographie, http://www.insd.bf/fr/

Base year reported by country: 1999

Base year reported by WDI: 1999

Burundi

In July 2011, a 2007 country estimate provided a GDP of 1,403 Burundi francs. The WDI databank reported GDP at 1,060 Burundi francs. These figures were verified on November 22, 2011, with no changes to report.

Source of country-level information: E-mail, Institut de Statistiques et d'Études Économiques, Bujumbura, Burundi, February 9, 2011

Base year reported by country: 2006

Base year reported by WDI: 1980

Cameroon

The country estimate for 2009 of 11,040.3 CFA francs was confirmed online on November 22, 2011. The WDI estimate for the same year was 10,474 CFA francs, as confirmed on November 22, 2011.

Source of country-level information: E-mail, Institut National de la Statistique, May 9, 2011

Country report: National Institute of Statistics, *Les Comptes Nationaux, 2009* (Yaoundé: Institut National de la Statistique, August 2010)

Base year reported by country: 2002

Base year reported by WDI: 2000

Cape Verde

I obtained the official country estimate of 107.25 Cape Verdean escudos for 2007 through direct contact on May 26, 2011, and confirmed that number through an online search on November 23, 2011. The WDI reported the same figure 107.25 Cape Verdean escudos on November 22, 2011.

Source of country-level information: E-mail, Instituto Nacional de Estatistica

Country report: Banco de Cape Verde, "Capitulo 1: Evolucao Economica Monetaria," in *Relatorio Anual de 2009* (Cidad de Praia: Instituto Nacional de Estatistica, 2010).

Base year reported by country: 1980

Base year reported by WDI: NA

Central African Republic

As of November 22, 2011, the country estimate for 2005 was 670.1 CFA francs. The WDI database recorded 662.1 CFA francs as the estimate for the same year.

Source of country-level information: http://www.stat-centrafrique.com/

Base year reported by country: 1985

Base year reported by WDI: 2000

Chad

The WDI reports 3,228 CFA francs for 2009. The country estimate for the same year was confirmed at 3,622 CFA francs as of November 22, 2011.

Source of country-level information: Secretariat General, Ministere de l'Economie, du Plan et de la Cooperation, Institut National de la Statistique, des Etudes Economiques et Demographiques, "Note to Cadrage Macroeconomique: Previsions Macroeconomiques, 2006–2009," Republique du Chad, Juin 2006

Base year reported by country: Not available

Base year reported by WDI: 1995

Republic of Congo

The country estimate of 3,869.8 CFA francs for 2009 and the corresponding estimate from the WDI of 4,523.4 CFA francs were confirmed on November 22, 2011.

Source of country-level information: Ministere de l'Economie, du Plan, de l'Amenagement du Territoire et de l'Integration, Centre National de la Statistique et des Etudes Economiques (CNSEE), *Annuaire Statistique du Congo, 2009* (Brazzaville: CNSEE, Juin 2011)

Base year reported by country: 1990

Base year reported by WDI: 1978

Cote d'Ivoire

On November 23, 2011, I obtained an official country estimate of 9,012 CFA francs for the year 2005. The WDI estimate for the same year was 8,631.19 CFA francs.

Source of country-level information: Institut National de la Statistique, "Tableau 27: Agrégats de la nation, selon le SCN 93 (en millards de f.cfa)," http://www.ins.ci/stats/Tableaux/TAB27.htm

Base year reported by country: 1996

Base year reported by WDI: 1996

Equatorial Guinea

The country reports a preliminary estimate for 2004 at 2,389.5 CFA francs. The most recent official country estimate of 1,572 CFA francs is for 2002. The WDI reports 1,496.3 CFA francs for 2002 and 4,334.3 CFA francs for 2005. Table 1.2 reports the comparison of the 2002 estimates.

Source of country-level information: Ministerio de Planificación, Desarrollo Económico e Inversions Públicas, http://www.dgecnstat-ge.org/

Base year reported by country: 1985

Base year reported by WDI: 2000

Gabon

The country estimate of 7,032.86 CFA francs for 2008 and the corresponding estimate from the WDI of 6,508.77 CFA francs were confirmed on November 22, 2011.

Source of country-level information: Direction Generale des Statistiques, Ministere de l'Economie, du Commerce de l'Industrie et du Tourisme, "Les Comptes Rapides du Gabon, 2006–2008," Republique Gabonaise, Juin 2010

Base year reported by country: 2001

Base year reported by WDI: 1991

Gambia

The country estimate of 23 dalasi for 2008 and the corresponding estimate from the WDI of 18.24 dalasi were confirmed on November 22, 2011.

Country report: Gambia Bureau of Statistics, www.gbos.gm

Base year reported by country: 2004

Base year reported by WDI: 1987

Ghana

When I compiled the table in July 2011, the official country estimate and the WDI estimate were both 36.9 Ghana cedi for the year 2009.

Source of country-level information: Ghana Statistical Service, Statistics for Development and Progress, "Revised Gross Domestic Product 2010," in *National Accounts Statistics* (Accra, May 2011); and a research visit in February 2010

Base year reported by country: 2006

Base year reported by WDI: 2006

Guinea

The country estimate of 20,982 Guinean francs for 2008 was confirmed online in November 23, 2011. The WDI reported 20,778 Guinean francs for the same year.

Source of country-level information: Ministere du Plan, Division de Statistiques Economiques et Sociales, Institute National de la Statistique, "Annuaire Statistique, 2011," Republique du Guinee, 2011.

Base year reported by country: 2003

Base year reported by WDI: 1996

Guinea-Bissau

The official country estimate of 172.3 CFA francs for 2006 was confirmed on November 22, 2011. The WDI estimate for 2006 was 312.11 CFA francs, downloaded on July 16, 2011. The November data from the WDI report was 302.5 CFA francs, so an update must have been made to this estimate.

Source of country-level information: Excel file entitled "Contas Nacionais," http://www.stat-guinebissau.com/dados_estrutural/dados_estru tural.htm

Base year reported by country: 1986

Base year reported by WDI: 2005

Kenya

The official country estimate for 2009 of 2,365.45 Kenyan shillings was confirmed on November 22, 2011. The WDI reported an estimate of 2,273.69 Kenyan shillings on the same date.

Source of country-level information: Kenya National Bureau of Statistics website, http://www.knbs.or.ke; and a research visit in October 2010.

Base year reported by country: 2001

Base year reported by WDI: 2001

Lesotho

Direct contact on May 9, 2011, revealed that the most recent official country estimate is for 2009 at 14.58 maloti. The WDI reported 13.76 maloti for 2009 on July 16, 2011. This estimated was updated to 14.58 maloti by November 22, 2011. An official estimate for 2009 was not found through a search at the country's website in November 2011 (the most recent was for 2008), so the estimate found through direct contact is being used instead.

Source of country-level information: E-mail, Bureau of Statistics, May 9, 2011; and a country report for the 2008 estimate: Bureau of Statistics, Ministry of Finance and Development Planning, *Statistical Yearbook, 2010* (Maseru: Bureau of Statistics, 2010).

Base year reported by country: 2004

Base year reported by WDI: 1995

Madagascar

I recorded a country estimate of 16,802 Malagasy ariaries in July 2011. Subsequently, the Madagascar statistical office made a minor revision; the number I found on November 22, 2011, was 16,803 Malagasy ariaries. The estimate from the WDI also changed slightly, from 16,802.95 Malagasy ariaries on July 16 to 16,604.25 Malagasy ariaries on November 22, 2011.

> Source of country-level information: Direction Generale, Institut National de la Statistique, "Tableau de Bord de l'Economie de Madagascar," Institut National de la Statistique de Madagascar, April 2011.
>
> Base year reported by country: 1984
>
> Base year reported by WDI: 1984

Malawi

On November 22, 2011, I confirmed the country estimate of 510.54 kwacha for 2007 and the corresponding estimate from the WDI of 484.02 kwacha that I had recorded in July 2011.

> Source of country-level information: National Statistical Office of Malawi, http://www.nso.malawi.net/index.php?option=com_content; and a research visit in November 2010.
>
> Base year reported by country: 2007
>
> Base year reported by WDI: 1994

Mauritania

I confirmed the official country estimate of 914.74 million ouguiyas for 2007 online on November 23, 2011. On November 22, 2011, I recorded the WDI's update of its 2007 estimate at 733.74 million ouguiyas.

> Source of country-level information: E-mail, Office National de la Statistique, July 3, 2011; and Office National de la Statistique, Ministere des Affaires Economiques et du Developpement, *Annuaire Statistique 2008* (Nouakchott: Office National de la Statistique, August 2009).
>
> Base year reported by country: 2005
>
> Base year reported by WDI: 1998

Mauritius

I confirmed the estimate I obtained through direct contact in March 2011—299.5 Mauritian rupees for 2010—through an online search on November 23, 2011. In July 2011, the WDI did not provide estimates for 2010, so I recorded the estimate of 274.5 Mauritian rupees from 2009 instead. On November 22, 2011, I updated this to the WDI's 2010 estimate of 299.5 Mauritian rupees.

> Source of country-level information: E-mail, Central Statistics Office, March 2011; and a country report: Central Statistics Office, Ministry of Finance and Economic Development, *National Accounts of Mauritius, 2010* (Port Luis: Central Statistics Office, June 2011)
>
> Base year reported by country: 2007
>
> Base year reported by WDI: 2006

Mozambique

I retrieved the country estimate of 266.21 Mozambican meticais for 2009 through direct contact on March 1, 2011. This number was confirmed online in November. The WDI estimate was unchanged at 263.26 Mozambican meticais as of November 23, 2011.

> Source of country-level information: Email, Instituto Nacional de Estatistica
>
> Base year reported by country: 2003
>
> Base year reported by WDI: 2003

Namibia

A search in July yielded a country estimate of 72.9 Namibian dollars for the year 2008. The Namibia statistical office subsequently updated this estimate; the search I performed November 23, 2011, revealed an estimate of 81.5 Namibian dollars for 2008. The WDI estimate was unchanged at 74 Namibian dollars for 2008.

> Source of country-level information: E-mail, National Planning Commission, Windhoek; Central Bureau of Statistics, National Planning

Commission, "National Accounts 2000–2010," Central Bureau of Statistics, September 2011

Base year reported by country: 2004

Base year reported by WDI: 2004

Niger

I confirmed the estimate I originally obtained through direct contact—2,748.2 CFA francs for 2010—during an online search on November 23, 2011. In July 2011, the WDI did not provide estimates for 2010, so I recorded the estimate of 2,542 CFA francs from 2009 instead. On November 22, 2011, I updated this to the WDI's estimate for 2010 of 2,748.2 CFA francs.

Source of country-level information: E-mail, Institut National de la Statistique, July 14, 2011; and Institute National de la Statistique, "Comptes Economiques de la Nation," Niamey, Institut National de la Statistique, November 2010.

Base year reported by country: 2006

Base year reported by WDI: 1987

Nigeria

I confirmed the country estimate for 2009 of 24,794.2 naira via e-mail. The most recent official country estimate is for 2008. That estimate is 24,665.24 naira; I located this number online on November 23, 2011. Subsequently, I obtained a provisional estimate of 29,205.78 naira for 2009. I confirmed the WDI's estimate of 25,760.58 naira for 2009 on November 22, 2011.

Source of country-level information: Online research; National Bureau of Statistics, "Gross Domestic Product for Nigeria," Abuja, Nigeria, November 2011; and a research visit in February 2010

Base year reported by country: 1990

Base year reported by WDI: 2002

Rwanda

The estimate I found online in July 2011—3,262 Rwandan francs for 2010—was confirmed through an online search on November 23, 2011. In July 2011, the WDI did not provide estimates for 2010, so I recorded its estimate of 2,964.07 Rwandan francs for 2009. On November 22, 2011, I updated this to the WDI's estimate for 2010 of 3,281.67 Rwandan francs.

> Source of country-level information: National Institute of Statistics, Rwanda, "GDP Annual Estimates (2010)," Kigali, Rwanda, October 2011.
>
> Base year reported by country: 2006
>
> Base year reported by WDI: 1995

São Tomé and Principe

The country estimate of 1,444.6 dobra for 2006 and the corresponding estimate from the WDI of 1,550.15 dobra that I recorded in July 2011 were confirmed on November 22, 2011.

> Source of country-level information: Instituto Nacional de Estatística, Democratic Republic of São Tomé and Principe, http://www.ine.st/ec onomia/economia.html
>
> Base year reported by country: 2001
>
> Base year reported by WDI: 2001

Senegal

I recorded the country estimate of 6,023 CFA francs for 2009 through direct contact on May 1, 2011, and through an online search in July 2011, but a search in November 2011 revealed that this was a provisional estimate. The updated information in the most recent search indicates that an estimate of 6,029 CFA francs is classified as "semi-definitive." I have used that number. The WDI estimate for 2009 was 6,037.88 CFA francs in July; by November 22, 2011, it had been updated to 6,023.21 CFA francs.

Source of country-level information: Ministere de l'Economie et des Finances, "Note d'Analyse des Comptes Nationaux Definitifs 2008, Semi-Definitifs 2009 et Provisoires 2010," Republique du Senegal, September 2011

Base year reported by country: 1999

Base year reported by WDI: 1999

Seychelles

The number I recorded in July 2011 of 10.75 Seychellois rupees for 2009 was found to be provisional when I searched in November 2011. In that month, the most recent official estimate was 9.1 Seychellois rupees for 2008. I made direct contact on April 29, 2011, but was unable to obtain an estimate from my source. The comparison with the WDI estimate has been updated to its 2008 estimate of 8.76 Seychellois rupees as of November 22, 2011.

Source of country-level information: E-mail, National Bureau of Statistics, April 29, 2011; and National Bureau of Statistics, "Statistical Abstract 2009," National Bureau of Statistics, Republic of Seychelles, 2010

Base year reported by country: 2006

Base year reported by WDI: 1986

Sierra Leone

The number recorded for 2009—7,868.8 leones—was supplied through e-mail correspondence. The most recent official estimate I found was 5,829.01 leones for 2007. The WDI estimate for this year was 4,966.47 leones as of November 22, 2011.

Source of country-level information: Email, Statistics Sierra Leone, November 2010; and Sierra Leone, Official Statistics Online, http://www.statistics.sl/gdp_archives.htm

Base year reported by country: 2001

Base year reported by WDI: 1990

South Africa

I confirmed the estimate provided in March—2,662.8 rand for 2010—through an online search on November 23, 2011. In July 2011, the WDI did not provide estimates for 2010, so I recorded its estimate of 2,407.69 rand from 2009. On November 22, 2011, I updated this to the WDI's 2010 estimate of 2,662.76 rand. Interestingly, the 2009 estimate the WDI reported is equal to the country official estimate for 2010 in basic prices.

> Source of country-level information: E-mail, March 2011; Excel file available at Statistics Africa, http://www.statssa.gov.za/
>
> Base year reported by country: 2005
>
> Base year reported by WDI: 2005

Tanzania

In July 2011, the country estimate of 32,293.5 Tanzanian shillings for 2010 was available at the website of the National Bureau of Statistics. In that month, the WDI did not provide estimates for 2010, so I recorded its estimate of 28,212.65 Tanzanian shillings from 2009 and compared it with the country estimate for the same year of 28,213 Tanzanian shillings. On November 22, 2011 the WDI's 2010 estimate of 32,492.87 Tanzanian shillings was available; that number is what I used on fable 1.2.

> Source of country-level information: National Bureau of Statistics, Ministry of Finance, *Tanzania in Figures 2010* (Dar es Salaam: National Bureau of Statistics, June 2011); and a research visit in October 2010
>
> Base year reported by country: 2001
>
> Base year reported by WDI: 1978

Uganda

I confirmed the estimate I found online in July—34,166 Ugandan shillings for 2010—through an online search on November 23, 2011. In July 2011, the WDI did not provide estimates for 2010, so I recorded its estimate of 30,556.8 Ugandan shillings from 2009. On November 22, 2011, I updated this to the WDI's 2010 estimate of 30,100.93 Ugandan shillings.

Source of country-level information: Summary of GDP at Market Prices, 2000–2009 found online at: http://www.ubos.org/; and a research visit in October 2010

Base year reported by country: 2002

Base year reported by WDI: 2003

Zambia

On November 22, 2011, I confirmed the country estimate of 55,210.6 Zambian kwacha for 2008 and the corresponding estimate from the WDI of 53,869.6 Zambian kwacha that I had recorded in July 2011.

Source of country-level information: Central Statistical Office website, www.zamstats.gov.zm; and a research visit in November 2010

Base year reported by country: 1994

Base year reported by WDI: 1994

APPENDIX B

DETAILS OF INTERVIEWS AND QUESTIONNAIRES

The first survey I used for all countries asked the following questions:

Question 1a: Which version of the United Nations Standard of National Accounts (SNA) do you currently follow?

Question 1b: Are there any deviations in method?

Question 1c: Does the statistical office publish a methods and sources?

Question 2:   What is the most recent GDP estimate (year and value in local current prices)?

Question 2a: Which year is used as the base year in the constant price estimates?

Question 2b: Which year was used in the previous constant price estimates?

Question 2c: When is the next rebasing planned?

Question 3:   When was the last revision (base year) of GDP?

Question 4:   How much were the current price estimates revised upwards with new methods and data?

Question 5:   What were the main sources of this upward revision?

Question 6:   Do you think that GDP is underestimated today?

Question 7:   What methods are used to prepare an estimate for the subsistence output and for the informal sector?

When there were particularly interesting responses or unclear answers, I followed up with additional questions by phone. I followed up in Burundi, Cameroon, Cape Verde, Guinea, Lesotho, Mali, Mauritania, Mauritius, Morocco, Namibia, Mozambique, Niger, Senegal, Seychelles, and South Africa. The e-mail survey took place in the spring and summer of 2011.

I also conducted in-person interviews in the spring and fall of 2010. When I conducted these interviews I used an extended version of this questionnaire to start off conversations in Ghana, Kenya, Malawi, Nigeria, Tanzania, Uganda, and Zambia.

By request, I have kept the names of technical advisors and other personnel confidential. I also have not quoted them directly in the book.

NOTES

Poor Numbers

1. Sally Engle Merry, "Measuring the World: Indicators, Human Rights, and Global Governance," *Current Anthropology* 52, no. 3 (2011): S85.

2. The countries surveyed were Ghana, Nigeria, Uganda, Kenya, Tanzania, Zambia, Malawi, Burundi, Cameroon, Cape Verde, Guinea, Lesotho, Mali, Mauritania, Mauritius, Namibia, Mozambique, Niger, Senegal, Seychelles, Sierra Leone, and South Africa. Details about the survey are in Appendix B.

3. It could thus be argued that the information is biased in two ways. First, we do not have information about the places where the situation may be worse (i.e., conflict and postconflict zones). Personal interviews with national statistical offices were conducted in only two countries in West Africa. Thus, the geographical focus on East and South-Central Africa is perhaps a bit narrow; we have less information about Francophone and Lusophone Africa. The structured survey data and discussions with experts who had knowledge of countries in those regions indicate that the same problems apply there, though with varying intensity. The variations in country-level problems are discussed in detail in chapter 4.

4. In chapters 3 and 4 the discussion is broadened to include population statistics, agricultural statistics, and social statistics. For slightly dated but still relevant surveys of all types of statistics, see R. A. Carr-Hill, *Social Conditions in Sub-Saharan Africa* (Basingstoke: Macmillan, 1990); and G. M. K. Kpedekpo and P. L. Arya, *Social and Economic Statistics for Africa: Their Source and Reliability* (London: Allen & Unwin, 1981).

5. As recently expressed in Peter Lawrence's response to the work of development economists Paul Collier, Jeffrey Sachs, and William Easterly in Lawrence's "Development by Numbers," *New Left Review* 62 (2010); or in Mike McGovern, "Popular Development Economics—An Anthropologist among the Mandarins," *Perspectives on Politics* 9, no. 2 (2011): 345–55.

6. Shanta Devarajan, "Africa's Statistical Tragedy," Africa Can … End Poverty blog, October 6, 2011, http://blogs.worldbank.org/africacan/africa-s-statistical-tragedy, accessed March 18, 2012.

Introduction

1. Roger C. Riddel, ed., *Manufacturing Africa: Performance and Prospects in Seven Countries in Sub-Saharan Africa* (London: James Currey, 1990), 10.

2. For one discussion of why and how "Africa" is a problematic yet important label, see James Ferguson, *Global Shadows: Africa in the Neoliberal World Order* (Durham, NC: Duke University Press, 2006), 25–49.

3. The phrase was attributed to the British politician Benjamin Disraeli by Mark Twain in his autobiography, according to Joel Best, *Damned Lies and Statistics: Untangling Numbers from the Media, Politicians, and Activists* (Berkeley, CA: University of California Press, 2001).

4. For a classic treatment of the inaccuracy of economic statistics, see Oskar Morgenstern, *On the Accuracy of Economic Observations* (Princeton, NJ: Princeton University Press, 1963). For issues pertaining to the general use of numbers in social sciences, see Theodore M. Porter, *Trust in Numbers: The Pursuit of Objectivity in Science and Public Life* (Princeton, NJ: Princeton University Press, 1995).

5. Gareth Austin, "Resources, Techniques and Strategies South of the Sahara: Revising the Factor Endowments Perspective on African Economic Development, 1500–2000," *Economic History Review* 61, no. 3 (2008): 587–624.

6. Sara Berry, "Debating the Land Question in Africa," *Comparative Studies in Society and History* 44 (2002): 638–68.

7. Jeffrey I. Herbst, *States and Power in Africa: Comparative Lessons in Authority and Control* (Princeton, NJ: Princeton University Press, 2000).

8. Frederick Cooper, *Africa since 1940: The Past of the Present* (New York: Cambridge University Press, 2002).

9. For how structural adjustment may have exacerbated this pattern by an increased dependence on foreign aid, see Nicolas van de Walle, *African Economies and the Politics of Permanent Crisis, 1979–1999* (New York: Cambridge University Press, 2001). For the link to natural resource rents and other nontax revenues, see Kevin M. Morrison, "Oil, Nontax Revenue, and the Redistributional Foundations of Regime Stability," *International Organization* 63, no. 1 (2009): 107–138. For other recent work that emphasizes the historical link between state capacity and taxation, see Morten Jerven, "African Growth Recurring: An Economic History Perspective on African Growth Episodes, 1690–2010," *Economic History of Developing Regions* 25, no. 2 (2010): 127–154; and Deborah A. Brautigam, Odd-Helge Fjeldstad, and Mick Moore, eds., *Taxation and State-Building in Developing Countries: Capacity and Consent* (New York: Cambridge University Press, 2008).

10. Porter, *Trust in Numbers*, 33.

11. In turn this means that most of the datasets we refer to as international or global are what Michael Ward has called "polystatist." This term reflects the fact that states collect and generate most of these data. Michael Ward, *Quantifying the World: UN Ideas and Statistics* (Bloomington, IN: Indiana University Press, 2004), 62, 245–52.

12. Charles Tilly, *Contention and Democracy in Europe, 1650–2000* (New York: Cambridge University Press, 2004), 15.

13. Peter Andreas and Kelly M. Greenhill, eds., *Sex, Drugs, and Body Counts: The Politics of Numbers in Global Crime and Conflict* (Ithaca: Cornell University Press, 2010), 7.

14. Ibid., 7.

15. Sally Engle Merry, "Measuring the World: Indicators, Human Rights, and Global Governance," *Current Anthropology* 52, no. 3 (2011): S84.

16. Merry draws on the theoretical insights that follow the work of Porter in *Trust in Numbers*.

17. For the importance of standards, see Martha Lampland and Susan Leigh Star, eds., *Standards and Their Stories: How Quantifying, Classifying and Formalizing Practices Shape Everyday Life* (Ithaca: Cornell University Press, 2009).

18. For a useful introduction to the relationship between policy and numbers, see Deborah Stone, *Policy Paradox: The Art of Political Decision Making* (New York: Norton, 2002), esp. Chapter 7.

19. For a basic introduction to why numbers are so important for international organizations, see Michael N. Barnett and Martha Finnemore, *Rules for the World: International Organizations in Global Politics* (Ithaca: Cornell University Press, 2004). The authors highlight the need for classification (31–32) and how quantification is linked to objectivity in decision making (68–71).

1. What Do We Know about Income and Growth in Africa?

1. Later renamed Organisation for Economic Co-operation and Development (OECD).

2. For a basic introduction to the changes in the guidelines, see Francios Lequiller and Derek Blades, *Understanding National Accounts* (Paris: OECD Publishing, 2007), Chapter 15.

3. Michael Ward, *Quantifying the World: UN Ideas and Statistics* (Bloomington: Indiana University Press, 2004), 45.

4. Yoshiko M. Herrera, *Mirrors of the Economy: National Accounts and International Norms in Russia and Beyond* (Ithaca: Cornell University Press, 2010), xi.

5. Oskar Morgenstern, *On the Accuracy of Economic Observations* (Princeton, NJ: Princeton University Press, 1963).

6. Dudley Seers, "The Political Economy of National Accounting," in *Employment, Income Distribution and Development Strategy: Problems of the Developing Countries*, edited by A. Caincross and M. Puri (New York: Holmes & Meier Publishers, 1976).

7. Brian van Arkadie, "National Accounting and Development Planning: A Review of Some Issues," *Development and Change* 4, no. 2 (1972–73): 15–31, 15.

8. Once again, the careful caveat noted in the preface should be added. Since I have not conducted field research in Francophone and Lusophone Africa, I must rely on secondary information and my e-mail survey results to fill in the gaps on the continent. The countries I have studied firsthand are in the middle of the quality range—some countries are poorer than others, and those that are more ravaged by war have deeper problems than the ones that I have studied. At the same time, I should also add that national account reporting and statistical training is a bit more standardized in the French-speaking countries (they all use the same software, and most statisticians from these countries are trained in Abidjan).

9. Republic of Kenya, Ministry of Economic Planning and Development, *Economic Survey 1967* (Nairobi: Ministry of Economic Planning and Development, 1968).

10. Annexes to Provisional Estimates, Consolidated National Accounts 1973–1978, Lusaka, Zambia, App. 2.1.2, Central Statistical Office, Lusaka, Zambia.

11. Despite the importance of this sector, it is usually poorly measured. See Owiti A K'Akumu, "Construction Statistics Review for Kenya," *Construction Management and Economics* 25, no. 3 (2007): 315–26.

12. Charles H. Feinstein, *Making History Count: A Primer in Quantitative Methods for Historians* (Cambridge: Cambridge University Press, 2002), Appendix B4.

13. I have of course already noted that the social and political meanings of this word are different. Numbers can gain importance or validity when powerful institutions such as nation-states use them as facts.

14. This is referred to as exhaustiveness of the measure. See, for instance, Adriaan M. Bloem and Manik L. Shrestha, "Exhaustive Measures of GDP and the Unrecorded Economy," International Monetary Fund Working Paper, Draft, October 2000.

15. The World Development Indicators dataset uses GDP per capita (in constant 1995 US$). The best equivalent from the Penn World Tables is real GDP per capita in 1996 International Geary Dollars. Finally, the Maddison dataset uses per capita GDP in 1990 International Geary-Khamis Dollars. Other sources of data such the OECD and Eurostat datasets exist, but these three are the most commonly used in scholarly work.

16. The indicators covered in the World Development Indicators were published in the statistical index of the World Bank's World Development Report from the 1970s until 1997, when the World Development Indicator became a publication in and of itself. The first report of 1997 covered 400 indicators (800 for the CD-ROM version) over the period 1970–1995 and covered nearly 150 countries. The World Bank published its data for the period 1960 to 1994 on a CD-ROM entitled *World*Data 1995*. Since the establishment of the Millennium Development Goals, the World Development Indicators have been used as a data source for tracking progress.

17. Thereby directly excluding Algeria, Egypt, Libya, Morocco, and Tunisia. In addition, the World Development Indicators dataset does not include data for Djibouti, Mayotte, Reunion, and Somalia. Note that Maddison lacks a separate estimate for Eritrea (his estimate for Eritrea and Ethiopia is considered to represent Ethiopia).

18. Maddison also expressed doubts about the validity of the estimates for the DRC when presenting his paper and dataset at the Comparative Economic History Seminar at the London School of Economics on December 6, 2008. MacGaffey suggested that the real economy might be three times larger than what the official statistics recorded. See Janet MacGaffey, *The Real Economy of Zaire: The Contribution of Smuggling & Other Unofficial Activities to National Wealth* (Philadelphia: University of Pennsylvania Press, 1991).

19. For further discussion of how this affects the analysis of economic development across time, see Morten Jerven, "The Relativity of Poverty and Income: How Reliable Are African Economic Statistics?" *African Affairs* 109, no. 434 (2010): 77–96.

20. The ranking matches country for country at the bottom and the top of the distribution. In the middle of the income distribution, Guatemala, Ecuador, Jamaica, the Dominican Republic, and Columbia jump a few places up and down from one source the other. The average of jumps in the ranking is less than one, compared to seven in the African sample.

21. A. Deaton and A. Heston, "Understanding PPPS and PPP-based National Accounts," *American Economic Journal: Macroeconomics* 2, no. 4 (2010): 1–35.

22. Maddison, Background Note on "Historical Statistics," (2010), http://www.ggdc.net/maddison, retrieved July 2011.

23. Ward, *Quantifying the World*, pp 96–97.

24. Kpedekpo and Arya, *Social and Economic Statistics*, 208.

25. Ward, *Quantifying the World*, 98. These were converted to U.S. dollars with the Atlas method in order to deal with volatile nominal exchange rates. The World Bank also made their own midyear population estimates. See 97–99 for the full account.

26. Ibid., 98.

27. Ibid., 99.

28. The topic of inadequate metadata is discussed in full in Chapter 4.

29. Alwyn Young, "The African Growth Miracle," (2010):1, http://www.econ.yale.edu/seminars/develop/tdw09/young-090924.pdf, retrieved 13 September 2012.

30. Ibid.

31. World Bank, "Method of Gap-Filling," http://web.worldbank.org/WBSITE/EXTER-NAL/DATASTATISTICS/EXTDECSTAMAN/0,contentMDK:20878854˜menuPK:2077987˜pagePK:64168445˜piPK:64168309˜theSitePK:2077967˜isCURL:Y,00.html, retrieved September 13, 2012.

32. Ibid.

33. For the full details of the provenance of these data, please see the appendix.

34. The World Bank does not report which base year they used for Madagascar and Somalia.

35. Personal communication, macroeconomic statistics advisor, East AFRITAC (IMF Africa Regional Technical Assistance Center), December 2010.

36. Ghana Statistical Service, "Rebasing of Ghana's National Accounts to Reference Year 2006," Accra, 2010, http://www.mofep.gov.gh/sites/default/files/reports/RebasingNationalAccounts Ghana_1.pdf.

37. Todd Moss, "Ghana Says, Hey, Guess What? We're Not Poor Anymore," Global Development: Views from the Centre, November 5, 2010, http://blogs.cgdev.org/globaldevelopment/2010/11/ghana-says-hey-guess-what-we%E2%80%99re-not-poor-anymore.php, accessed July 2011.

38. Charles Kenny and Andy Sumner, "How 28 Poor Countries Escaped the Poverty Trap," Poverty Matters Blog, *The Guardian*, July 12, 2011, http://www.guardian.co.uk/global-development/poverty-matters/2011/jul/12/world-bank-reclassifies-28-poor-countries.

39. News reports claim that mobile phone usage has reached 70 percent of the population; see "Mobile Phone Users to Reach 70 Percent," *Ghanaian Chronicle*, October 14, 2010. However, according to the United Nations Conference on Trade and Development (UNCTAD), only about 50 percent of the population used cell phones as of 2008; see UNCTAD, *Information Economy Report 2009: Trends and Outlook in Turbulent Times* (New York: UNCTAD, 2009), 97.

40. Personal Communication, Ghana Statistical Services, Accra, Ghana, February 2010.

41. World Bank, "Changes in Country Classifications, 1 July," http://data.worldbank.org/news/2010-GNI-income-classifications, retrieved August 2011.

42. Personal Communication, Ghana Statistical Services, Accra, Ghana, February 2010.

43. Tim Cocks, "Analysis—Nigeria GDP Rebase May Pose Challenge to SAfrica," Reuters, November 11, 2011.

44. The countries surveyed were Ghana, Nigeria, Uganda, Kenya, Tanzania, Zambia, Malawi, Burundi, Cameroon, Cape Verde, Guinea, Lesotho, Mali, Mauritania, Namibia, Mozambique, Niger, Senegal, Seychelles, Sierra Leone, and South Africa.

45. From South Africa it was stated that it was not the mandate of the Statistical Office to give an answer to this question, while the response from Lesotho was that it was difficult to say.

46. The World Bank does have data for 2009, as noted, whereas the country data are older. The comparison is made between the most recent year for which each source has current GDP estimates.

47. Personal communication, Institut de Statistiques et d"Études Économiques, Burundi, February 2011.

48. *The Economist*, "Measuring Growth from Outer Space," August 6, 2009, referring to J. V. Henderson, A. Storeygard, and D. N. Weil, "Measuring Economic Growth from Outer Space," NBER Working Paper Series no. 15199 (2009); and Xi Chen and William D. Nordhaus, "Using Luminosity as a Proxy for Economic Statistics," *Proceedings of the National Academy of Sciences* 108, no. 21 (2011): 8589–8594.

49. E. Miguel, S. Shanker, and S. Ernest, "Economic Shocks and Civil Conflict: An Instrumental Variables Approach," *Journal of Political Economy* 112, no. 4 (2004): 725–53. Yet others suggest the use of different measures, such as heights. See, for example, Alexander Moradi, "Towards an Objective Account of Nutrition and Health in Colonial Kenya: A Study of Stature in African Army Recruits and Civilians, 1880–1980," *Journal of Economic History* 69, no. 3 (2009): 720–55.

50. J. W. Dawson, J. P. DeJuan, J. J. Seater, and E. F Stephenson, "Economic Information versus Quality Variation in Cross-Country Data," *Canadian Journal of Economics* 34, no. 3 (2001): 988–1009.

51. S. Johnson, W. Larson, C. Papageorgiou, and A. Subramanian, "Is Newer Better? The Penn World Table Revisions and the Cross-Country Growth Literature," NBER Working Paper 15455 (2009).

52. S. Durlauf, P. Johnson, and J. Temple, "Growth Econometrics," in *Handbook of Economic Growth*, edited by P. Aghion and S. Durlauf (Amsterdam: Elsevier, 2005): 555–667.

53. J. S. Arbache and J. Page, "Patterns of Long Term Growth in Sub-Saharan Africa," World Bank Policy Research Working Paper 4398 (2007).

54. Morten Jerven, "Random Growth in Africa? Lessons from an Evaluation of the Growth Evidence on Botswana, Kenya, Tanzania and Zambia, 1965–1995," *Journal of Development Studies* 46, no. 2 (2010): 274–94.

55. T. N. Srinivasan, "The Data Base for Development Analysis: An Overview," *Journal of Development Economics* 44 (1994): 4–5.

56. A. Heston, "A Brief Review of Some Problems in Using National Accounts Data in Level Comparisons and Growth Studies," *Journal of Development Economics* 44, no. 1 (1994): 31.

57. Derek Blades, *Non-Monetary (Subsistence) Activities in the National Accounts of Developing Countries* (Paris: OECD, 1975); and "What Do We Know about Levels and Growth of Output in Developing Countries? A Critical Analysis with Special Reference to Africa," in *Economic Growth and Resources: Proceedings of the Fifth World Congress, International Economic Association, Tokyo*, vol. 2, *Trends and Factors*, edited by R. C. O. Mathews(New York: St. Martin's Press, 1980), 60–77.

58. Ibid., 70.

59. Ibid., 72.

60. Miguel, Shanker, and Ernest, "Economic Shocks and Civil Conflict," 740.

61. Angus Deaton, "Understanding the Mechanisms of Economic Development," *Journal of Economic Perspectives* 24 (2010): 14.

62. Morten Jerven, "The Quest for the African Dummy: Explaining African Post-Colonial Economic Performance Revisited," *Journal of International Development* 23, no. 2 (2011): 288–307.

63. P. Collier, *The Bottom Billion: Why the Poorest Countries Are Failing and What Can Be Done About It* (New York: Oxford University Press, 2009), 9.

2. Measuring African Wealth and Progress

1. "Users and Producers of Statistics" was the name chosen for seminars organized by the Federal Office of Statistics in Nigeria in the 1980s and 1990s, which aimed to provide a consultation between data providers and data users. See Morten Jerven, "Users and Producers of African Income: Measuring African Progress," *African Affairs* 110, no. 439 (April 2011): 169–90.

2. William Easterly, "The Lost Decades: Developing Countries' Stagnation In Spite of Policy Reform, 1980–1998," *Journal of Economic Growth* 6, no. 2 (2001): 135–57.

3. Theodore M. Porter, *Trust in Numbers: The Pursuit of Objectivity in Science and Public Life* (Princeton, NJ: Princeton University Press, 1995).

4. Referred to as the "growth regression industry" in S. Durlauf, P. Johnson, and J. Temple, "Growth Econometrics," in *Handbook of Economic Growth*, edited by P. Aghion and S. Durlauf (Amsterdam: Elsevier, 2005), 555–667, quote on 599. For a discussion of Africa specifically, see Morten Jerven, "The Quest for the African Dummy: Explaining African Post-Colonial Economic Performance Revisited," *Journal of International Development* 23, no. 2 (2011): 288–307; and Morten Jerven, "A Clash of Disciplines? Economists and Historians Approaching the African Past," *Economic History of Developing Regions* 26, no. 2 (2011): 111–24.

5. Indeed, a much-noted strategy of the World Bank is its practice of moving country economists around frequently so they will not become too immersed in a local economy. See Michella Wrong, *It's Our Turn To Eat: The Story of a Kenyan Whistle Blower* (New York: Harper Collins Publishers, 2009), 189–90; and H. Stein, *Beyond the World Bank Agenda. An Institutional Approach to Development* (Chicago: University of Chicago Press, 2008).

6. R. Herring, "Data as Social Product," in *Q-Square: Combining Qualitative and Quantitative Methods in Poverty Appraisal*, edited by R. Kanbur (New Delhi: Permanent Black, 2001), 141.

7. Frederick Cooper, "Modernizing Bureaucrats, Backward Africans, and the Development Concept," in *International Development and the Social Sciences: Essays on the History and Politics of Knowledge*, edited by Frederick Cooper and Randall Packard (Berkeley, CA: University of California Press, 1997), 64–92. For a specific study of development planning under the colonial state, see Toyin Falola, *Development Planning and Decolonization in Nigeria* (Gainesville: University Press of Florida, 1996).

8. With some notable exceptions, such as Rwanda, Ethiopia, and Botswana, but in most cases the colonial borders did not fully coincide with the borders of precolonial states. In other cases, such as Eritrea and Southern Sudan, the borders have remained unchanged in the postcolonial period. See P. Englebert, "Pre-Colonial Institutions, Post-Colonial States, and Economic Development in Tropical Africa," *Political Research Quarterly* 53, no.1 (2000): 7–36; and Jeffrey I. Herbst, *States and Power in Africa: Comparative Lessons in Authority and Control* (Princeton, NJ: Princeton University Press, 2000).

9. Thus, the historian Frederick Cooper argues that modern African history should take 1940 as its starting point rather than 1960. See Frederick Cooper, *Africa since 1940: The Past of the Present* (New York: Cambridge University Press, 2002).

10. For a classic empirical study, see Tony. Killick, *Development Economics in Action: A Study of Economic Policies in Ghana* (New York: Routledge, 2010).

11. N. van de Walle, *African Economies and the Politics of Permanent Crisis, 1979–1999* (Cambridge: Cambridge University Press, 2001).

12. The Angus Maddison dataset provides data back to 1950.

13. Dudley Seers, "The Role of National Income Estimates in the Statistical Policy of an Under-Developed Area," *Review of Economic Studies* 20, no. 3 (1952–53): 160.

14. For a study of the application of social sciences to British Africa, see Helen Tilley, *Africa as Living Laboratory: Empire, Development and the Problem of Scientific Knowledge* (Chicago: University of Chicago Press, 2011). She puts great emphasis on the African Research Survey, a project undertaken in the 1930s. For a similar account that focuses on the first national income estimates, see Daniel Speich, "The Use of Global Abstractions: National Income Accounting in the Period of Imperial Decline," *Journal of Global History* 6, no. 1 (2011): 7–28.

15. Federation of Rhodesia and Nyasaland, *Monthly Digest of Statistics* (Salisbury, 1955).

16. Seers, "Role of National Income Estimates."

17. G. Donald Wood, Jr., "Problems of Comparisons in Africa with Special Regard to Kenya," *Review of Income and Wealth* 19, no. 1 (1973): 105–116.

18. Peter H. Ady, "Uses of National Accounts in Africa," in *African Studies in Income and Wealth*, edited by L. H. Samuels (London: Bowes & Bowes, 1963), 62.

19. Seers, "Role of National Income Estimates," 161.

20. S. Herbert Frankel, "'Psychic' and 'Accounting' Concepts of Income and Welfare," *Oxford Economic Papers* 4, no. 1 (1952): 1–17.

21. Phyllis Deane, *The Measurement of Colonial National Income: An Experiment* (Cambridge: Cambridge University Press, 1948), 127.

22. Republic of South Africa, Department of Statistics, *National Accounts of the Black States, 1972 to 1976* (Pretoria: South Africa Department of Statistics, 1980).

23. Alan R. Prest and Ian. G. Stewart, *The National Income of Nigeria, 1950–51*, Colonial Research Studies no. 11 (London: Her Majesty's Stationery Office, 1953).

24. Pius N. C. Okigbo, *Nigerian National Accounts, 1950–57* (Enugu: Government Printer, 1962).

25. I. I. U. Eke, "The Nigerian National Accounts—A Critical Appraisal," *Nigerian Journal of Economic and Social Studies* 8 (1966): 334.

26. Ady, "Uses of National Accounts in Africa," 55.

27. S. Herbert Frankel, *The Economic Impact on Under-Developed Societies: Essays on International Investment and Social Change* (Cambridge, MA: Harvard University Press, 1953), 37.

28. Dudley Seers, "An Approach to the Short-Period Analysis of Primary Producing Economies," *Oxford Economic Papers,* new series 11, no. 1 (1959): 1–36.

29. Ibid., 36.

30. Prest and Stewart, *The National Income of Nigeria*; and Alan T. Peacock and Douglas G. M. Dosser, *The National Income of Tanganyika 1952–54* (London: Her Majesty's Stationery Office, 1958).

31. G. C. Billington, "A Minimum System of National Accounts for Use by African Countries and Some Related Problems," *Review of Income and Wealth* 1 (1962): 1–51.

32. Douglas Rimmer, "Learning about Economic Development from Africa," *African Affairs* 102 (2003): 471.

33. Okigbo, *Nigerian National Accounts*, 65.

34. For an indication of the openness of the debate on the accuracy and usefulness of national income accounts in Africa, see L. H. Samuels, ed., *African Studies in Income and Wealth* (London: Bowes & Bowes, 1963), a collection of the papers given in a conference organized by the International Organization for Research in Income and Wealth and the Economic Commission of Africa that took place in Addis Ababa, Ethiopia, from the January 4–10, 1961.

35. Porter, *Trust in Numbers*, 90.

36. Phyllis Deane, "Domestic Income and Product in Kenya: A Description of Sources and Methods with Revised Calculations from 1954–1958; The National Income of the Sudan, 1955–1956, by C. H. Harvie and J. G. Kleve; Comptes Économiques Togo, 1956–1957–1958, by G. Le Hégarat" (book review), *The Economic Journal* 71, no. 283 (1961): 630–31.

37. Republic of Zambia, Central Statistical Office, *National Accounts 1964–1967* (Lusaka: Central Statistical Office, 1967), 37.

38. The example of the population census in Nigeria in chapter 3 illustrates the upside of being counted in Nigeria following independence versus the downside of being counted before independence.

39. Republic of Zambia, Central Statistical Office, *National Accounts 1964–1967*, 37.

40. United Republic of Tanzania, *National Accounts of Tanzania, 1966–68* (Dar es Salaam: G.P., 1970), 2.

41. Similarly, Killick reports that for Ghana, the assumption during the 1960s was a constant real per capita consumption of locally produced goods. See Tony Killick, *Development Economics in Action: A Study of Economic Policies in Ghana* (New York: Routledge, 2010), 93.

42. Derek Blades, "What Do We Know about Levels and Growth of Output in Developing Countries? A Critical Analysis with Special Reference to Africa," in *Economic Growth and Resources: Proceedings of the Fifth World Congress, International Economic Association, Tokyo*, vol. 2, *Trends and Factors*, edited by R. C. O. Mathews (New York: St. Martin's Press, 1980), 60–77.

43. Ibid., 69.

44. Morten Jerven, "Accounting for the African Growth Miracle: The Official Evidence, Botswana 1965–1995," *Journal of Southern African Studies* 36, no. 1 (2010): 73–94.

45. Republic of Kenya, Central Bureau of Statistics, Ministry of Finance and Planning, *Sources and Methods Used for the National Accounts of Kenya* (Nairobi: Central Bureau of Statistics, Ministry of Finance and Planning, 1977).

46. Gerald K. Helleiner, *Peasant Agriculture, Government and Economic Growth in Nigeria* (Homewood, IL: R. D. Irwin, 1966), 392.

47. Helleiner, *Economic Growth in Nigeria*, 391.

48. The Nigerian-Biafran War, July 6, 1967–January 15, 1970.

49. Federal Ministry of Planning, *National Accounts of Nigeria, 1973–1975* (Lagos, Nigeria, 1981), 47.

50. Ibid.

51. R. H. Bates, *Markets and States in Tropical Africa: The Political Basis of Agricultural Policies* (Berkeley, CA: University of California Press, 1981).

52. Easterly, "The Lost Decades."

53. Stephen Ellis, "Writing Histories of Contemporary Africa," *Journal of African History* 43, no. 1 (2002): 1–26; and Paul Nugent, *Africa since Independence: A Comparative History* (New York: Palgrave Macmillan, 2004).

54. Personal communication, National Accounts Branch, Central Statistical Office, Lusaka, March 2007.

55. Personal communication, Institute of Social, Statistical and Economic Research, Legon, Ghana, February 2010.

56. Personal communication, Central Bureau of Statistics, Nairobi, April 2007.

57. This information was conveyed to me in conversations at the University Library, Lusaka, and the National Archives, Lusaka, during February 2007.

58. Personal communication, the Institute of Statistical, Social and Economic Research (ISSER), Legon, Ghana, February 15, 2010, and the National Bureau of Statistics, Abuja, Nigeria, February 23, 2010.

59. E. A. Brett, "State Failure and Success in Uganda and Zimbabwe: The Logic of Political Decay and Reconstruction in Africa," *Journal of Development Studies* 44, no. 3 (2008): 339–64, quote on 350.

60. E. S. K. Muwanga-Zake, "Statistics Reform," in *Uganda's Economic Reforms: Insider Accounts*, edited by F. Kuteesa, E. Tumusiime-Mutebile, A. Whitworth, and T. Williamson (New York: Oxford University Press, 2010), 247.

61. J. Barkan, ed., *Beyond Capitalism vs. Capitalism in Kenya and Tanzania* (London: Lynne Rienner, 1994).

62. Beatrice Hibou, ed., *Privatizing the State*, translated from French by Jonathan Derick (New York: Columbia University Press, 2004), 7.

63. Odd-Helge Fjeldstad and Mick Moore, "Tax Reform and State-Building in a Globalised World," in *Taxation and State-Building in Developing Countries: Capacity and Consent*, edited by Deborag A. Brautigam, Odd-Helge Fjeldstad, and Mick Moore (Cambridge, NY: Cambridge University Press, 2008), 235–63.

64. Some scholars argue that this downsizing of state functions directly undermines state capacity. See, for instance, Thandika Mkandawire, "Thinking about Developmental States in Africa," *Cambridge Journal of Economics* 25 (2001): 289–313. Others see it as a response to states that are incapable of managing or unwilling to manage development polices, interpreting states as either neopatrimonial or simply failed. See Anne Pitcher, Mary H. Moran, and Michael Johnston, "Rethinking Patrimonialism and Neopatrimonialism in Africa," *African Studies Review* 52, no. 1 (2009): 125–56; and P. Collier, *The Bottom Billion: Why the Poorest Countries Are Failing and What Can Be Done About It* (New York: Oxford University Press, 2009).

65. Republic of Zambia, National Accounts Statistics, GDP Revision of Benchmark 1994 Estimates, Central Statistical Office, Lusaka.

66. Ibid.

67. Ibid.

68. Ibid.

69. Ibid.

70. United Republic of Tanzania, Bureau of Statistics, *Report on the Revised National Accounts of Tanzania 1987–96* (Dar es Salaam: Bureau of Statistics, 1997), 1.

71. Ibid.

72. Ibid.

73. International Labour Organization, *Employment, Incomes and Equality: A Strategy for Increasing Production Employment in Kenya* (Geneva: International Labour Organization, 1972): 97–108; and Keith Hart, "Informal Income Opportunities and Urban Employment in Ghana," *Journal of Modern African Studies* 11, no. 1 (1973): 61–89.

74. For recent reviews of the literature on the informal sector, see Kenneth King, "Africa's Informal Economies: Thirty Years On," *SAIS Review* 11, no. 1 (2001); Keith Hart, "On the Informal Economy: The Political History of an Ethnographic Concept," CEB Working Paper no. 09/042, Centre Emile Bernheim, 2009, http://www2.solvay.edu/EN/Research/Bernheim/documents/wp09042.pdf; and Kate Meagher, *Identity Economics: Social Networks and the Informal Economy in Nigeria* (London: James Currey, 2010).

75. Tilley describes how beginning in the 1930s, surveys attempted to fill this gap in administrative data. See Helen Tilley, *Africa as a Living Laboratory: Empire, Development, Scientific Knowledge, 1870–1950* (Chicago: Chicago University Press, 2011).

76. Muwanga-Zake, "Statistics Reform," 247.

77. Personal communication, Uganda Bureau of Statistics, Kampala, Uganda, October 2010.

78. Uganda Bureau of Statistics, "Informal Cross Border Trade Qualitative Baseline Study," UBOS, February 2009, 53.

79. Tony Killick, *Development Economics in Action: A Study of Economic Policies in Ghana*, 2nd ed. (New York: Routledge, 2010). This title was first published in 1978.

80. Killick, *Development Economics in Action*, 397

81. Ward, *Quantifying the World*, 100

82. Which is the how data are produced today, as will be described in chapter 4.

83. Ward, *Quantifying the World*, 100

84. Killick, *Development Economics in Action*, 397

85. Collier, *Bottom Billion*, 9.

86. Particularly after the availability of the Penn World Tables, which Stern referred to as "an important statistical event." N. Stern, "The Economics of Development: A Survey," *Economic Journal* 99, no. 597 (1989): 600.

87. For example, B. J. Ndulu, S. A. O'Connell, J. P. Azam, R. H. Bates, A. K. Fosu, J. W. Gunning, and D. Njinkeu, eds., *The Political Economy of Economic Growth in Africa, 1960–2000: An Analytic Survey*, vol. 1 (Cambridge: Cambridge University Press, 2008); and B. J. Ndulu, S. A. O'Connell, J. P. Azam, R. H. Bates, A. K. Fosu, J. W. Gunning, and D. Njinkeu, eds., *The Political Economy of Economic Growth in Africa, 1960–2000*, vol. 2, *Case Studies* (Cambridge: Cambridge University Press, 2008).

88. Ward, *Quantifying the World*, 101

3. Facts, Assumptions, and Controversy

1. In the field of historical economic investigation, it is common practice to turn to estimates of population growth, population size, or population densities when data on economic growth or income levels is not available.

2. A. Okolo, "The Nigerian Census: Problems and Prospects," *American Statistician* 53, no. 4 (1999): 321–25.

3. Polly Hill, *Population, Prosperity and Poverty: Rural Kano, 1900 and 1970* (Cambridge: Cambridge University Press, 1977), 322.

4. Ibid., 18.

5. For a basic introduction to the political rivalry between South and North, see Tom Forrest, *Politics and Economic Development in Nigeria* (Boulder, CO: Westview Press, 1993).

6. Tony Falola and Matthew Heaton, *A History of Nigeria* (Cambridge: Cambridge University Press, 2008), 168.

7. Ibid, 186.

8. Okolo, "The Nigerian Census," 323.

9. B. A. Ahonsi, "Deliberate Falsification and Census Data in Nigeria," *African Affairs* 87 (1988): 561.

10. F. Mimiko, "Census in Nigeria: The Politics and the Imperative of Depoliticization," *African and Asian Studies* 5, no. 1 (2006): 14.

11. National Population Commission, "Nigeria 2005 Census Awareness and Attitude Survey (CAAS)," Abuja, Nigeria, 2005.

12. Personal Communication, Federal Ministry of Planning (FOS) and National Population Commission (NPC), Abuja, Nigeria, February 22–25, 2010.

13. National Population Commission, "Report on the Census 2006 Final Result to the President of the Federal Republic of Nigeria," Abuja, Nigeria, 2008, 11.

14. S. Yin, "Objections Surface over Nigerian Census Results," Population Reference Bureau website, http://www.prb.org/Articles/2007/ObjectionsOverNigerianCensus.aspx, April 2007.

15. Hill, *Population, Prosperity and Poverty*, 18.

16. J. C. Caldwell and C. Okonjo, *The Population of Tropical Africa* (London: Longman, 1968), 85.

17. W. Arthur Lewis, *Reflections on Nigeria's Economic Growth* (Paris: Development Centre of the Organisation for Economic Co-operation and Development, 1967), 9

18. O. E. Umoh, "Demographic Statistics in Nigeria," in *Population Growth and Economic Development in Africa*, edited by D. H. Ominde and C. N. Ejiogu (Nairobi: Heinemann, 1972), 21.

19. Previously the Federal Office of Statistics, as it was called when it was based in Lagos.

20. Interviews at FOS and NPC, Abuja, Nigeria, February 22–25, 2010.*

21. William F. Stolper, *Planning without Facts: Lessons in Resource Allocation from Nigeria's Development* (Cambridge: Harvard University Press, 1966).

22. Paul Collier, "Oil Shocks and Food Security in Nigeria," *International Labour Review* 127 (1988): 762.

23. Collier, "Oil Shocks and Food Security," 763.

24. Ibid.

25. Paul Mosley, "Policy Making without Facts: A Note on the Assessment of Structural Adjustment Policies in Nigeria, 1985–1990," *African Affairs* 91, no. 363 (1992): 227–40.

26. Federal Republic of Nigeria, *Annual Abstract of Statistics* (Abuja: Federal Office of Statistics, Abuja, 1995); Federal Republic of Nigeria, *Annual Abstract of Statistics* (Abuja: Federal Office of Statistics, Abuja, 1999).

27. For a complete discussion of the evidence on economic growth in Tanzania, see Morten Jerven, "Growth, Stagnation or Retrogression? On the Accuracy of Economic Observations, Tanzania, 1961–2001," *Journal of African Economies* 20, no. 3 (2011): 377–394.

28. The most notable competitors are Ghana, Nigeria, and Kenya.

29. A.M. Tripp, *Changing the Rules: The Politics of Liberalization and the Urban Informal Economy in Tanzania* (Berkeley: University of California Press, 1997); and T. L. Maliyamkono and M. S. D. Bagachwa, *The Second Economy in Tanzania* (London: James Currey, 1990).

30. Maliyamkono and Bagachwa, *The Second Economy in Tanzania.*

31. Paul Collier, S. Radwan, and S. Wangwe (with A. Wagner), *Labour and Poverty in Rural Tanzania: Ujamaa and Rural Development in the United Republic of Tanzania* (Oxford: Clarendon Press, 1986), 134–35.

32. Tripp, *Changing the Rules.*

33. Maliyamkono and Bagachwa, *The Second Economy in Tanzania*, 133.

34. United Republic of Tanzania, Bureau of Statistics, Report on the Revised National Accounts, 1986–87, Dar es Salaam, 1.

35. Ibid., 3.

36. B. J. Ndulu and C. K. Mutalemwa, *Tanzania at the Turn of the Century—Background Papers and Statistics* (Washington, DC: World Bank, 2002).

37. S. Durlauf, P. Johnson, and J. Temple, "Growth Econometrics," in *Handbook of Economic Growth*, edited by P. Aghion and S. Durlauf (Amsterdam: Elsevier, 2005), 574.

38. B. J. Ndulu, S. A. O'Connell, J. P. Azam, R. H. Bates, A. K. Fosu, J. W. Gunning, and D. Njinkeu, eds., *The Political Economy of Economic Growth in Africa, 1960–2000: An Analytic Survey*, vol. 1 (Cambridge: Cambridge University Press, 2008); and B. J. Ndulu, S. A. O'Connell, J. P. Azam, R. H. Bates, A. K. Fosu, J. W. Gunning, and D. Njinkeu, eds., *The Political Economy of Economic Growth in Africa, 1960–2000*, vol. 2, *Case Studies* (Cambridge: Cambridge University Press, 2008).

39. Ndulu et al., *The Political Economy of Economic Growth in Africa*, 2:7.

40. Patrick Manning, "African Population. Projections 1850–1960," in *The Demographics of Empire: The Colonial Order and the Creation of Knowledge*, edited by Karl Ittmann, Dennis D. Cordell, and Gregory Maddox (Athens: Ohio University Press, 2010), 245–75.

41. "Kenya: Census Will Reveal Key Data for Planners," *Daily Nation* (Nairobi), August 24, 2009.

42. "Options after Census Results Quashed," *Daily Nation*, September 28, 2010.

43. "Kenya: Controversy over Inclusion of Tribal Identity in Census," *Daily Nation*, June 27, 2009.

44. "Kenya's Census Figures Contested," Wanted in Africa website, September 4, 2010.

45. "Kenya: Census Changes Flow of Sh14 Billion CDF Money," *Daily Nation*, September 12, 2010.

46. "Kenya: State Puts Final touches on 2009 Census Results," *Daily Nation*, December 31, 2009.

47. Ibid.

48. "Kenya's Census Figures Contested."

49. Ibid.

50. "Kenya Somalis Population Explosion Cancelled in Census Results," *Alshahid Network*, August 31, 2010, http://english.alshahid.net/archives/12080.

51. "Kenya: Rescind Census Decision, Community Demands," *Daily Nation*, September 11, 2010.

52. Ibid.

53. "Kenya's Census Figures Contested."

54. For a further discussion of the bias in the methods and controversy surrounding previous censuses in Kenya, see Lars Bondestam, "Some Notes on African Statistics Collection—Reliability and Interpretation," Research Report no. 18, Uppsala, Scandinavian Institute of African Studies, 1973.

55. Particularly since the widely disseminated finding of Easterly and Levine, who found that linguistic fragmentation in 1965 was correlated with slow growth from 1965 to 1990. W. Easterly

and R. Levine, "Africa's Growth Tragedy: Policies and Ethnic Divisions," *Quarterly Journal of Economics* 112, no. 4 (1997): 1203–1250.

56. See Daniel Thorner and Alice Thorner, *Land and Labour in India* (Bombay: Asia Publishing House, 1962), 133–153 for a study of how agricultural relations were redefined in the 1951 census in India.

57. Patrick Manning, "African Population Projections 1850–1960," in *The Demographics of Empire: The Colonial Order and the Creation of Knowledge*, edited by Dennis D. Cordell and Gregory Maddox (Athens: Ohio University Press, 2010), 245–75.

58. Mathew James Connelly, *Fatal Misconception: The Struggle to Control World Population* (Cambridge, MA: Belknap Press of Harvard University Press, 2008).

59. For a classic study and critique of the overpopulation thesis and misguided policy interventions, see Mahmood Mamdani, *The Myth of Population Control: Family, Caste and Class in an Indian Village* (New York: Monthly Review Press, 1973).

60. Martina Santschi, "Briefing: Counting "New Sudan,"" *African Affairs* 107, no. 429 (2008): 631–40.

61. According to Jeffrey Sachs, Bingu wa Mutharika of Malawi "broke old donor-led shibboleths by establishing new government programs to get fertilizer and high-yield seeds to impoverished peasant farmers who could not afford these inputs. Farm yields soared once nitrogen got back into the depleted soils." Jeffrey Sachs, "Homegrown Aid," New York Times, April 8, 2009, A23.

62. National Statistics Office, Malawi, *National Census of Agriculture and Livestock (NACAL)* (Zomba: NSO, 2010).

63. Malawi, "Peer Review of Malawi National Statistical System," January 2009, Republic of Malawi and Partnership in Statistics for Development in the 21st Century, 26–30.

64. Ibid.

65. Personal communication, International Monetary Fund, 2010.

66. Personal communication, Malawi, National Statistics Office, 2010

67. Personal communication, IMF, 2010; and personal communication, NORAD, 2010.

68. N. Lea and L. Hanmer, "Constraints to Growth in Malawi" Policy Research Working Paper 5097, World Bank, Africa Region: Southern Africa Poverty Reduction and Economic Management Unit, 2009.

69. Africa Research Institute, "Making Fertiliser Subsidies Work in Malawi," Briefing Note 0703 (2007, December); and International Food Policy Research Institute, "Fertilizer Subsidies in Africa. Are Vouchers the Answer?" *IFPRI Issue Brief* 60 (2009).

70. Personal communication, National Statistics Office of Malawi, November, 2010; and personal communication, Malawi Reserve Bank, November 2010.

71. R. Chambers, "Beyond the Green Revolution: A Selective Essay," in *Understanding Green Revolutions: Agrarian Change and Development Planning in South Asia: Essays in Honour of B. H. Farmer*, edited by B.H. Farmer, S. Wanmali, and T. Bayliss-Smith (New York: Cambridge University Press, 1984), 362.

72. T. N. Srinivasan A. Vaidyanathan, "Agricultural Statistics," in *Data Base of Indian Economy; Review and Appraisal*, vol. 1, edited by C. R. Rao (Calcutta: Eka Press, 1972), 33–62. This phenomenon is fundamental to economic planning, as is persuasively argued by Janos Kornai with reference to the USSR and other centrally planned economies; see Janos Kornai, *The Socialist System: The Political Economy of Communism* (Oxford: Oxford University Press, 1992).

73. See, for instance, Sarah Berry, "The Food Crisis and Agrarian Change in Africa: A Review Essay," *African Studies Review* 27, no. 2 (1984): 59–112; and Roy A. Carr-Hill, *Social Conditions in Sub-Saharan Africa* (Houndmills: MacMillan, 1990), esp. 39–51.

74. Polly Hill, *Development Economics on Trial: The Anthropological Case for Prosecution* (Cambridge: Cambridge University Press, 1986).

75. Hill, *Development Economics on Trial*, 34.

76. Ibid.

77. For a particularly bold effort, see Steven Block, "The Decline and Rise of Agricultural Productivity in Sun-Saharan Africa since 1961," NBER Working Paper no. 16481, National Bureau of Economic Research, 2010.

78. Edward Miguel, Shanker Satyanath, and Ernest Sergenti, "Economic Shocks and Civil Conflict: An Instrumental Variables Approach," *Journal of Political Economy* 122 (2004): 740 Miguel, Shanker, and Ernest cite Jere R. Behrman and Mark R. Rosenzweig, "Caveat Emptor" Cross-Country Data on Education and the Labor Force," *Journal of Developmental Economy* 44 (June 1994): 147–71; and Alan Heston, "A Brief Review of Some Problems in Using National Accounts Data in Level Comparisons and Growth Studies," *Journal of Development Economics* 44, no. 1 (1994): 29–52.

79. Angus Deaton, "Instruments, Randomization, and Learning about Development," *Journal of Economic Literature* 48, no. 2 (2010): 424–55; and Thad Dunning, "Model Specification in Instrumental-Variables Regression," *Political Analysis* 16 (2008): 290–302.

80. Derek Blades, "What Do We Know about Levels and Growth of Output in Developing Countries? A Critical Analysis with Special Reference to Africa," in *Economic Growth and Resources: Proceedings of the Fifth World Congress, International Economic Association, Tokyo*, vol. 2, *Trends and Factors*, edited by R. C. O. Mathews (New York: St. Martin's Press, 1980), 69.

81. For a description of different methods in measuring maize output, see P. Mosley, "Policy and Capital Market Constraints to the African Green Revolution: A Study of Maize and Sorghum Yields in Kenya, Malawi and Zimbabwe, 1960–91," Innocenti Occasional Papers, Economic Policy Series no. 38 (1993). Mosley's publication is part of a special subseries on Structural Adjustment in Africa by the UNICEF International Child Development Centre.

82. Miguel, Satyanath, and Sergenti, "Economic Shocks and Civil Conflict," 740.

83. Sachs, "Homegrown Aid."

84. Paul Nugent, *Africa since Independence: A Comparative History* (New York: Palgrave Macmillan, 2004), 328. For other studies of the difficulty of assessing the economic growth effects of policy reform, see Thandika P. Mkandawire and Charles C. Soludo, *Our Continent, Our Future: African Perspectives on Structural Adjustment* (Trenton, N.J.: Africa World Press, 1999), esp. chapter 3; and Trevor W. Parfitt, "Review: Lies, Damned Lies and Statistics: The World Bank/ECA Structural Adjustment Controversy," *Review of African Political Economy* 47 (1990): 128–41.

85. Heston, "A Brief Review of Some Problems in Using National Accounts Data," 37.

86. Personal communication, Ghana Statistical Services, Accra, Ghana, February 2010.

87. Personal communication, Central Statistical Office, Lusaka, Zambia, November 2010.

88. Chijioke Ohuocha, "Exclusive: Nigeria GDP Rebasing May See Big Upward Revision—Stats Chief," Reuters Africa, November 10, 2011.

89. Personal communication, Federal Statistical Office, Abuja, Nigeria, February 2010.

90. It is hard to say exactly how normal this practice is. The only way one can find out is to the compare revised time series with old ones. Sometimes the changes can be significant, as in Botswana, where a backward revision in the late 1980s caused a rewriting of the history of agricultural growth since the late 1970s. See Morten Jerven, "Accounting for the African Growth Miracle: The Official Evidence, Botswana 1965–1995," *Journal of Southern African Studies* 36, no. 1 (2010): 73–94.

91. As discussed further in Morten Jerven, "Random Growth in Africa? Lessons from an Evaluation of the Growth Evidence on Botswana, Kenya, Tanzania and Zambia, 1965–1995," *Journal of Development Studies* 46, no. 2 (2010): 274–94. For a country study of Kenya, see Morton Jerven, "Revisiting the Consensus on Kenyan Economic Growth, 1964–1995," *Journal of Eastern African Studies* 5, no. 1 (2011): 2–23.

4. Data for Development

1. Representatives from the statistical offices of Burundi, Cameroon, Cape Verde, Guinea, Lesotho, Mali, Mauritania, Mauritius, Morocco, Namibia, Mozambique, Niger, Senegal, Seychelles, and South Africa have participated in the e-mail survey. I also conducted in-depth interviews in Ghana, Kenya, Malawi, Nigeria, Tanzania, Uganda, and Zambia. Further details are provided in the appendix.

2. As summarized by Robert H. Bates in *Making Aid Work*, edited by A. Banerjee (Cambridge, MA: MIT Press, 2007), 67–73.

3. R. Bates, *Markets and States in Tropical Africa: The Political Basis of Agricultural Policies* (Berkeley: University of California Press, 1981).

4. For how this perspective conflates states and individuals, see Jon Elster, "Review: Rational Choice History: A Case of Excessive Ambition," *American Political Science Review* 94, no. 3 (2000): 685–95.

5. As expressed in typologies of the African states as "neopatrimonial." See Michael Bratton and Nicolas Van de Walle, "Neopatrimonial Regimes and Political Transitions in Africa," *World Politics* 46, no. 4 (1994): 453–89.

6. An example of such promises is the last election campaign successfully ran by Jay Kikwete in Tanzania in 2010; personal communication, Central Bank, Tanzania, Dar es Salaam, November 2010. For the absence of labor market data, see John Sender, Christopher Cramer, and Carlos Oya, "Unequal Prospects: Disparities in the Quantity and Quality of Labour Supply in Sub-Saharan Africa," World Bank Social Protection Discussion Paper Series no. 0525, 2005, 5.

7. Theodore M. Porter, *Trust in Numbers: The Pursuit of Objectivity in Science and Public Life* (Princeton, NJ: Princeton University Press, 1995), 33.

8. Lourdes Beneria, "Accounting for Women's Work: The Progress of Two Decades," *World Development* 20, no. 11 (1992): 1547–60.

9. Dudley Seers, "The Political Economy of National Accounting," in *Employment, Income Distribution and Development Strategy: Problems of the Developing Countries*, edited by A. Caincross and M. Puri (New York: Holmes & Meier Publishers, 1976).

10. A. C. Kulshreshtha and Gulab Singh, "Valuation of Non-Market Household Production," Central Statistical Organisation, New Delhi, 1999.

11. However, this is not always true. The GDP series for Zambia used 1970 constant prices. Following large downward price swings, such as those experienced in Zambia as a result of its copper exports in the 1970s, the economy was much smaller when copper output was measured at current prices than if the output was measured at constant prices.

12. Personal communication, National Statistical Office; personal communication, IMF Malawi; personal communication, Reserve Bank, Malawi, all in Lilongwe, Malawi, November 2011.

13. Personal communication, Uganda Bureau of Statistics, Kampala, Uganda, October 2011.

14. Although the methods from country to country may differ. See Jean Le Nay and Jean Mathis, "The Impact of Drought on the National Accounts for Livestock in Sahelian Countries," *Review of Income and Wealth* 35, no. 2 (June 1989): 209–24.

15. E. S. K. Muwanga-Zake, "Statistics Reform," in *Uganda's Economic Reforms: Insider Accounts*, edited by F. Kuteesa, E. Tumusiime-Mutebile, A. Whitworth, and T. Williamson (New York: Oxford University Press, 2010), 257.

16. Klaus Deininger, Calogero Carletto, Sara Savastano, and James Muwonge, "Can Diaries Help Improve Agricultural Production Statistics? Evidence from Uganda," World Bank Development Research Group Policy Research Working Paper 5717, June 2011, http://www-wds.worldbank.org/servlet/WDSContentServer/WDSP/IB/2011/06/30/000158349_20110630105553/Rendered/PDF/WPS5717.pdf, accessed September 13, 2012.

17. Ibid., 11.

18. Elliot Berg, *Accelerated Development in sub-Saharan Africa: An Agenda for Action*, World Bank Report no. 14030 (Washington, DC: World Bank, 1981).

19. Ibid., 142.

20. Ibid., 187–88.

21. Ibid., 31–32.

22. Ibid., 34–35.

23. A. Banerjee, *Making Aid Work* (Cambridge, MA: MIT Press, 2006), 16.

24. Ibid., 6.

25. Frederick Cooper and Randall Packard, "Introduction," in *International Development and the Social Sciences: Essays on the History and Politics of Knowledge*, edited by Frederick Cooper and Randall Packard (Berkeley, CA University of California Press, 1997), 27.

26. Two recent publications favor this line. See Dean Karlon and Jacob Appel, *More Than Good Intentions: How a New Economics Is Helping to Solve Global Poverty* (New York: Dutton, 2011); and A. V. Banerjee and Esther Duflo, *Poor Economics: A Radical Rethinking of the Way to Fight Global Poverty* (New York: PublicAffairs, 2011).

27. Esther Duflo, Michael Kremer, and Jonathan Robinson, "How High Are Rates of Return to Fertilizer? Evidence from Field Experiments in Kenya," *American Economic Review: Papers and Proceedings* 98, no. 2 (2008): 487.

28. "Forum: Angus Deaton," in *Making Aid Work*, edited by A. Banerjee (Cambridge, MA: MIT Press, 2006), 55–65; and Angus Deaton, "Understanding the Mechanisms of Economic Development," *Journal of Economic Perspectives* 24, no. 3 (2010): 14.

29. Ritva Reinikka and Jacob Svensson, "Explaining Leakage of Public Funds," Policy Research Working Paper Series no. 2709, World Bank, 2001.

30. In the research for this book I have not studied how development statistics enters parliamentary debates and legislative bodies.

31. Organization for Economic Co-operation and Development, *Measuring the Non-Observed Economy: A Handbook* (Paris: OECD, 2002).

32. Financial-sector reforms have been a major priority for both the World Bank and the IMF.

33. Personal communication, Ghana Statistical Office, Accra, Ghana, February 2010; personal communication, Federal Office of Statistics, Abuja, Nigeria, February 2010.

34. Personal communication, National Statistical Office, Zambia, November 2010.

35. Personal communication, National Statistical Office, Lilongwe, Malawi, November 2010. The debate was about the preliminary growth numbers, and the IMF and the premier were not able to agree. The distance between the parties was about 1.5 percent (the IMF wanted just above 5 percent, while the premier wanted the growth data to be about 7 percent). Both parties were of course guessing.

36. Don Cohen and Bruno Laporte, "The Evolution of the Knowledge Bank," *KM Magazine*, March 2004.

37. Devesh Kapur "The 'Knowledge' Bank," in *Rescuing the World Bank: A CGD Working Group Report and Select Essays*, edited by Nancy Birdstall (Washington, DC: Center for Global Development, 2006), 159–70.

38. Christopher Gilbert, Andrew Powell, and David Vines, "Positioning the World Bank," *Economic Journal* 109 (November 1999): F598–F633.

39. R. Wade, "US Hegemony and the World Bank: The Fight for People and Ideas," *Review of International Political Economy* 9, no. 2 (2002): 215–42.

40. William Easterly, "Planners versus Searchers in Foreign Aid," *Asian Development* 23, no. 1 (2006): 1–35.

41. David Ellerman, "Should Development Agencies Have Official Views?" *Development in Practice* 12, nos. 3–4 (August 2002).

42. James Ferguson, *Global Shadows: Africa in the Neoliberal World Order* (Durham, NC: Duke University Press, 2006).

43. Michael Ward, *Quantifying the World: UN Ideas and Statistics* (Bloomington, IN.: Indiana University Press, 2004), 100; Michael Barnett and Martha Finnemore, *Rules for the World: International Organizations in Global Politics* (Ithaca: Cornell University Press, 2004), chapter 3.

44. Personal communication, Ghana Statistical Office, Accra, Ghana, February 2010; personal communication, Federal Office of Statistics, Abuja, Nigeria, February 2010; personal communication, National Statistical Office, Zambia, November 2010.

45. The only regional empirical study of statistical training lends support to this claim. There is a need for more training that is oriented to the practical. See M. Woodward, N. Dourmashkin, E. Twagirumukiza, M. Mbago, and A. S. Ferreira da Cunha, "Statistics Training in Eastern and Southern Africa: A Study of Supply and Demand," *Journal of the Royal Statistical Society: Series D (The Statistician)* 46, no. 3 (1997): 371–86.

46. Personal communication, World Bank, October 2010; personal communication, UK Department for International Development, Tanzania, October 2010. Also see Valéry Ridde, "Per Diems Undermine Health Interventions, System and Research in Africa: Burying Our Heads in the Sand," *Tropical Medicine and International Health* (July 28, 2010): 1–4.

47. Personal communication, UK Department for International Development, Zambia, November 2010.

48. For example, two officers have been trained, but when I visited in November 2010, one of them had already left for another position. Personal communication, National Statistical Office, Lilongwe, Malawi, November 2010.

49. Personal communication, Malawi Reserve Bank, Lilongwe, Malawi, November 2010. For a similar account of macro-economic modeling efforts in Burkina Faso, see Boris Samuel, "Calcul macroéconomique et modes de gouvernement: Les cas du Burkina Faso et de la Mauritanie," *Politique Africaine* 124 (February 2012): 101–26.

50. Howard Stein, *Beyond the World Bank Agenda: An Institutional Approach to Development* (Chicago: University of Chicago Press, 2008), 25–51.

51. For a history, see Bjorn Wold, "A Social Statistics System for the Millennium Development Goals?" *Forum for Development Studies* no. 1 (2005): 219–42.

52. David Booth and Henry Lucas, "Monitoring Progress Towards the Millennium Development Goals at Country Level," in *Targeting Development: Critical Perspectives on the Millennium Development Goals*, edited by R. Black and H. White (New York: Routledge, 2003), 101.

53. Ibid., 102.

54. Sebastian Levine, "Measuring Progress Towards Global Poverty Goals: Challenges and Lessons from Southern Africa," *African Statistical Journal* 3 (November 2006): 89–110.

55. R. Black and H. White, "Millennium Development Goals," in *Targeting Development: Critical Perspectives on the Millennium Development Goals*, edited by R. Black and H. White (Routledge, 2003), 11.

56. UNDP, "Capacity Development for Democratic Governance: Assessments and Measurements," A Global Program Report, 2010, 5.

57. The observations that are used for the start and end dates of 1990 and 2009 are only projected estimates, not factual observations. Gonzalo Duenas Alvarez, Mary Tran, and Raj Raina, "MDGS: Sub-Saharan Africa: Overcoming Data Gaps and Ranking Progress" Fordham University, Department of Economics Discussion Paper Series no. 2011–01, 2011.

58. Charlotte Guenard and Sandrine Mesple-Somps, "Measuring Inequalities: Do Household Surveys Paint a Realistic Picture?" *Review of Income and Wealth* 56, no. 3 (2010): 519–38.

59. United Nations, *The Millennium Development Goals Report, 2011* (New York: United Nations, 2011).

60. Jan Vandemoortele, "The MDG Story: Intention Denied," *Development and Change* 42, no. 1 (2011): 1–21.

61. Dimitri Sanga, "The Challenges of Monitoring and Reporting on the Millennium Development Goals in Africa by 2015 and Beyond," *African Statistical Journal* 12 (May 2011): 104–18.

62. World Bank Database, http://data.worldbank.org/, accessed August 2011.

63. World Bank, Statistical Manual, National Accounts, http://web.worldbank.org, accessed August 2011.

64. E-mail correspondence with the World Bank Development Data Group, September 8, 2009. When I presented this information to the Data Group in a talk at the Centre of Global Development in November 2011, the director denied that these data were confidential and claimed that I had been misinformed or was asking the wrong question. When I showed them the e-mail with my question and the response, it was conceded that indeed some of this data are not shared. I have since re-requested access to raw data (specifically for Ghana and Tanzania to see what changes have been made to the long-term growth series) but I have not been granted access.

65. UNData, http://data.un.org/, accessed August 2011.

66. E-mail correspondence with the World Bank Development Data Group, September 10, 2009.

67. E-mail correspondence with Data Dissemination and Client Services Team, Statistical Information Management Division, Statistics Department, International Monetary Fund, September 16, 2009.

68. E-mail correspondence with the Center for International Comparisons, University of Pennsylvania, September 21, 2009.

69. E-mail correspondence with the Center for International Comparisons University of Pennsylvania, September 22, 2009.

70. Personal communication with representatives from UK Department for International Development, 2010; personal communication, Lusaka, 2010; personal communication, World Bank, Dar es Salaam, November 2010.

71. E-mail correspondence with Macroeconomic Statistics Advisor, IMF East AFRITAC, November 22, 2010.

72. E-mail correspondence with Macroeconomic Statistics Advisor, IMF East AFRITAC, December 7, 2010.

73. E-mail correspondence with Macroeconomic Statistics Advisor, IMF East AFRITAC, December 13, 2010.

74. Ibid.

75. This is a general problem with the type of country evaluations the IMF and World Bank use, as James Ferguson points out in *The Anti-Politics Machine: "Development," Depoliticization, and Bureaucratic Power in Lesotho* (New York: Cambridge University Press, 1990), 258–59.

76. IMF, Report on the Observance of Standards and Codes, various years, various countries. The full list is available in the references.

77. E-mail correspondence with World Bank Development Data Group, fall 2005.

78. Muwanga-Zake, "Statistics Reform," 246–63.

79. Personal communication, UK Department for International Development, Zambia, November 2010.

80. Ibid.

81. World Bank, STATCAP, "Statistical Capacity: Overview," http://web.worldbank.org/, accessed August 2011.

82. Ibid.

83. Personal communication, National Statistical Office, Lilongwe, Malawi, November 2010; personal communication, Malawi Reserve Bank, Lilongwe, Malawi, November 2010.

84. Personal communication, Federal Office of Statistics, Abuja, Nigeria, February 2010; personal communication, National Statistical Office, Zambia, November 2010; personal

communication, World Bank Consultants, Dar es Salaam, October 2010; e-mail correspondence with National Bureau of Statistics in Kenya, spring 2011.

85. Economic Commission for Africa, *Manual on Improving the Quality of Statistics in Africa* (Addis Ababa: UN Economic Commission for Africa, 1998). This is a report from a UN ECA Regional Workshop on Improving the Quality of African Statistics for English Speaking Countries that was held in Addis Ababa on 14–18 December 1998.

86. This (or a version of it) was an oft-repeated answer when I asked about interaction and political pressure at statistical offices in Ghana, Nigeria, Kenya, Tanzania, Malawi and Zambia.

87. A recent example comes from Zambia in 2007. The statistical office applied for funding for an economic census, and the money was granted from the government. The office then began compiling a list of all the businesses in Zambia. By the end of the year, all the funds for data collection had been used. The list was never finished, and no results were ever published.

88. As argued by Guenard and Mesple-Somps in "Measuring Inequalities," 519–38. The surveys favored by the World Bank today are more expensive in terms of data collection and need more resources for analysis than were used a decade ago. For more on per diems, see Ridde, "Per Diems Undermine Health Interventions, System and Research in Africa."

Conclusion

1. William Easterly, "Can Foreign Aid Buy Growth?" *Journal of Economic Perspectives* 17, no. 3 (2003): 23–48.

2. For a powerful critique of inferential statistics, see Stephen T. Ziliak and Deirdre N. McCloskey, *The Cult of Statistical Significance: How the Standard Error Costs Us Jobs, Justice and Lives* (Ann Arbor: University of Michigan Press; 2008).

3. Maynard Keynes, *The General Theory of Employment, Interest and Money* (Basingstoke, England: Palgrave Macmillan for the Royal Economic Society, 2007).

4. Morten Jerven, "An Unlevel Playing Field: National Income Estimates and Reciprocal Comparison in Global Economic History," *Journal of Global History* 7, no. 1 (2012): 107–28.

5. Joseph Stiglitz, Amartya Sen, and Jean-Paul Fitoussi, *Mismeasuring Our Lives: Why GDP Doesn't Add Up* (New York: New Press, 2010).

6. Pius N. C. Okigbo, *Nigerian National Accounts, 1950–57* (Enugu: Government Printer, 1962), 65.

7. Ibid., 63.

8. Ibid., 174.

9. Federal Ministry of National Planning, *National Accounts of Nigeria, 1973–1975* (Lagos: Federal Ministry of National Planning), 53.

10. John Harriss, "The Case for Cross-Disciplinary Approaches in International Development," *World Development* 30 (2002): 487–96.

11. For good overviews, see Sudhir Anand, Paul Segal, and Joseph E. Stiglitz, eds., *Debates on the Measurement of Global Poverty* (Oxford: Oxford University Press, 2010); and Richard Black and Howard White, eds., *Targeting Development: Critical Perspectives on the Millennium Development Goals* (New York: Routledge, 2004).

12. Robert M. Solow, "A Contribution to the Theory of Economic Growth," *Quarterly Journal of Economics* 70, no. 1 (1956): 65–94; and Robert Solow, "Technical Change and the Aggregate Production Function," *Review of Economics and Statistics* 39, no. 3 (1957): 312–20.

13. For a basic introduction, see Elhanan Helpman, *The Mystery of Economic Growth* (Cambridge, Mass.: Harvard University Press, 2004).

14. Paul M. Romer, "Increasing Returns and Long-Run Growth," *Journal of Political Economy* 94, no. 5 (1986): 1002–37; Robert E. Lucas, Jr., "On the Mechanics of Economic Development," *Journal of Monetary Economics* 22, no. 1 (1988): 3–42.

15. Robert J. Barro, "Economic Growth in a Cross Section of Countries," *Quarterly Journal of Economics* 106, no. 2 (1991): 407–43.

16. The Penn World Tables provided economic growth data adjusted for purchasing power parity, following the work of Robert Summers and Alan Heston. For a discussion of the significance of these datasets when they appeared, see Nicholas Stern, "The Economics of Development: A Survey," *The Economic Journal* 99, no. 397 (1989): 597–685. For a contemporary evaluation of the datasets, see Angus Deaton and Alan Heston, "Understanding PPPS and PPP-Based National Accounts," *American Economic Journal: Macroeconomics,* 2, no. 4 (2010): 1–35.

17. A dummy variable takes a value of 1 or 0. In this case, it takes 1 if the country in question is African. What these first regressions found was that slow growth was systematically correlated with the country being African.

18. Barro, "On the Mechanics of Economic Development," 437.

19. Durlauf et al., "Growth Econometrics." The title of X. Sala-i-Martin's article, "I Just Ran Two Million Regressions," also describes the volume of permutations that appeared in studies of growth regression; see *American Economic Review* 87, no. 2 (1997): 178–83. Kenny and Williams argued that despite the scholarly effort, the "current state of the understanding about causes of economic growth is fairly poor" and that "we are in a weak position to explain why some countries have experienced economic growth and others not." See Charles Kenny and David Williams, "What Do We Know about Economic Growth? Or, Why Don't We Know Very Much?" *World Development* 29, no. 1 (2001): 15. The argument for pleading ignorance was recently summarized by one of the central participants in the growth regression industry, William Easterly, in a lecture held at London School of Economics on 19 May 2010: "We don't know how to solve global poverty, and that's a good thing."

20. Jonathan Temple, "Initial Conditions, Social Capital and Growth in Africa," *Journal of African Economies* 7, no. 3 (1998): 309–47.

21. Paul Collier and Jan W. Gunning, "Why Has Africa Grown So Slowly?" *Journal of Economic Perspectives* 13, no. 3 (1999): 3–22.

22. For a review pertaining to Africa in particular, see Morten Jerven, "A Clash of Disciplines? Economists and Historians Approaching the African Past," *Economic History of Developing Regions* 26, no. 2 (2011): 111–24.

23. Christopher Cramer, *Violence in Developing Countries: War, Memory, Progress* (Bloomington: Indiana University Press, 2007), esp. 51–84.

24. Havard Hegre and Nicholas Sambanis, "Sensitivity Analysis of Empirical Results on Civil War Onset," *Journal of Conflict Resolution* 50, no. 4 (2006): 508–35.

25. Particularly related to the Correlates of War project. See Nicholas Sambanis, "What Is Civil War? Conceptual and Empirical Complexities of an Operational Definition," *Journal of Conflict Resolution* 48, no. 6 (2004): 814–58.

26. The efforts to quantify the trends in war and conflict in the world are summarized in Human Security Report Group Project, *Human Security Report 2009/2010: The Causes of Peace and Shrinking Costs of War* (New York: Human Security Report Project, 2010).

27. As for instance the widely used data from the Economist Intelligence Unit. See Stephen Knack, "Measuring Corruption: A Critique of Indicators in Eastern Europe and Central Asia," *Journal of Public Policy* 27, no. 3 (2007): 261.

28. There are more; Munck reviews nine different datasets. See Gerardo Luis Munck, *Measuring Democracy: A Bridge between Scholarship and Politics* (Baltimore, Md.: Johns Hopkins University Press, 2009).

29. While Polity IV data shows trends with rather dramatic peaks and drops (which are to be expected given the basic criteria upon which a country is classified as democratic or autocratic), the results from Freedom House present trends with more gradual changes. See Yury V. Bosin,

"Measuring Democracy: Approaches and Challenges Associated with Developing Democratic Indices," William and Kathy Hybl Democracy Studies Fellowship Paper, 2007.

30. Raymond June, Afroza Chowdhury, Nathaniel Heller and Jonathan Werve, *A User's Guide to Measuring Corruption* (Oslo: Global Integrity and UNDP, 2008).

31. Knack, "Measuring Corruption."

32. Toke S. Aidt, "Corruption and Sustainable Development," Cambridge Working Papers in Economics 1601, University of Cambridge, November 2010.

33. Christine Arndt and Charles Oman, *Uses and Abuses of Governance Indicators* (Paris: Development Centre Studies, OECD, 2006).

34. Frane Adam, "Mapping Social Capital across Europe: Findings, Trends and Methodological Shortcomings of Cross-National Surveys," *Social Science Information* 47 (2008): 159–86.

35. June et al., *A User's Guide to Measuring Corruption*, 28.

36. Aidt, "Corruption and Sustainable Development," 16.

37. Gareth Austin reminds us that the literal interpretation of the word data is "things that are given" in "'The "Reversal of Fortune' Thesis and the Compression of History: Perspectives from African and Comparative Economic History," *Journal of International Development* 20, no. 8 (2008): 1002.

38. Kpedekpo, *Social and Economic Statistics*.

39. Sarah Berry, "The Food Crisis and Agrarian Change in Africa: A Review Essay," *African Studies Review* 27, no. 2 (1984): 60.

40. Polly Hill, *Development Economics on Trial: The Anthropological Case for Prosecution* (Cambridge: Cambridge University Press, 1986), 34.

41. R. Carr-Hill, *Social Conditions in Sub-Saharan Africa* (MacMillan: London, 1990), 210.

42. I took these quotes to meetings with statistical officers, who generally agreed with these claims.

REFERENCES

Official Documents

Central Statistical Office, Zambia. Annexes to Provisional Estimates, Consolidated National Accounts 1973–1978, Lusaka, Zambia.

Economic Commission for Africa. Manual on Improving the Quality of Statistics in Africa. Report from Regional Workshop on Improving the Quality of African Statistics for English Speaking Countries, Addis Ababa, 14–18 December 1998.

Federal Republic of Nigeria, Department of Statistics. *Annual Abstract of Statistics, 1995*. Abuja: Federal Office of Statistics, 1995.

——. *Annual Abstract of Statistics, 1999*. Abuja: Federal Office of Statistics, 1999.

Federal Republic of Nigeria, Federal Ministry of Planning. *National Accounts of Nigeria, 1973–1975*. Lagos, Nigeria, 1981.

Federation of Rhodesia and Nyasaland. *Monthly Digest of Statistics*. Salisbury, 1955.

Ghana Statistical Service. "Rebasing of Ghana's National Accounts to Reference Year 2006." Accra, 2010. http://www.mofep.gov.gh/sites/default/files/reports/Rebasing-NationalAccountsGhana_1.pdf.

The Human Security Report Group Project. *Human Security Report 2009/2010: The Causes of Peace and Shrinking Costs of War*. New York: Human Security Report Project, 2010.

International Monetary Fund. "Burkina Faso: Report on the Observance of Standards and Codes—Data Module, Response by the Authorities, and Detailed Assessment Using the Data Quality Assessment Framework (DQAF)." IMF Country Report no. 04/287. March 2004. http://www.imf.org/external/pubs/ft/scr/2004/cr0487.pdf.

——. "Botswana: Report on the Observance of Standards and Codes—Data Module, Response by the Authorities, and Detailed Assessment Using the Data Quality Assessment Framework (DQAF)." IMF Country Report 07/139. April 2007. http://www.imf.org/external/pubs/ft/scr/2007/cr07139.pdf.

——. "Cameroon: Report on Observance of Standards and Codes—Data Module." IMF Country Report no. 01/150. August 2001. http://www.imf.org/external/pubs/ft/scr/2001/cr01150.pdf.

——. "Chad: Report on the Observance of Standards and Codes—Data Module, Response by the Authorities, and Detailed Assessment Using the Data Quality Assessment Framework (DQAF)." IMF Country Report no. 07/300. August 2007. http://www.imf.org/external/pubs/ft/scr/2007/cr07300.pdf.

——. "Experimental IMF Report on Observance of Standards and Codes: Uganda." August 1999. http://www.imf.org/external/np/rosc/uga/index.htm.

——. "The Gambia: Report on the Observance of Standards and Codes—Data Module, Response by the Authorities, and Detailed Assessment Using the Data Quality Assessment Framework (DQAF)." IMF Country Report no. 05/421. November 2005. http://www.imf.org/external/pubs/ft/scr/2005/cr05421.pdf.

——. "Kenya: Report on the Observance of Standards and Codes—Data Module, Response by the Authorities, and Detailed Assessment Using the Data Quality Assessment Framework (DQAF)." IMF Country Report no. 05/300. October 2005. http://www.imf.org/external/pubs/ft/scr/2005/cr05388.pdf.

——. "Malawi: Report on the Observance of Standards and Codes—Data Module, Response by the Authorities, and Detailed Assessment Using the Data Quality Assessment Framework (DQAF)." IMF Country Report no. 05/60. February 2005. http://www.imf.org/external/pubs/ft/scr/2005/cr0560.pdf.

——. "Mauritius: Report on the Observance of Standards and Codes—Data Module, Response by the Authorities, and Detailed Assessment Using the Data Quality Assessment Framework (DQAF)." IMF Country Report no. 08/277. August 2008. http://www.imf.org/external/pubs/ft/scr/2008/cr08277.pdf.

——. "Namibia: Report on the Observance of Standards and Codes—Data Module—Substantive Update on Monetary Statistics, Response by the Authorities, and Detailed Assessments Using the Data Quality Assessment Framework." IMF Country Report no. 05/317. September 2005. http://www.imf.org/external/pubs/ft/scr/2005/cr05317.pdf.

——. "Niger: Report on the Observance of Standards and Codes—Data Module, Response by the Authorities, and Detailed Assessment Using the Data Quality Assessment Framework (DQAF)." IMF Country Report no. 06/236. June 2006. http://www.imf.org/external/pubs/ft/scr/2006/cr06236.pdf.

——. "Republic of Mozambique: Report on the Observance of Standards and Codes—Data Module—Update." IMF Country Report no. 05/278. August 2005. http://www.imf.org/external/pubs/ft/scr/2005/cr05278.pdf.

———. "Senegal: Report on Observations of Standards and Codes—Data Module, Response by the Authorities, and Detailed Assessments Using the Data Quality Assessment Framework." IMF Country Report no. 02/259. November 2002. http://www.imf.org/external/pubs/ft/scr/2002/cr02259.pdf.

———. "South Africa: Report on Observations of Standards and Codes—Data Module; Response by the Authorities, and Detailed Assessments Using the Data Quality Assessment Framework." IMF Country Report no. 01/80. October 2001. http://www.imf.org/external/pubs/ft/scr/2001/cr01180.pdf.

———. "Tanzania: Report on Observations of Standards and Codes—Data Module, Response by the Authorities, and Detailed Assessments Using the Data Quality Assessment Framework." IMF Country Report no. 04/82. March 2004. http://www.imf.org/external/pubs/ft/scr/2004/cr0482.pdf.

———. "Zambia: Report on the Observance of Standards and Codes (ROSC)—Data Module, Response by the Authorities, and Detailed Assessments Using the Data Quality Assessment Framework." IMF Country Report no. 05/30. January 2005. http://www.imf.org/external/pubs/ft/scr/2005/cr0530.pdf.

National Population Commission of Nigeria. "Nigeria 2005 Census Awareness and Attitude Survey (CAAS)." Abuja, Nigeria, 2005.

———. "Report on the Census 2006 Final Result to the President of the Federal Republic of Nigeria." Abuja, Nigeria, 2008.

Organization for Economic Co-operation and Development. *Measuring the Non-Observed Economy: A Handbook*. Paris: OECD, 2002.

Republic of Kenya, Central Bureau of Statistics, Ministry of Finance and Planning. Sources and Methods Used for the National Accounts of Kenya. Nairobi: Central Bureau of Statistics, Ministry of Finance and Planning, 1977.

Republic of Kenya, Ministry of Economic Planning and Development. *Economic Survey 1967*. Nairobi: Ministry of Economic Planning and Development, 1968.

Republic of Malawi. "Peer Review of the Malawi National Statistical System, 26–30 January 2009." Republic of Malawi and Partnership in Statistics for Development in the 21st Century. http://www.paris21.org/sites/default/files/Malawi_peer_review_Feb_2009.pdf.

Republic of Malawi, National Statistics Office. *National Census of Agriculture and Livestock (NACAL)*. Zomba: National Statistics Office, 2010.

Republic of South Africa, Department of Statistics. *National Accounts of the Black States, 1972 to 1976*. Pretoria: South Africa Department of Statistics, 1980.

Republic of Zambia, Central Statistical Office. *National Accounts 1964–1967*. Lusaka: Central Statistical Office, 1967.

———. National Accounts Statistics GDP Revision of Benchmark 1994 Estimates. Central Statistical Office, Lusaka.

Uganda Bureau of Statistics. Informal Cross Border Trade Qualitative Baseline Study. February 2009.

United Nations. *The Millennium Development Goals Report, 2011*. New York: United Nations, 2011.

United Nations Conference on Trade and Development. *Information Economy Report 2009: Trends and Outlook in Turbulent Times*. New York and Geneva: United Nations, 2009.

United Nations Development Program. "Capacity Development for Democratic Governance: Assessments and Measurements." A Global Program Report, 2010.

United Republic of Tanzania. *National Accounts of Tanzania, 1966–68*. Dar es Salaam: G.P., 1970.

United Republic of Tanzania, Bureau of Statistics. *Report on the Revised National Accounts of Tanzania 1987–96*. Dar es Salaam: Bureau of Statistics, 1997.

World Bank. "Accelerating Malawi's Growth: Long-Term Prospects and Transitional Problems." Washington, D.C.: World Bank Southern Africa Department, 1997.

——. "Data: Changes in Country Classifications, 1 July." Retrieved August 2011 from http://data.worldbank.org/news/2010-GNI-income-classifications.

——. "Malawi, Fertilizer Subsidies and the World Bank." [Web Post]. Retrieved from http://go.worldbank.org/KIGRBOO0B0

——. "Method of Gap Filling." Retrieved July 2011 from the World Bank data website http://go.worldbank.org/.

——. STATCAP, "Overview." Retrieved August 2011 from http://web.worldbank.org/.

——. World Bank Statistical Manual, National Accounts. Retrieved August 2011 from http://web.worldbank.org.

——. World Development Indicators. Retrieved 2011 from http://data.worldbank.org/.

Secondary Sources

Ady, Peter H. "Uses of National Accounts in Africa." In *African Studies in Income and Wealth*, edited by L. H. Samuels. London: Bowes & Bowes, 1963.

Africa Research Institute. "Making Fertiliser Subsidies Work in Malawi." Briefing Note 0703. December 2007.

Ahonsi, B. A. "Deliberate Falsification and Census Data in Nigeria." *African Affairs* 87 (1988): 553–62.

Aidt, Toke S. "Corruption and Sustainable Development." Cambridge Working Papers in Economics 1601. University of Cambridge, November 2010.

Alvarez, Gonzalo Duenas, Mary Tran, and Raj Raina. "MDGs: Sub-Saharan Africa: Overcoming Data Gaps and Ranking Progress." Department of Economics Discussion Paper Series no. 2011–01. Fordham University, 2011.

Anand, Sudhir, Paul Segal, and Joseph E. Stiglitz, eds. *Debates on the Measurement of Global Poverty*. Oxford: Oxford University Press, 2010.

Andreas, Peter, and Kelly M. Greenhill, eds. *Sex, Drugs and Body Counts: The Politics of Numbers in General Crime and Conflict*. Ithaca: Cornell University Press, 2010.

Arbache, J. S., and J. Page. "Patterns of Long Term Growth in Sub-Saharan Africa." World Bank Policy Research Working Paper 4398, 2007.

Arkadie, Brian van. "National Accounting and Development Planning: Some Issues." *Development and Change* 4, no. 2 (1973): 15–31.

Arndt, Christine, and Charles Oman. "Uses and Abuses of Governance Indicators." Development Centre Studies, OECD, 2006.

Austin, Gareth. "Resources, Techniques and Strategies South of the Sahara: Revising the Factor Endowments Perspective on African Economic Development, 1500–2000." *Economic History Review* 61, no. 3 (2008): 587–624.

———. "The 'Reversal of Fortune' Thesis and the Compression of History: Perspectives from African and Comparative Economic History." *Journal of International Development* 20, no. 8 (2008): 996–1027.

Banerjee, A. *Making Aid Work*. Cambridge, MA: MIT Press, 2007.

Banerjee, A. V., and Esther Duflo. *Poor Economics: A Radical Rethinking of the Way to Fight Global Poverty*. New York: Public Affairs, 2011.

Barkan, J., ed. *Beyond Capitalism vs. Capitalism in Kenya and Tanzania*. London: Lynne Rienner, 1994.

Barnett, Michael N., and Martha Finnemore. *Rules for the World: International Organizations in Global Politics*. Ithaca: Cornell University Press, 2004.

Barro, R. J. "Economic Growth in a Cross Section of Countries." *Quarterly Journal of Economics* 106, no. 2 (1991): 407–43.

Bates, R. *Markets and States in Tropical Africa: The Political Basis of Agricultural Policies*. Berkeley: University of California Press, 1981.

———. "Forum: Robert H. Bates." In *Making Aid Work*, edited by A. V. Banerjee, pp. 67–72. Cambridge, MA: MIT Press, 2007.

Beneria, Lourdes. "Accounting for Women's Work: The Progress of Two Decades." *World Development* 20, no. 11 (1992): 1547–60.

Berg, Elliot. "Accelerated Development in Sub-Saharan Africa: An Agenda for Action." World Bank report no. 14030, 1981.

Berry, Sara. "The Food Crisis and Agrarian Change in Africa: A Review Essay." *African Studies Review* 27, no. 2 (1984): 59–112.

———. "Debating the Land Question in Africa." *Comparative Studies in Society and History* 44 (2002): 638–68.

Best, Joel. *Damned Lies and Statistics: Untangling Numbers from the Media, Politicians, and Activists*. Berkeley: University of California Press, 2001.

Billington, G. C. "A Minimum System of National Accounts for Use by African Countries and some Related Problems." *Review of Income and Wealth,* no. 1 (1962): 1–51.

Black, Richard, and Howard White. "Millennium Development Goals." In *Targeting Development: Critical Perspectives on the Millennium Development Goals*, edited by Richard Black and Howard White. New York: Routledge, 2003.

Black, Richard, and Howard White, eds. *Targeting Development: Critical Perspectives on the Millennium Development Goals*. New York: Routledge, 2004.

Blades, Derek. *Non-Monetary (Subsistence) Activities in the National Accounts of Developing Countries*. Paris: OECD, 1975.

———. "What Do We Know about Levels and Growth of Output in Developing Countries? A Critical Analysis with Special Reference to Africa." In *Trends and Factors*, edited by R. C. O. Mathews, 60–70. Vol. 2 of *Economic Growth and Resources: Proceedings of the Fifth World Congress, International Economic Association, Tokyo*. New York: St. Martin's Press, 1980.

Blades, Derek, and Francois Lequiller. *Understanding National Accounts*. Paris: OECD, 2006.

Bloem, Adriaan M., and Manik L Shrestha. "Exhaustive Measures of GDP and the Unrecorded Economy." International Monetary Fund Working Paper, Draft, October 2000.

Booth, David, and Henry Lucas. "Monitoring Progress Towards the Millennium Development Goals at Country Level." In *Targeting Development: Critical Perspectives on the Millennium Development Goals*, edited by R. Black and H. White, 96–123. New York: Routledge, 2003.

Bondestam, Lars. *Some Notes on African Statistics: Collection, Reliability and Interpretation*. Research Report no. 18. Uppsala: Scandinavian Institute of African Studies, 1973.

Bosin, Yury V. "Measuring Democracy: Approaches and Challenges Associated with Developing Democratic Indices." William and Kathy Hyble Democracy Studies Fellowship Paper, 2007.

Bratton, Michael, and Nicolas Van de Walle. "Neopatrimonial Regimes and Political Transitions in Africa." *World Politics* 46, no. 4 (1994): 453–89.

Brautigam, Deborah A., Odd-Helge Fjeldstad, and Mick Moore, eds. *Taxation and State-Building in Developing Countries: Capacity and Consent*. Cambridge: Cambridge University Press, 2008.

Brett, E. A. "State Failure and Success in Uganda and Zimbabwe: The Logic of Political Decay and Reconstruction in Africa." *Journal of Development Studies* 44, no. 3 (2008): 339–64.

Caldwell, J. C., and C. Okonjo. *The Population of Tropical Africa*. London: Longman, 1968.

Carr-Hill, Roy A. *Social Conditions in Sub-Saharan Africa*. MacMillan, 1990.

Chambers, R. "Beyond the Green Revolution: A Selective Essay." In *Understanding Green Revolutions: Agrarian Change and Development Planning in South Asia: Essays in Honour of B. H. Farmer*, edited by B. H. Farmer, S. Wanmali, and T. Bayliss-Smith, 362–80. New York: Cambridge University Press, 1984.

Chen, Xi, and William D. Nordhaus. "Using Luminosity as a Proxy for Economic Statistics." *Proceedings of the National Academy of Sciences* 108, no. 21 (2011): 8589–94.

Chirwa, E. W., J. Kydd, and A. Dorward. "Future Scenarios for Agriculture in Malawi: Challenges and Dilemmas." The Future Agricultures Consortium, Research Paper 3, 2006.

Cocks, Tim. "Analysis—Nigeria GDP Rebase May Pose Challenge to SAfrica." Reuters Africa, November 11, 2011.

Cohen, Don, and Bruno Laporte. "The Evolution of the Knowledge Bank." *KM Magazine*, March 2004.

Connelly, Mathew James. *Fatal Misconception: The Struggle to Control World Population*. Cambridge, MA: Belknap Press of Harvard University Press, 2008.

Cooper, Frederick. *Africa since 1940: The Past of the Present*. New York: Cambridge University Press, 2002.

———. "Modernizing Bureaucrats, Backward Africans, and the Development Concept." In *International Development and the Social Sciences: Essays on the History and Politics of Knowledge*, edited by Frederick Cooper and Randall Packard, 64–92. Berkeley: University of California Press, 1997.

Cooper, Frederick, and Randall Packard. "Introduction." In *International Development and the Social Sciences: Essays on the History and Politics of Knowledge*, edited by Frederick Cooper and Randall Packard, 1–63. Berkeley: University of California Press, 1997.

Collier, Paul. *The Bottom Billion. Why the Poorest Countries Are Failing and What Can Be Done about It*. New York: Oxford University Press, 2007.

———. "Oil Shocks and Food Security in Nigeria." *International Labour Review* 127 (1988): 761–82.

Collier, Paul, and Jan W. Gunning. "Why Has Africa Grown So Slowly?" *Journal of Economic Perspectives* 13, no. 3 (1999): 3–22.

Collier, P., S. Radwan, and S. Wangwe with A. Wagner. *Labour and Poverty in Rural Tanzania: Ujamaa and Rural Development in the United Republic of Tanzania*. Oxford: Clarendon Press, 1986.

Conroy, A. C., M. J. Blackie, A. Whiteside, J. C. Malewezi and J. D. Sachs. *Poverty, Aids and Hunger: Breaking the Poverty Trap in Malawi*. New York: Palgrave Macmillan, 2006.

Cramer, Christopher. *Violence in Developing Countries: War, Memory, Progress*. Bloomington: Indiana University Press, 2007.

Daily Nation. "Kenya: Census Changes Flow of Sh14 Billion CDF Money." September 12, 2010.

———. "Kenya: Census Will Reveal Key Data for Planners." August 24, 2009.

———. "Kenya: Controversy over Inclusion of Tribal Identity in Census." June 27, 2009.

———. "Kenya: Rescind Census Decision, Community Demands." September 11, 2010.

———. "Kenya: State Puts Final Touches on 2009 Census Results." December 31, 2009.

———. "Options after Census Results Quashed." September 28, 2010.

Dawson, J. W., J. P. DeJuan, J. J. Seater, and E. F. Stephenson. "Economic Information versus Quality Variation in Cross-Country Data." *Canadian Journal of Economics* 34 no. 3 (2001): 988–1009.

Deane, Phyllis. *The Measurement of Colonial National Income: An Experiment*. Cambridge: Cambridge University Press, 1948.

———. Domestic Income and Product in Kenya: A Description of Sources and Methods with Revised Calculations from 1954–1958; The National Income of the Sudan, 1955–1956, by C. H. Harvie and J. G. Kleve; Comptes Économiques Togo, 1956–1957–1958, by G. Le Hégarat." Book Review. *Economic Journal* 71, no. 283 (1961): 630–31.

Deaton, Angus. "Forum: Angus Deaton." In *Making Aid Work*, edited by A. V. Banerjee, pp. 55–62. Cambridge, MA: MIT Press, 2007.

———. "Understanding the Mechanisms of Economic Development." *Journal of Economic Perspectives* 24, no. 3 (2010): 3–16.

Deaton, A., and A. Heston. "Understanding PPPS and PPP-Based National Accounts." *American Economic Journal: Macroeconomics* 2, no. 4 (2010): 1–35.

Duflo, Esther, M. Kremer, and J. Robinson. "How High Are Rates of Return to Fertilizer? Evidence from Field Experiments in Kenya." *American Economic Review* 98, no. 2 (2008): 482–88.

Durlauf, S., P. Johnson, and J. Temple. "Growth Econometrics." In *Handbook of Economic Growth*, edited by P. Aghion and S. Durlauf, 555–667. Amsterdam: Elsevier, 2005.

Easterly, William. "Can Foreign Aid Buy Growth?" *Journal of Economic Perspectives* 17, no. 3 (2003): 23–48.

——. "The Lost Decades: Developing Countries' Stagnation in Spite of Policy Reform 1980–1998." *Journal of Economic Growth* 6, no. 2 (June 2001): 135–57.

——. "Planners versus Searchers in Foreign Aid." *Asian Development* 23, no. 1 (2006): 1–35.

Eke, I. I. U. "The Nigerian National Accounts—A Critical Appraisal." *Nigerian Journal of Economic and Social Studies* 8 (1966): 333–60.

Ellis, Stephen. "Writing Histories of Contemporary Africa." *Journal of African History* 43, no. 1 (2002): 1–26.

Elster, Jon. "Rational Choice History: A Case of Excessive Ambition." *American Political Science Review* 94, no. 3 (2000): 685–95.

Ellerman, David. "Should Development Agencies Have Official Views?" *Development in Practice* 12, nos. 3–4 (2002): 285–97.

Englebert, P. "Pre-Colonial Institutions, Post-Colonial States, and Economic Development in Tropical Africa." *Political Research Quarterly* 53, no. 1 (2000): 7–36.

Falola, Tony, and Matthew Heaton. *A History of Nigeria*. Cambridge: Cambridge University Press, 2008.

Feinstein, Charles H. *Making History Count: A Primer in Quantitative Methods for Historians*. Cambridge: Cambridge University Press, 2002.

Ferguson, James. *Global Shadows: Africa in the Neoliberal World Order*. Durham, NC: Duke University Press, 2006.

——. *The Anti-Politics Machine: "Development," Depoliticization, and Bureaucratic Power in Lesotho*. New York: Cambridge University Press, 1990.

Fjeldstad, Odd-Helge, and Mick Moore. "Tax Reform and State-Building in a Globalised World." In *Taxation and State-Building in Developing Countries: Capacity and Consent*, edited by Deborag A. Brautigam, Odd-Helge Fjeldstad, and Mick Moore, 235–63. Cambridge: Cambridge University Press, 2008.

Forrest, Tom. *Politics and Economic Development in Nigeria*. Boulder, CO: Westview Press, 1993.

Frane, Adam. "Mapping Social Capital across Europe: Findings, Trends and Methodological Shortcomings of Cross-National Surveys." *Social Science Information* 47 (2008): 159–86.

Frankel, Herbert S. *The Economic Impact on Under-Developed Societies: Essays on International Investment and Social Change*. Cambridge, MA: Harvard University Press, 1953.

——. "Psychic and Accounting Concepts of Income and Welfare." *Oxford Economic Papers* 4, no. 1 (1952): 1–17.

Ghanaian Chronicle. "Mobile Phone Users to Reach 70 Percent." October 14, 2010.

Guenard, Charlotte, and Sandrine Mesple-Somps. "Measuring Inequalities: Do Household Surveys Paint a Realistic Picture?" *Review of Income and Wealth* 56, no. 3 (2010): 519–38.

Gilbert, Christopher, Andrew Powell, and David Vines. "Positioning the World Bank." *Economic Journal* 109 (November 1999): F598–F633.

Harriss, John. "The Case for Cross-Disciplinary Approaches in International Development." *World Development* 30 (2002): 487–96.

Hart, Keith. "Informal Income Opportunities and Urban Employment in Ghana." *Journal of Modern African Studies* 11, no. 1 (1973): 61–89.

———. "On the Informal Economy: The Political History of an Ethnographic Concept." CEB Working Paper no. 09/04, Centre Emile Bernheim, 2009.

Hegre, Havard, and Nicholas Sambanis. "Sensitivity Analysis of Empirical Results on Civil War Onset." *Journal of Conflict Resolution* 50, no. 4 (2006): 508–35.

Helleiner, Gerald K. *Peasant Agriculture, Government and Economic Growth in Nigeria.* Homewood, IL: R. D. Irwin, 1966.

Helpman, Elhanan. *The Mystery of Economic Growth.* Cambridge, MA: Harvard University Press, 2004.

Henderson, J. V., A. Storeygard, and D. N. Weil "Measuring Growth from Outer Space." NBER Working Paper 15199, 2009.

Herbst, Jeffrey I. *States and Power in Africa: Comparative Lessons in Authority and Control.* Princeton, NJ: Princeton University Press, 2000.

Herrera, Yoshiko M. *Mirrors of the Economy: National Accounts and International Norms in Russia and Beyond.* Ithaca: Cornell University Press, 2010.

Herring, R. "Data as Social Product." In *Q-Squared: Combining Qualitative and Quantitative Methods in Poverty Appraisal*, edited by R. Kanbur, 141–17. New Delhi: Permanent Black, 2001.

Heston, A. "A Brief Review of Some Problems in Using National Accounts Data in Level Comparisons and Growth Studies." *Journal of Development Economics* 44, no. 1 (1994): 29–52.

Heston, A., R. Summers, and B. Aten. Penn World Table Version 6.2. Center for International Comparisons of Production, Income and Prices at the University of Pennsylvania, 2006.

Hibou, Beatrice, ed. *Privatizing the State.* Translated from the French by Jonathan Derick. New York: Columbia University Press, 2004.

Hill, Polly. *Development Economics on Trial: The Anthropological Case for Prosecution.* Cambridge: Cambridge University Press, 1986.

———. *Population, Prosperity and Poverty: Rural Kano, 1900 and 1970.* Cambridge: Cambridge University Press, 1977.

International Labour Organization. *Employment, Incomes and Equality: A Strategy for Increasing Production Employment in Kenya.* Geneva: International Labour Organization, 1972.

Jerven, Morten. "Accounting for the African Growth Miracle: The Official Evidence, Botswana 1965–1995." *Journal of Southern African Studies* 36, no. 1 (2010): 73–94.

———. "African Growth Recurring: An Economic History Perspective on African Growth Episodes, 1690–2010." *Economic History of Developing Regions* 25, no. 2 (2010): 127–54.

———. "A Clash of Disciplines? Economists and Historians Approaching the African Past." *Economic History of Developing Regions* 26, no. 2 (2011): 111–24.

———. "Counting the Bottom Billion: Measuring the Wealth and Progress of African Economies." *World Economics* 12, no. 4 (2011): 35–52.

———. "Growth, Stagnation or Retrogression? On the Accuracy of Economic Observations, Tanzania, 1961–2001." *Journal of African Economies* 20, no. 3 (2011): 377–94.

———. "Random Growth in Africa? Lessons from an Evaluation of the Growth Evidence on Botswana, Kenya, Tanzania and Zambia, 1965–1995." *Journal of Development Studies* 42, no. 2 (2010): 274–94.

———. "Revisiting the Consensus on Kenyan Economic Growth, 1964–1995." *Journal of Eastern African Studies* 5, no. 1 (2011): 2–23

———. "The Quest for the African Dummy: Explaining African Post-Colonial Economic Performance Revisited." *Journal of International Development* 23, no. 2 (2011): 288–307.

———. "Social Capital as a Determinant of Economic Growth in Africa." *Africa Review* 2, no. 2 (2010): 139–62.

———. "The Relativity of Poverty and Income: How Reliable Are African Economic Statistics?" *African Affairs* 109, no. 434 (2010): 77–96.

———. "An Unlevel Playing Field: National Income Estimates and Reciprocal Comparison in Global Economic History." *Journal of Global History* 7, no. 1 (2012): 107–28.

———. "Users and Producers of African Income: Measuring African Progress." *African Affairs* 110, no. 439 (April 2011): 169–90.

Jerven, Morten, Beatrice Hibou, and Boris Samuel. "Un demi-siècle de fictions de croissance en Afrique." *Politque Africaine* 124 (2011): 29–43.

Johnson, W. Larson, C. Papageorgiou, and A. Subramanian. "Is Newer Better? The Penn World Table Revisions and the Cross-Country Growth Literature." NBER Working Paper 15455, 2009.

June, Raymond, Afroza Chowdhury, Nathaniel Heller, and Jonathan Werve. *A User's Guide to Measuring Corruption*. Oslo: Global Integrity and UNDP, 2008.

K'Akumu, Owiti A. "Construction Statistics Review for Kenya." *Construction Management and Economics* 25, no. 3 (2007): 315–26.

Kapur, Devesh. "The 'Knowledge' Bank." In *Rescuing the World Bank: A CGD Working Group Report and Select Essays*, edited by Nancy Birdstall, 159–70. Washington, DC: Brookings Institution Press, 2006.

Karlon, Dean and Jacob Appel. *More Than Good Intentions: How a New Economics Is Helping to Solve Global Poverty*. New York: Dutton, 2011.

Kenny, Charles, and Andy Sumner. "How 28 Poor Countries Escaped the Poverty Trap." Poverty Matters blog, July 12, 2011. Retrieved July 2011 from http://www.guardian.co.uk

Kenny, Charles, and David Williams. "What Do We Know about Economic Growth? Or, Why Don't We Know Very Much?" *World Development* 29, no. 1 (2001): 1–22.

"Kenya's Census Figures Contested." Wanted in Africa website. September 4, 2010.

Keynes, Maynard. *The General Theory of Employment, Interest and Money*. Basingstoke, England: Palgrave Macmillan for the Royal Economic Society, 2007.

Killick, Tony. *Development Economics in Action: A Study of Economic Policies in Ghana*. New York: Routledge, 2010.

King, Kenneth. "Africa's Informal Economies: Thirty Years On." *SAIS Review* 11, no. 1 (2001): 97–108.

Knack, Stephen. "Measuring Corruption: A Critique of Indicators in Eastern Europe and Central Asia." *Journal of Public Policy* 27, no. 3 (2007): 255–91.

Kornai, Janos. *The Socialist System: The Political Economy of Communism.* Clarendon, Oxford: Oxford University Press, 1992.

Kpedekpo, G. M. K., and P. L. Arya. *Social and Economic Statistics for Africa: Their Source and Reliability.* London: Allen & Unwin, 1981.

Kulshreshtha, A. C., and Gulab Singh. "Valuation of Non-Market Household Production." Central Statistical Organization, New Delhi, 1999.

Lawrence, Peter. "Development by Numbers." *New Left Review* 62 (2010): 143–53.

Le Nay, Jean, and Jean Mathis. "The Impact of Drought on the National Accounts for Livestock in Sahelian Countries." *Review of Income and Wealth* 35, no. 2 (June 1989): 209–24.

Lea, N., and L. Hanmer. "Constraints to Growth in Malawi." Policy Research Working Paper 5097. Southern African Poverty Reduction and Economic Management Unit, World Bank, 2009.

Lequiller, Francois, and Derek Blades. *Understanding National Accounts.* Paris: OECD Publishing, 2007.

Levine, Sebastian. "Measuring Progress towards Global Poverty Goals: Challenges and Lessons from Southern Africa." *African Statistical Journal* 3 (November 2006): 89–110.

Lewis, W. Arthur. *Reflections on Nigeria's Economic Growth.* Paris: Development Centre of the Organisation for Economic Co-operation and Development, 1967.

Lucas, Robert E., Jr. "On the Mechanics of Economic Development." *Journal of Monetary Economics* 22, no. 1 (1988): 3–42.

MacGaffey, Janet. *The Real Economy of Zaire: The Contribution of Smuggling & Other Unofficial Activities to National Wealth.* Philadelphia: University of Pennsylvania Press, 1991.

Maddison, A. "Background Note on 'Historical Statistics.'" 2010. http://www.ggdc.net/maddison. Retrieved July 2011.

———. Historical Statistics of the World Economy: 1–2006 AD. Copyright Angus Maddison, 2009.

Maliyamkono, T. L., and M. S. D. Bagachwa. *The Second Economy in Tanzania.* London: James Currey, 1990.

Mamdani, Mahmood. *The Myth of Population Control: Family, Caste and Class in an Indian Village.* New York: Monthly Review Press, 1973.

Manning, Patrick. "African Population: Projections 1850–1960." In *The Demographics of Empire: The Colonial Order and the Creation of Knowledge*, edited by K. Ittmann, D. D. Cordell, and G. Maddox, 245–75. Athens: Ohio University Press, 2010.

McGovern, Mike. "Popular Development Economics—An Anthropologist among the Mandarins." *Perspectives on Politics* 9, no. 2 (2011): 345–55.

Meagher, Kate. *Identity Economics: Social Networks and the Informal Economy in Nigeria.* London: James Currey, 2010.

Merry, Sally Engle. "Measuring the World: Indicators, Human Rights, and Global Governance." *Current Anthropology* 52, no. 3 (2011): S83–S95.

Miguel, E., S. Shanker, and S. Ernest. "Economic Shocks and Civil Conflict: An Instrumental Variables Approach." *Journal of Political Economy* 112, no. 4 (2004): 725–53.

Mimiko, F. "Census in Nigeria: The Politics and the Imperative of Depoliticization." *African and Asian Studies* 5 no. 1 (2006): 1–21.

Mkandawire, Thandika. "Thinking about Developmental States in Africa." *Cambridge Journal of Economics* 25 (2001): 289–313.

Mkandawire, Thandika P., and Charles C. Soludo. *Our Continent, Our Future: African Perspectives on Structural Adjustment*. Trenton, NJ: Africa World Press, 1999.

Moradi, Alexander. "Towards an Objective Account of Nutrition and Health in Colonial Kenya: A Study of Stature in African Army Recruits and Civilians, 1880–1980." *Journal of Economic History* 69, no. 3 (2009): 720–55.

Morgenstern, Oskar. *On the Accuracy of Economic Observations*. Princeton, NJ: Princeton University Press, 1963.

Morrison, Kevin M. "Oil, Nontax Revenue, and the Redistributional Foundations of Regime Stability." *International Organization* 63, no. 1 (2009): 107–38.

Mosley, P. "Policy and Capital Market Constraints to the African Green Revolution: A Study of Maize and Sorghum Yields in Kenya, Malawi and Zimbabwe, 1960–91." Innocenti Occasional Papers, Economic Policy Series no. 38, 1993.

——. "Policy Making without Facts: A Note on the Assessment of Structural Adjustment Policies in Nigeria, 1985–1990." *African Affairs* 91, no. 363 (1992): 227–40.

Moss, Todd. "Ghana Says, Hey, Guess What? We're Not Poor Anymore." Global Development: Views from the Centre, November 5, 2010. http://blogs.cgdev.org/globaldevelopment/2010/11/ghana-says-hey-guess-what-we%E2%80%99re-not-poor-anymore.php. Accessed July 2011.

Mouyelo-Katoula, Michel. "Rethinking Statistics for National Development in Africa." *African Statistical Journal* 7 (May 2006): 19–29.

Munck, Gerardo Luis. *Measuring Democracy: A Bridge between Scholarship and Politics*. Baltimore, MD: Johns Hopkins University Press, 2009.

Muwanga-Zake, E. S. K. "Statistics Reform." In *Uganda's Economic Reforms: Insider Accounts*, edited by F. Kuteesa, E. Tumusiime-Mutebile, A. Whitworth, and T. Williamson, pp. 246–63. London: Oxford University Press, 2010.

Ndulu, B. J., and C. K. Mutalemwa. *Tanzania at the Turn of the Century: Background Papers and Statistics*. Washington, DC: World Bank, 2002.

Ndulu, B. J., S. A. O. Connell, J. P. Azam, R. H. Bates, A. K. Fosu, J. W. Gunning, and D. Njinkeu, eds. *The Political Economy of Economic of Growth in Africa 1960–2000: An Analytic Survey*. Cambridge: Cambridge University Press, 2008.

——. *The Political Economy of Economic of Growth in Africa 1960–2000: Case Studies*. Cambridge: Cambridge University Press, 2008b.

Ngaruko, Floribert. "The World Bank's Framework for Statistical Capacity Measurement: Strengths, Weaknesses, and Options for Improvement." *African Statistical Journal* 2 (November 2008): 149–69.

Nugent, Paul. *Africa since Independence: A Comparative History*. New York: Palgrave Macmillan, 2004.

Nurkse, R. *Problems of Capital Formation in Underdeveloped Countries*. London: Oxford University Press, 1953.

Ohuocha, Chijioke. "Exclusive: Nigeria GDP Rebasing May See Big Upward Revision—Stats Chief." Reuters Africa, November 10, 2011.

Okigbo, Pius N. C. *Nigerian National Accounts, 1950–57*. Enugu, Government Printer, 1962.

Okolo, A. "The Nigerian Census: Problems and Prospects." *American Statistician* 53, no. 4 (1999): 321–25.

Parfitt, Trevor W. "Review: Lies, Damned Lies and Statistics: The World Bank/ECA Structural Adjustment Controversy." *Review of African Political Economy* 47 (1990): 128–41.

Peacock, Alan T., and Douglas G. M. Dosser. *The National Income of Tanganyika, 1952–54*. London: Her Majesty's Stationery Office, 1958.

Pitcher, Anne, Mary H. Moran, and Michael Johnston. "Rethinking Patrimonialism and Neopatrimonialism in Africa." *African Studies Review* 52, no. 1 (2009): 125–56.

Porter, Theodore M. *Trust in Numbers: The Pursuit of Objectivity in Science and Public Life*. Princeton, NJ: Princeton University Press, 1995.

Prest, Alan, and Ian G. Stewart. *The National Income of Nigeria, Colonial Office*. Colonial Research Studies no. 11. London: Her Majesty's Stationery Office, 1953.

Rao, C. R. *Data Base of Indian Economy: Review and Appraisal*. Vol. 1. Calcutta: Eka Press, 1972.

Reinikka, Ritva, and Jacob Svensson. "Explaining Leakage of Public Funds." Policy Research Working Paper Series no. 2709, 2001.

Riddel, Roger C., ed. *Manufacturing Africa: Performance and Prospects in Seven Countries in Sub-Saharan Africa*. London: James Currey, 1990.

Rimmer, Douglas. "Learning about Economic Development from Africa." *African Affairs* 102 (2003): 469–91.

Romer, Paul M. "Increasing Returns and Long-Run Growth." *Journal of Political Economy* 94, no. 5 (1986): 1002–37.

Sachs, J. "Homegrown Aid." *New York Times*, April 8, 2009, A23.

Sala-i-Martin, X. "I Just Ran Two Million Regressions." *American Economic Review* 87, no. 2 (1997): 178–83.

Sambanis, Nicholas. "What Is Civil War? Conceptual and Empirical Complexities of an Operational Definition." *Journal of Conflict Resolution* 48, no. 6 (2004): 814–58.

Samuels, L. H. ed. *African Studies in Income and Wealth*. London: Bowes & Bowes, 1963.

Sanga, Dimitri. "The Challenges of Monitoring and Reporting on the Millennium Development Goals in Africa by 2015 and Beyond." *African Statistical Journal* 12 (May 2011): 104–18.

Santschi, Martina. "Briefing: Counting 'New Sudan.'" *African Affairs* 107, no. 429 (2008): 631–40.

Seers, Dudley. "An Approach to the Short-Period Analysis of Primary Producing Economies." Oxford Economic Paper 11, no. 1, 1959.

———. "The Political Economy of National Accounting." In *Employment, Income Distribution and Development Strategy: Problems of the Developing Countries*, edited by A. Caincross and M. Puri. New York: Homes & Meier Publishers, 1976.

———. "The Role of National Income Estimates in the Statistical Policy of an Under-Developed Area." *Review of Economic Studies* 20, no. 3 (1952–1953): 159–68.

Sender, John, Christopher Cramer, and Carlos Oya. *Unequal Prospects: Disparities in the Quantity and Quality of Labour Supply in Sub-Saharan Africa*. Social Protection

Discussion Paper Series no. 0525. Human Development Network, World Bank, 2005.

Solow, Robert M. "A Contribution to the Theory of Economic Growth." *Quarterly Journal of Economics* 70, no. 1 (1956): 65–94.

———. "Technical Change and the Aggregate Production Function." *Review of Economics and Statistics* 39, no. 3 (1957): 312–20.

Srinivasan, T. N. "The Data Base for Development Analysis: An Overview." *Journal of Development Economics* 44, no. 1 (1994): 3–27.

Srinivasan, T. N., and A. Vaidyanathan. "Agricultural Statistics." In *Data Base of Indian Economy: Review and Appraisal*, vol. 1, edited by C. R. Rao, 33–62. Calcutta: Eka Press, 1972.

Stein, Howard. *Beyond the World Bank Agenda: An Institutional Approach to Development*. Chicago: University of Chicago Press, 2008.

Stern, N. "The Economics of Development: A Survey." *Economic Journal* 99, no. 397 (1989): 597–685.

Stiglitz, Joseph, Amartya Sen, and Jean-Paul Fitoussi. *Mismeasuring Our Lives: Why GDP Doesn't Add Up*. New York: New Press, 2010.

Stolper, William F. *Planning without Facts: Lessons in Resource Allocation from Nigeria's Development*. Cambridge, MA: Harvard University Press, 1966.

Stone, Deborah, *Policy Paradox: The Art of Political Decision Making*. New York: Norton, 2002.

Suberu, R. T. I. *Federalism and Ethnic Conflict in Nigeria*. Washington, DC: Institute of Peace Press, 2001.

Thorner, Daniel, and Alice Thorner. *Land and Labour in India*. Bombay: Asia Publishing House, 1962.

Tilly, Charles. *Contention and Democracy in Europe, 1650–2000*. New York: Cambridge University Press, 2004.

Tilley, Helen. *Africa as a Living Laboratory: Empire, Development, Scientific Knowledge, 1870–1950*. Chicago: University of Chicago Press, 2011.

Tripp, A. M. *Changing the Rules: The Politics of Liberalization and the Urban Informal Economy in Tanzania*. Berkeley: University of California Press, 1997.

Udo, R. K. "Geography and Population Censuses in Nigeria." In *Fifty Years of Geography in Nigeria: The Ibadan Story*, edited by Olusegun Areola and Stanley I. Okafor. Ibadan: Ibadan University Press, 1998.

Vandemoortele, Jan. "The MDG Story: Intention Denied." *Development and Change* 42, no. 1 (2011): 1–21.

Van de Walle, N. *African Economies and the Politics of Permanent Crisis, 1979–1999*. New York: Cambridge University Press, 2001.

Wade, R. "US Hegemony and the World Bank: The Fight for People and Ideas." *Review of International Political Economy* 9, no. 2 (2002): 215–42.

Ward, Michael. *Quantifying the World: UN Ideas and Statistics*. Bloomington: Indiana University Press, 2004.

Wold, Bjorn. "A Social Statistics System for the Millennium Development Goals?" *Forum for Development Studies* no. 1 (2005): 219–42.

Wood, G. Donald, Jr. "Problems of Comparisons in Africa with Special Regard to Kenya." *Review of Income and Wealth* 19, no. 1 (1973): 105–16.

Woodward, M., N. Dourmashkin, E. Twagirumukiza, M. Mbago, and A. S. Ferreira da Cunha. "Statistics Training in Eastern and Southern Africa: A Study of Supply and Demand." *Journal of the Royal Statistical Society: Series D (The Statistician)* 46, no. 3 (1997): 371–86.

Wrong, Michella. *It's Our Turn to Eat: The Story of a Kenyan Whistle Blower*. New York: Harper Collins, 2009.

Yin, S. "Objections Surface Over Nigerian Census Results." Population Reference Bureau, April 2007.

Young, Alwyn. "The African Growth Miracle." Department of Economics, London School of Economics, 2010.

Ziliak, Stephen T., and Deirdre N. McCloskey. *The Cult of Statistical Significance: How the Standard Error Costs Us Jobs, Justice and Lives*. Ann Arbor: University of Michigan Press; 2008.

INDEX

Aboyade, A., 42, 114
Ady, Peter, 38–39
African Governance Indicators, 118
African national statistics: availability
  of, 22–24; concerns about quality of,
  30; inadequacy of western economic
  concepts for, 38–39, 78; methodologies
  used to generate, ix–x, xvi, 84; recommendations for improving, 106–108;
  unreliability of, 21–22; weak capacity
  of African nations to generate, ix–xi,
  xvi, 2–3, 96–96. *See also* constraints on
  statistical capacity; national statistics
  offices; political factors; revisions of
  GDP data series; statistical capacity of
  African nations; courses for national
  statisticians.
Afrobarometer, 119
agricultural sector: assumptions about
  growth of, 42–43, 75–77; history of sta-

tistical measurement of, 85; inaccuracy
  of statistics for, 51, 61–65; methods used
  to estimate production in, ix, 29, 75, 79,
  87–88; and production method of estimating GDP, 12; sources of data about,
  13, 62; statisticians exclude subsistence
  farming, 37, 42, 61, 103–104; value of
  underestimated in colonial era, 50.
  See also crop-cutting surveys; eye estimates; fertilizer subsidies; rainfall data;
  subsistence.
Angola, 18–19, 24, 102, 124
Arusha Declaration, 69
Asian Barometer, 119

Benin, 18–19, 23–25, 124–125
Berg report, 88–89. *See also* structural
  adjustment.
Blades, Derek, 30–32, 43
Blue Books, 50

Kenya: absence of information about national accounting methodology after 1977, 44–45; annual Integrated Rural Survey of, 43; applies for STATCAP funding, 103; colonial-era estimates of national income in, 37; controversy over population census in, 73–74; country estimate of GDP of, 130; errors in national accounts of, 31; fertilizer subsidies in, 90; IMF and World Bank evaluate national statistics of, 100–101; method of compiling national income of, 12; outdated baseline year of for GDP estimates, 26, 103; poor statistical capacity of, 91; relation of statistical office to ministry of finance, 92; survey of informal sector in, 46

Kpedekpo, G. M. K., 21

Latinobarómetro, 119
Lesotho, 18–19, 23–24, 93, 130
Liberia, 18–19, 23–25, 95, 102, 124
Local Authority Transfer Fund (Kenya), 73
lost decades, 34, 44–45. *See also* structural adjustment.

MacGaffey, Janet, 17
macroeconomic data, 47, 52, 90, 98
Madagascar: absence of information about which base year World Bank uses, 145n34; country estimate of GDP of, 130–131; differences between national accounts data and World Bank reports, 24; in GDP rankings, 18; World Bank does not report base year for, 145n34
Maddison, Angus, 16, 20
Maddison datasets: begins in 1950, 147n12; discrepancies with other databases of African statistics, 16–20, 30, 65–67, 71–72, 144n15; used by economic historians and economists, 17
Malawi: census of agriculture of, 75–76; conflicting sources of agricultural data for, 76–77; country estimate of GDP of, 131; differences between national

accounts data and World Bank reports, 23–24; IMF and World Bank evaluate national statistics of, 100–101; central bank judges national statistics inaccurate, 87; Norway provides funding to improve statistical capacity, 94, 103, 106; relation of statistical office to ministry of finance, 92; training programs for national statisticians of, 94; weak capacity of national statistical office of, 91, 101
Mali, 18, 23, 25, 124
Mauritania, 18, 131–132
Mauritius, 19, 23–24, 100–101
metadata: defined, 97; gaps in for international datasets, 97–98, 101, 107–108; need for, 104, 117–119
methodology of this book, xii, 83, 86, 102, 139–140
Millennium Development Goals: donors prioritize, x; create pressure for national statistical offices, x–xi, 6, 95–96, 105–106; incomplete data for, 95; sets development agenda, 6, 9; and use of World Development Indicators, 144n16
Mills, John Atta, 27
ministries of agriculture, 13, 75–77, 91
ministries of finance, 91–93, 102, 104
Mosley, Paul, 63–64
Mozambique, 18–19, 47, 100–101, 132

Namibia, 25, 28–29, 100–101, 132–133
National Census of Agriculture and Livestock (Malawi), 75–76
National Council of Nigeria and the Cameroons, 58
national income estimates: and data quality, 12–13, 16; discrepancies in methods used to produce in Africa, 12, 30, 36, 40, 64, 106; effect of more recent base year on, 86; history of, 40–41; impact of structural adjustment policies on, 46–49; inadequacy of western models of for African context, 38–39; and measurement errors, 78; and production boundary, 11; production method, 12; relationship of to estimates of economic

Tanzania *(continued)*
centralization of economy on national
statistics, 44–45; errors in international
databases about GDP of, 70–71; errors
in national accounts of, 31; in GDP
rankings, 17–18; growth of formal sector in, 70; growth rate data for, 65–69;
household budget surveys in, 42, 80;
IMF and World Bank evaluate national
statistics of, 100–101; informal economy
of, 80; interest of donors and scholars in,
69; outdated baseline year of for GDP
estimates, 103; poor statistical capacity
of, 91, 100; relation of statistical office to
ministry of finance, 92; revises national
accounts, 42, 48, 69–70, 79–80; role of
parastatal companies in, 44–45, 49, 68, 80
taxation: and capacity of African states,
2–3, 35; and colonial-era population
censuses, 57; during colonial era, 50,
57; and formal economy, 46; revenue
from excluded from African national
accounts, 47; and statistical capacity,
142n9; and women's unpaid labor, 86;
and World Bank's definition of GDP, 97
Togo, 18, 23, 25, 102, 124
training courses for national statisticians,
xi, 93–94, 99, 143n8, 157n45, 157n48.
See also statistical capacity of African
nations.
Turkana community (Kenya), 73–74

Uganda: applies for STATCAP, 103;
colonial-era estimates of national income of, 37; country estimate of GDP
of, 136–137; differences between national accounts data and World Bank
reports, 23, 25; estimates agricultural
production, 43, 87–88; expenditures
on primary schools in, 90; history of
national accounts of, 31, 48, 102; IMF
and World Bank evaluate national statistics of, 100–101; impact of collapse of
formal economy in 1970s on statistical
office, 46; in GDP rankings, 18; incomplete collection of data on external trade
before 2008, 51; meets IMF standards

for national statistical capacity, 100–101;
problems with dissemination of national statistics of, 100; relation of statistical office to ministry of finance, 92
Uganda Board of Trade, 51
Uganda Bureau of Statistics, 51
United Nations Development Program,
95, 118
United Nations Statistical Office, 21
United Nations System of National Accounts (SNA): creates global standard,
3; history of, 9–10; and production
boundary, 11; recommends methodology for aggregating GDP, 12, 36–37, 70;
revised to include nonmonetary activities, 86
unobserved economy, 48, 92. *See also* informal sector.
unpaid housework, 86
unrecorded economy, 86, 113. *See also* informal sector.

validity of statistical data: defined, 16;
equated with comprehensiveness, 107;
factors that limit, 117; IMF and World
Bank defend, xvii; relationship of to
power, 3, 35, 144n13; and unknowable
factors, 120

Ward, Michael, 10, 21–22, 52
women's economic contributions, 11, 86
World Bank: dangers of role as knowledge producer, 93; failure of to establish
baseline estimate for assessing structural
adjustment, 5; lack of openness of about
methodology used to generate statistical
series, xvii, 97–98; and liberalization
of markets under structural adjustment, 69; neglect of national statistical
services during structural adjustment,
35; one-way communication style of, 93;
provides justification for structural adjustment, 88; questions about evaluation
of structural adjustment of, 80; refuses
to provide STATCAP funding to Zambia, 102–103; role of in national policymaking processes, 91; slowness of to

reform collection of national statistical data after structural adjustment, 52; structural adjustment policies of, 47. *See also* gap filling; International Development Association; poverty reduction programs; Reports on the Observance of Standards and Codes (ROSC); STATCAP; structural adjustment.

World Bank Development Data Group, 16, 97–98

World Bank Governance and Anti-Corruption Diagnosis, 118

World Bank Statistics Manual, 22

World Development Indicators: absence of metadata about, 97–98; base years used for GDP, 124–137; becomes major source for scholars, 34; described, 16; excludes some African countries, 144n17; GDP rankings of African countries, 18–19; lack of consistency of with country-level data, 23, 24–25, 28; lack of historical knowledge about, 22; and practice of gap filling, 22, 32; rejects Nigeria's population estimate, 58, 60; rejects revised data from Tanzanian Central Bureau of Statistics, 70–71; reports different growth rates for African countries than other databases, 30, 67; used for assessments of output volatil-

ity, 29–30; uses different cash values in GDP series from other databases, 20; uses GDP per capita, 144n15; warnings about quality of data of, 30–31

World Governance Indicators, 118

World Values Survey, 118–119

Zambia: absence of national account reports for 1970s and 1980s, 44; country estimate of GDP of, 137; effect of centralization of economy on national statistics, 44, 46; exclusion of informal sector data before 1990s, 47; in GDP rankings, 18–19; household budget surveys of, 43; IMF and World Bank evaluate national statistics of, 100–101; impact of structural adjustment on growth statistics of, 47; irregularity of donor funding for national statistics, 81; lack of institutional memory at Central Statistical Office of, ix; outdated baseline year of for GDP estimates, 103; relation of statistical office to ministry of finance, 92; revises national accounts, ix, 41–42, 47–48; weak statistical capacity of, ix–xi, 91; World Bank refuses to provide STATCAP funding to, 102–103

Zimbabwe, 18–19, 23, 25, 102, 124